THE DREAM OF REVOLUTION

PRAISE FOR THE BOOK

'A riveting account of the life of the greatest keeper, after Gandhi, of India's political conscience, who died, like his guide, in the loneliness of shattered dreams, betrayed ideals, forsaken covenants. JP's incredible life needs to be studied, restudied, told, retold. And who better than Bimal Prasad's daughter'
—Gopalkrishna Gandhi

'If an institution, as Ralph Waldo Emerson wrote, is the lengthened shadow of one man, Jayaprakash Narayan's touched an entire arc of history. From his battle of ideas in the Congress, shaped by Bihar as much as Berkeley, to his rallying cry of Total Revolution against the Emergency, JP was, and remains to this day, the talismanic face for the opposition in a deeply divided democracy. His journey lies at the heart of Sujata Prasad and Bimal Prasad's remarkable biography *The Dream of Revolution*. The book is a labour of love, a deeply felt and yet dispassionate analysis, invaluable for scholars and students. Blending personal and political, public and private, the authors explain how JP galvanized an entire generation of midnight's children, helping them find, in democratic politics, a cause larger than themselves. There couldn't be a more relevant political life story than this'—Raj Kamal Jha

'Sujata Prasad's biography of Jayaprakash Narayan sketches a vivid picture of his life and times in the nationalist movement and in independent India. Its elegant prose brings to life his revolutionary ideas and socialist beliefs, juxtaposed with political realities that tormented him with unanswered questions. Even so, his dissenting voice and moral stature provided critical checks and balances for our political democracy, which are sorely missed in these difficult times. *The Dream of Revolution* is an engaging must-read for anyone interested in the history and politics of democracy in India'—Deepak Nayyar

THE DREAM OF REVOLUTION

A biography of

JAYAPRAKASH NARAYAN

BIMAL PRASAD
SUJATA PRASAD

VINTAGE

An imprint of Penguin Random House

VINTAGE

USA | Canada | UK | Ireland | Australia
New Zealand | India | South Africa | China

Vintage is part of the Penguin Random House group of companies
whose addresses can be found at global.penguinrandomhouse.com

Published by Penguin Random House India Pvt. Ltd
4th Floor, Capital Tower 1, MG Road,
Gurugram 122 002, Haryana, India

First published in Vintage by Penguin Random House India 2021

ISBN 9780670096176

Typeset in Adobe Garamond Pro by Manipal Technologies Limited, Manipal
Printed at Thomson Press India Ltd, New Delhi

www.penguin.co.in

'Freedom is always, and exclusively, freedom for the one who thinks differently'—Rosa Luxemburg

'We need a protest against forgetting'—Eric Hobsbawm

Contents

Introduction

Jayaprakash Narayan needs to be rescued from the condescension of posterity and a curious historical amnesia. He was a political force for nearly half a century. Self-effacing, yet so visible that he was known by his initials, JP. He was the face of the student revolution in 1974. It was high-energy politics, personal and political, very of the moment, mobilizing and energizing large groups of people and shaping the political discourse with its own nuances. Several student leaders cut their teeth in the tumult of the movement and became characters in a drama they never seriously auditioned for. It brought the romance of barricades back to our lives, and imbued our lived experience with something akin to what Raymond Williams has described as 'a new structure of feeling'.

Jayaprakash's dream of revolution collapsed under the weight of its own contradictions, but like many of my generation, I was caught in a swirl of admiration. I saw in him an embodiment of intellectual elegance at a time when politics was raw, angry and out of control. His vision of a society untethered from capitalism seemed to open up new possibilities. His ideas continue to echo in the waves of protests and civil unrest that sweep across the world, as they have during the 2010 anti-government protests that rocked countries in North Africa and the Middle East, in the Indignados protests in Spain, in the Occupy Wall Street and its sister movements for economic justice that spread to 951 cities in eighty-two countries and in the fires of social revolt in Latin America in 2019.

Jayaprakash's pursuit of freedom and an equitable and just order was the quintessential revolutionary's quest (the title of one of my father, Bimal Prasad's books on his selected writings). His ideas were in a state of perpetual unrest, and the quest led him from Gandhi to Marx and then back again to Gandhi, never completely forsaking one for the other. In an entry in his 1975 book *Prison Diary*, Jayaprakash confessed that he was bitten by the 'bug of revolution' when he was in high school. He studied the inner life of revolutions and revolutionary movements while reading for his master's at the University of Wisconsin. He devoured Marx's masterpiece on political economy, *Das Kapital*, that laid bare the exploitation at the heart of the capitalist mode of production. He also read *The Communist Manifesto* (more Engels than Marx), the *Grundrisse* and an enormous body of theoretical work by Marxists like Rosa Luxemburg, Karl Liebknecht and Karl Kautsky, and soon became a prominent Marxist voice on the campus.

Socialism gained legitimacy, both as an idea and as political ambition, when Jayaprakash returned to India and threw in his lot with the Congress. No one could question his radical politics and his high-wire acts of dissent. His contagious confidence about the future of Marxian socialism led to the formation of the Congress Socialist Party (CSP) in 1934. Seeing the CSP as the vanguard of the nationalist left, he struggled to build socialism as a powerful countervailing political force within the Congress. He remained an anathema, a quintessential rebel frequently at odds with the very side he was supposed to represent. During this phase, he saw very little potential in Gandhism as a tool of political praxis. He considered it a dangerous doctrine that hushed up real issues, deceived the masses and facilitated continued domination by the upper classes. But he was also not particularly enamoured by the Bolshevik-style state socialism. He felt it was imperative to build a socialist movement within the framework of Marxist thought, of world history since Marx's death and India's own political history, aware that there were multiple constructions of Marxism that needed contextualization.

Jayaprakash pioneered the idea of an independent left, unbeholden to the Comintern that was dominated by the Communist Party of the Soviet Union. He took up the challenge of forging left unity, but the quibbles were far too many, and the odds were against him. Marx's aphorism about history repeating itself, 'first as tragedy, then as farce', stood on its head during Jayaprakash's engagement with the Communist Party of India (CPI), patterning itself as farce first, and then, tragedy. The farcical side emerged when the CPI started a venal campaign against the CSP, characterizing the latter as the left manoeuvre of the bourgeoisie and projecting itself as the only genuine Marxist party in India. If Jayaprakash felt let down by the CPI's intellectual turpitude, the horrors of Stalin's debased version of Marxism compounded the sense of tragedy. Nothing, he felt, could historically justify what was happening in Russia.

Radicalized by his long spells in prison, Jayaprakash's political thinking took a dramatic turn in 1942 when he turned to a spikier version of Marxism–Leninism and built an underground network of armed revolutionaries. The unpredictability and arbitrariness of his combative call to arms, that many in the Congress considered a misstep, was explained in a letter addressed to students with detailed blueprints on guerrilla strategy and tactics—somewhat like Che Guevara's *Guerrilla Warfare*, the bible of revolutionary movements in Latin America. His brief flirtation with guerrilla insurgency ended with his arrest, but he continued to exhort his followers to prepare for the last offensive: the struggle for liberty, national unity and bread, organized by strengthening peasant and labour unions, volunteer corps, student and youth organizations, weaver cooperatives and other grassroots organizations.

By 1944–45, Jayaprakash swerved again. This time it was a nonviolent ideological detour prompted by the conviction that orthodox Marxism needed Gandhian antibodies to remain immune to violent assaults on democratic norms. That Marx himself did not exclude the possibility that revolution could be peaceful encouraged this thinking. At this point, he also saw the potential for social revolution in the postwar European social democratic safety nets. But even when his thoughts were aligned with the democratic socialist vision, he viewed the state as a coercive instrument that could be perverted to produce dystopian ends. His own revolutionary praxis was grounded in grassroots-participatory democracy and Gandhian economics.

Gandhi's critique of the modern state remained central to the evolution of his political thought.

The early 1950s saw Jayaprakash formally renounce power politics and move towards a fundamental rethink on the mechanical, positivist elements in dialectical materialism (a distortion in Marxism, commonly attributed to Marx's co-author, Engels). For someone schooled in Hegelian and Marxist dialectics, this was a major intellectual and ideological shift towards a humanist approach to socialism, of looking at human agency and the role of ethics and values. It involved a deliberate distancing from the version of Marxism inherited from Sovietism and Maoism. In a sense, by distancing himself from materialism, Jayaprakash was embracing an open and critical mode of thinking guided by Marx's famous directive to doubt everything.

In a bruising struggle of ideas, the 1940s and '50s also saw the rebel excoriating Nehru for reneging on many of his socialist promises. Angry exchanges peppered their debates, with intimations of widening cracks in their relationship. The resultant brouhaha, however, did not stop Nehru from admiring Jayaprakash's ability and integrity, foreseeing a time when the latter would play a leading role in shaping India's destiny and perhaps succeed him.

Jayaprakash's solidarity with labour and peasant organizations was legion. He was the president of several large unions of government employees and played a decisive role in creating the nucleus of a strong and independent socialist opposition, eventually finding his ground zero in the Gandhian Bhoodan–Gramdan movement that remained his muse for two decades. But Marx never really left him, despite the prophecy of many a Sarvodaya warrior. He remained caught up with the revolutionary-romantic dimensions of Marxism, attempting to locate in Gandhian Sarvodaya the kernels of the ideal communist society that Marx dreamt of. Dismayed by the banality of conventional politics, he also tried to create an ideational framework for a radical democratic consensus that would lead to shared decision-making amongst a range of political actors, across a plurality of institutions. Perhaps even an ideological convergence on issues that needed to be addressed urgently. It was an incredible tightrope walk, destined to fail. One of the issues was the accretion of hatred against the minorities.

He cautioned that Hindu communalism was more pernicious than others because of the ease with which it could masquerade as nationalism and treat opposition to it as anti-national.

Through all this, Jayaprakash worked tirelessly against the drowning of dissenting voices. Taking on status-quoists with barely concealed derision, he continued to lead an uncompromising struggle against oppression and injustice. His long sojourn across villages in the Musahari area of Muzaffarpur, a hotbed of Naxalism, brought him close to the armed agrarian struggle of marginalized peasants and landless agricultural labourers. Looking at their grinding poverty and the clear possibility of a protracted people's war, he openly took sides and stated: 'I say with a due sense of responsibility that if convinced that there is no deliverance of people except through violence, Jayaprakash Narayan will also take to violence.' In an open letter to the villagers of Musahari (25 October 1972), he confessed that the portentous and tired Sarvodaya movement had failed to address the issue of landlessness, or any other important aspect of the raging agrarian crisis.

A prisoner of conscience, Jayaprakash's movement against the entitlement, nepotism, corruption, vacuity and venality of the governing elite came with the promise of social revolution. By 1973–74, Jayaprakash grew tired of waiting for the political cognoscenti to support him. He began looking at university campuses as sites of powerful dissent. Student anger was fuelling an unprecedented political radicalism and a profound sense of the dawn of a new era. Crusading with them, Jayaprakash was once again the man of the season. The movement may have moved in leaps and ruptures, but Jayaprakash found echoes of 1942 in what was happening on the streets of Bihar, the primary theatre of resistance. He believed that 'Sampoorna Kranti' (total revolution) was around the corner.

It was in the revolutionary space created by Jayaprakash that the definitive 1978 Bodh Gaya struggle for land rights for the landless was born. Positioned as a non-violent movement, the visceral struggle against the evasion of land ceiling laws nurtured a new spirit of militancy. Its underlying ideas and anarchical praxis may have been borrowed from the total revolution manifesto, but the movement was rooted in class struggle. Women were at the forefront of the movement.

Their decade-long struggle was the first in the history of social movements in South Asia to secure land rights for women. It addressed gender inequality at multiple levels, using a feminist lens to look at unwaged domestic labour and gendered violence.

There were some disturbing ambiguities in Jayaprakash's political stances. He betrayed himself when he acquiesced to Indira Gandhi's challenge of allowing the issue of the dissolution of the Bihar Assembly to be decided in the parliamentary arena through the ballot box. His decision to involve himself in the elections was questionable, as it foreclosed the possibility of a new kind of politics. He told my father that his aim was to restore freedom and democracy before radicalizing politics. But the momentum of revolution dissipated by 1978, betrayed by its own cheerleaders. What happened had an undeniably dark underbelly. Joseph Lelyveld's words about Gandhi came back to haunt Jayaprakash. Whatever his ideology stood for disappeared in a Kafkaesque maze. He was ultimately forced, like Lear, to see the limits of his ambition to remake the world. Emotionally bruised, he lost his energy and hope. No more a revolutionary figure, he retreated into history. Eventually even his words seemed to dry up.

Jayaprakash was not a textbook revolutionary, but he delighted in debunking received orthodoxies and revitalized new ways of thinking. The fact that he dreamt impossible dreams, pushed against certitudes, shunned power and remained an unputdownable dissident all his life is key to his relevance. The socialist and Gandhian ideas that he lived and died for certainly seem to be our best hopes in what Naomi Klein has called the make-or-break times.

This book is an ode to memory and its tenacious hold. If my father could rewind time, he would probably have gone back to being a socially gauche twenty-year-old when he met Jayaprakash and fell under his spell. His hero remained part of his life for what felt like his whole lifetime. The ten volumes of Jayaprakash's *Selected Works*, which he put together in his eighties, remain an ambitious tour de force, containing correspondence dense in political history and autobiographical fragments, pages from his diary with the minutiae of his preoccupations, economic and social treatises and nearly all his political writings. Studied linearly, they read like the history of a

major part of the last century. My father was at death's door when
he started this project. Our home was an incubator of JP memories,
inconsequential and profound, feeding my inchoate hunger for details.
After my father's death, it was left to me to glue the broken fragments
of his narrative.

My writing rests on my father's voluminous archive, paper trails
rich in knotty political details, a raft of books on Jayaprakash's writings
and thoughts, research at the National Archives and the private papers
and oral history section of the Nehru Memorial Museum and Library.
It was a hard ride, but my father's outline sandpapered the cracks in
my text. A part of Jayaprakash's hidden love life and other forgotten
personal nuggets that my father intended to keep outside the narrative
scaffold of the biography crept into mine. It was the living, breathing,
conflicted man that absorbed me: the tireless revolutionary who was
tormented by his own unanswered questions. Hence, even at the risk
of violating my father's innate sense of what was right, I decided to
retain them, hoping that the bones of the essential story would remain
the same.

April 2021   Sujata Prasad

1

The Formative Years

Jayaprakash Narayan was born on 11 October 1902. The British Empire was at its zenith and freedom from years of colonial repression seemed like a faraway dream. However, this was also when a more strident, unapologetic form of assertiveness against colonial policies started gaining traction, heralding revolutionary changes that no one could have foreseen.

Not much is known about Jayaprakash's childhood. A joining-of-the-dots quest starts at Sitabdiara, a quiet, bucolic village, susceptible to floods, situated near the confluence of the Ganga and the Saryu, 118 kilometres by road from Patna. The diaras are shifting geographical formations brimming with layers of history and hermetically sealed culture. Sitabdiara gets its name from a clever eighteenth-century zamindar, Sitab Rai, who was at war with the king of Awadh, but made a truce with the East India Company and settled here.

The village had a population of about 40,000, divided into several caste-based *tolas*. Jayaprakash's ancestral home was part of the 'Lala Tola', an area occupied by the educated Kayastha community. With the passing of the Tenancy Act of 1885, his ancestors received rights over a small portion of land leased to them by one of the rajas of Dumraon, an old princely state. But they were not part of the landed aristocracy. Rather, his forebears derived their income from government jobs. Jayaprakash's grandfather, Devkinandan Lal, a sub-inspector of police, was a radical, outspoken provocateur. According to a family anecdote, when faced with lacerating barbs, he once assaulted a white superintendent of police, escaping retribution only because the British officer did not want to own up to being beaten by a 'native' subordinate.

Jayaprakash's father, Harsu Dayal, was a well-educated man with more than a working knowledge of Arabic, Persian and English. He worked as a ziladar, a relatively minor officer in the irrigation department of the state government, charged with revenue collection in Shahabad district of Bihar. He was also a social activist and took a keen interest in the national movement. Jayaprakash's mother, Phulrani Devi, was from a landed family of Amardah, a village in the Chhapra (now Saran) district of Bihar. A strong opponent of women's seclusion, she too was exceptionally progressive.

At the time of Jayaprakash's birth, his family moved to their small home in a village in the Ballia district to escape the scourge of plague that had enveloped Sitabdiara. Jayaprakash's early days were unexceptional. He was late in cutting his milk teeth, leading his mother to remark that he was 'baul', the toothless one, innocent to the point of being a simpleton. The name stuck and he was called 'Baulji' by relatives and family friends, who occasionally taunted him for his long silences and inability to communicate.

As the oldest surviving son, he was cosseted by his mother and grandmother. Not one for the outdoors, he spent hours by himself creating imaginary alter egos. He created impenetrable walls of silence when it came to his father, forcing the latter to rather deprecatingly remark that Jayaprakash was an 'old' child. Their relationship remained in a perpetual flux of unravelling and remaking. It took years before Jayaprakash was able to look at the ambiguities of his father's life with some empathy.

Even as his solitariness enveloped him like an aura, Jayaprakash found his slice of paradise in playing with his younger siblings and in communion with birds and animals. He had two white pigeons, gifted to him by his father. When one of them died of heatstroke, he was inconsolable. He also adopted furry rabbits and yappy little mongrels living near his home and a pony who could not be tamed, but whom he loved unconditionally nonetheless.

His early education began at home. There were telling signs of a precocious intellect by the time Jayaprakash entered the primary school at Sitabdiara. One of the young teachers of his school, who was also a bodybuilder, became his role model and encouraged him to crawl out of his shell. He told him stories of young revolutionaries like Khudiram Bose, who was hanged at the age of eighteen. His stories seeped into Jayaprakash's consciousness. In 1912, when he was still a socially awkward boy of ten, he was sent to study at the Patna Collegiate School. Founded in 1835 by the East India Company, this was one of the best secondary schools in Bihar, known for legendary headmasters like Amjad Ali Khan and Professor Raas Masood, grandson of the founder of Aligarh Muslim University (AMU), Sir Syed Ahmed Khan.

To begin with, Jayaprakash stayed with a close relative, Shambhu Sharan, in Saraswati Bhawan, a hostel that was also an incubator of nationalist dreams. Many of the hostellers went on to become prominent public figures in Bihar.[1] Forbidden, subversive, political literature, smuggled in by visiting student leaders, shaped the political culture of the place. As he listened to political debates and occasional verbal fisticuffs, he let go of some of his reticence and reserve, and his oratorial skills began to develop. Historian Sir Jadunath Sarkar, who at that point was teaching at Patna College, lived close by. His house, the hub of young Bengali revolutionaries, was often raided by the police. The political churn in Saraswati Bhawan and Jadunath Sarkar's house foreshadowed Jayaprakash's own deeply nationalistic fervour.

Jayaprakash moved out of Saraswati Bhawan after some time to lead a more sequestered life with his elder sister, Chandramukhi, and brother-in-law, Braj Bihari Sahay. He developed a close bond with them. With the exception of an occasional afternoon spent watching a football match at the Patna Lawn (renamed Gandhi Maidan in 1948), he spent most of his time reading and writing and assisting his sister in housework. Rambriksh Benipuri has lovingly recorded the minutiae of Jayaprakash's life at this stage.[2] His Muslim English teacher inculcated in him a love for reading as a crucial dimension of living. In his spare time, Jayaprakash found nothing more enjoyable than browsing in the school library, or the personal library of his English teacher, rich with romantic poetry and fiction in Urdu, Hindi and English. He discovered the fire in Maithili Sharan Gupt's poetry and developed a love for new writing in journals like Mahabir Dwivedi's *Saraswati*, G.S. Vidyarthi's *Pratap* and Madan Mohan Malaviya's political weekly *Maryada*. His teacher also helped Jayaprakash understand the events and movements that were shaping the twentieth century. Jayaprakash's own essays, written for school competitions, were ground-breaking in style and content, and his teachers never ceased to express incredulity at the maturity of his teenage writing.

The political developments in India, too, were leaving an indelible impact on Jayaprakash. Inspired by the Swadeshi movement, he gave up the use of foreign cloth and footwear, turning to simple, coarse khadi kurtas and handmade shoes. In a quaint spirit of political baptism, he began studying the Bhagavad Gita and embraced its core message of selfless action. When Gopal Krishna Gokhale died in 1915, an emotional Jayaprakash wrote a long poem, styled as an obituary. Soon after, when Bal Gangadhar Tilak was passing through Patna, Jayaprakash bunked his classes in order to go to the railway station, a transgression for which he was severely admonished by the principal of his school.

Jayaprakash was fascinated by young revolutionaries who were laying down their lives for freedom from colonial rule. One of his classmates, Chhottan Singh, seemed to know the hideouts of these revolutionaries in Patna. On Jayaprakash's request, Chhottan arranged clandestine meetings with them; either at deserted ghats or at a derelict place near the university campus. Chhottan, however, was arrested, ending Jayaprakash's brief tryst with revolutionary struggle.

Jayaprakash completed his matriculation in 1919 with distinction, doing well enough to get a government scholarship of Rs 15 a month. Despite his keen interest in literature and politics, he opted to study science at Patna College. With his classic good looks, brooding eyes, a romantic-revolutionary persona and several scholarly attributes, he soon achieved an important place in the intellectual life of his college. When he was in his second year in college, Shambhu Sharan took him to meet Rajendra Prasad at the latter's residence. This chance meeting was a momentous event in Jayaprakash's life. It was here that he met Braj Kishore Prasad, a legendary social reformer, lawyer and freedom fighter, who at that point was searching for a suitable boy for his daughter, Prabhavati. When he saw Jayaprakash, he was convinced that his search was over.

Jayaprakash married fourteen-year-old Prabhavati on 14 October 1920.[3] This was a turning point in their lives. A feisty girl, Prabhavati was encouraged by her father to think independently and question convention. Braj Kishore Prasad was at the vanguard of a movement to break caste barriers and promote women's education. She accompanied him to his public meetings and was herself a passionate crusader for social justice. Growing up in a liberal household, she even dressed androgynously in a dhoti and short tunic. Prabhavati adored Gandhi and remained a diehard supporter of his throughout her life. Jayaprakash, too, had followed Gandhi's moves from the time he arrived at the Apollo Bunder in Bombay in January 1915. He was especially interested in the 1917 Champaran movement, when for nearly a year, Gandhi, Braj Kishore Prasad, Gorakh Prasad, Chandrabhaga Sahay and Babu Dharnidhar carried out the largest peasant survey in Indian history, recording more than 4000 oral testimonies.

The turning point in Jayaprakash and Prabhavati's life coincided with a major inflection point in history. India was in the throes of non-cooperation, a surging mass movement for 'Swaraj'. Non-cooperation was launched as a protest against the Rowlatt Act, the government's disregard of the demand put forward by the Khilafat movement, and incidents like the Jallianwala Bagh massacre, the failure of the Montague–Chelmsford Reforms and the dismemberment of Turkey by Britain and France.

The first phase of the struggle was to consist of non-cooperation with British courts, offices and educational institutions. Several eminent lawyers gave up their practice. Hundreds of students left college campuses and began eating, sleeping and dreaming politics. This marked the beginning of a new phase in the history of India's struggle for freedom, under the leadership of Gandhi, and was a remarkable testimony to what a movement could achieve against all odds.

Gandhi visited Patna with the message of non-cooperation in December 1920. Jayaprakash, present at the public meetings addressed by him, wanted to invest all his time, energy and passion into political work but was held back by a nagging sense of apprehension.

His misgivings disappeared a month later when the young and charismatic Maulana Abul Kalam Azad visited Patna and exhorted students to give up English education. In a powerful speech, Azad argued that if someone realized that he were sipping poison, he could not continue doing so on the grounds that no other drink was available. Education imparted in institutions run by the government, thundered Azad, was nothing but poison and students must renounce it immediately, regardless of the existence or non-existence of alternative arrangements for their studies.

Intoxicated by Azad's fiery speech and the heady possibilities of Swaraj, Jayaprakash cut his teeth in student politics by quitting college twenty days before his exams. He was convinced that non-cooperation was more worthy of his attention than the relentless pursuit of education. Several students of Patna College and BN College joined him. That was, indeed, the turning point in Jayaprakash's life. He felt 'lifted up to the skies' by a strong sense of exhilaration. 'That brief experience of soaring up with the winds of a great idea,' he observed later, 'left imprints on the inner being that time and much familiarity with the ugliness of reality have not removed.' He added, 'It was then that freedom became one of the beacon lights of my life, and it has remained so ever since. Freedom, with the passing of the years, transcended the mere freedom of my country and embraced freedom of man everywhere and from every sort of trammel—above all, it meant freedom of the human personality, freedom of the mind, freedom of the spirit.'[4]

Jayaprakash's decision was a jolt for his family. His father-in-law cautioned him against tempestuousness and pointed out that the Congress party's directive was only to boycott British-run educational institutions. He was persuaded to join Bihar Vidyapeeth,[5] an institution founded by Mahatma Gandhi on land donated by the eminent lawyer and Congress leader Maulana Mazharul Haque. Jayaprakash obtained an ISC degree from the Vidyapeeth, securing a first division.

Following the Chauri Chaura incident,[6] the non-cooperation movement petered out. Many students who had walked out of government-controlled educational institutions returned to them, but not Jayaprakash. The Vidyapeeth could only provide education up to the intermediate level. Given his hardwired sense of what was right, he was conflicted about studying at a place that received grants from the government. For a few months, he lived and studied science at the residence of a family friend, Phuldeva Sahay, a professor of chemistry at the Banaras Hindu University (BHU). But he refused to join the university since it received grants from the government. It was around this time that he met Bhola Pant, a young Garhwali student seeking to study in America. Their friendship deepened, and eventually Jayaprakash was also attracted to the idea of studying there. A lecture delivered by Swami Satyadev Parivrajak on his experience of working his way through college in America was an added inspiration.

Jayaprakash's decision was, however, a severely discomfiting one for his parents. His mother was especially distraught and he had to work hard to convince her. He received strong support from an unexpected quarter. His wife, Prabhavati, then only sixteen, recognized the potentially transformative aspect of her husband's decision. She wrote to him saying that she was happy with his decision and hoped that on his return he would devote himself to the national cause. If there were any heartaches, questions and doubts, she kept them to herself. Lively and exuberant, she accepted his decision with impressive calmness. She and Jayaprakash were slowly getting to know each other. She had visited his home for what was known as the 'gauna ceremony'[7] very briefly but met him frequently at her parents' place. She treasured her time with him, mirrored many of his commitments and shared his nationalistic fervour. Even so, she declined his proposal to accompany him, knowing instinctively that it would stretch him no end!

At this point, Jayaprakash's father was posted as ziladar in a place called Nasriganj in the Shahabad district. It is from there that Jayaprakash set out for Calcutta to begin his sea voyage to the United States aboard a small cargo liner, *Janus*, which began its journey to Kobe on 16 May 1922. From its second-class deck in the ambient daylight, attired in Western clothes hurriedly bought in Calcutta, Jayaprakash watched India's vanishing coastline with some trepidation and hope. The expenses of travel up to Kobe were met partly by a grant from an educational foundation in Calcutta. His father paid the rest of the travel cost, in addition to giving him $600 to take care of contingent expenses.

A viscerally intense experience, it was long-haul travel in a no-frills option. He had four travelling companions: one from Telangana, one from Hyderabad and two from Bengal.[8] The sea was rough and at one point in the South China Sea, *Janus* found itself in the tail of a typhoon. Despite severe seasickness, Jayaprakash survived the ordeal and tried to make the most of brief halts at Rangoon, Penang, Singapore and Hong Kong. From Kobe, he went to Osaka, and then to the glistening seafront of Yokohama, from where he set sail for the United States after an interlude of several weeks spent travelling and proofreading for the Japanese national daily, the *Mainichi*. His German liner, *Taiyo Maru*, entered the San Francisco Bay on 8 October, three days before his twentieth birthday, after an eighteen-day voyage through vivid blue seas.

The campus of the University of California, Berkeley, a haven of calm with lush lawns and beautiful buildings, worked its serendipitous magic on Jayaprakash. He found temporary shelter in the attic of the Nalanda Club, a den of Indian students. The academic term had however already begun. Since he needed to wait until the following January, he thought it prudent to earn some money. While hunting for a job in Marysville, a neighbourhood town, he met Sikh activists from the Ghadar Party, headquartered in San Francisco. They persuaded him to stay back for a few days, eager to get details of the non-cooperation movement. On his third day in Marysville, he ran into Sher Khan, a Pathan overseer, externed from India. Khan directed him to a large orchard near Yuba City. A little off the beaten track, but somewhat idyllic, his job involved sun-drying large quantities of grapes to turn them into raisins. He worked there for about a month, at 40 cents an hour. Working nine hours per day—with half an hour's break for lunch and Sundays off—Jayaprakash earned $21.60 per week.

Jayaprakash's living space was scruffy and basic. It consisted of a long wooden shed without furniture but with a raised platform along the walls, covered with straw. The entire team of workers slept there, sharing an intimate space. It was old-fashioned community living with three dozen workers, mostly Pathans from the North-West Frontier

Province. They liked the young man from India and crowded around him in the evenings for thought-provoking conversations about the freedom struggle. Out of regard for him, they stopped bringing beef into their common kitchenette. As no agricultural work was available near Marysville in winter, Jayaprakash returned to Berkeley to wash dishes and wait tables at restaurants. On Sundays, he moved around town, taking up whatever odd jobs were available.

In January, he was directly admitted into the second year, getting a year's credit for his intermediate science degree. After completing his first term as a student of mathematics, chemical engineering and biology at Berkeley, Jayaprakash moved out again at the end of May, to work first as a grape picker at a scenic vineyard in the Sacramento Valley, and then as a packer and carton mender in a fruit and jam canning factory at San Jose. He enjoyed his time at Berkeley but had to leave when non-Californian citizens were forced to pay nearly double the fees, amounting to $300 a year. He was persuaded by his friend Bhola Pant, studying at the State University of Iowa, to migrate there. Iowa's tuition fee of about $80 was far more affordable. So, after studying in California for two terms, Jayaprakash moved to the 1700-acre university campus at Iowa, a Midwestern US state positioned between the Missouri and Mississippi rivers. He shared Bhola's room. The adjoining rooms too had Indian inmates. Jyoti Basu's brother Kiran was one of them. They cooked their meals together and bonded over cups of coffee. In addition to his science curriculum, Jayaprakash studied French and German.

During the winter and summer breaks, the search for employment took Jayaprakash to Chicago, a city witnessing explosive growth. Several Indian students formed themselves into groups and rented shacks in the gritty slums of Chicago. They paid $10 per month, usually two persons to a room, sharing a weathered double bed. Rooms were not easy to get due to the colour prejudice and xenophobia. During weeks that hinged on uncertainty, Jayaprakash worked in a terracotta factory, a steel foundry with walls of jagged iron sheets, a butcher house (looking after refrigeration plants), in restaurants and departmental stores, once even as a vendor of a whitening cream in the narrow alleys inhabited by African Americans. By and large, coloured people were an anathema and had to strictly play by the rules. Very few people knew about India. He was once asked if he was from Honduras.

At Iowa, Jayaprakash did exceptionally well academically, getting straight A's in all subjects except in drawing, which was a part of the course of chemical engineering that he was registered for, his only failure as a student. After spending about a year at Iowa, he felt the need for a more stimulating environment. At that time, the University of Wisconsin at Madison had in its faculty scholars known for their iconoclastic, progressive outlook. Wisconsin was also considered one of the most liberal states in the US—deriving its reputation from senators like Robert Follette, who pushed through a historic resolution demanding investigation into the most infamous scandal involving a presidential administration. Jayaprakash moved to Madison in the summer of 1924. He studied there for the next couple of years, while continuing to earn a living doing odd jobs like spring cleaning, clearing snow and washing dishes.

Jayaprakash drew a richly textured portrait of his time at Madison for my father. The campus, vibrant and infused with radical politics, opened its arms to him. He suddenly had a lot to look forward to. It was here that he was exposed to Marxism. One of his closest friends was Abram Landy, a Polish Jew, who was a member of the student wing of the American Communist Party. He loaned Jayaprakash Marxist literature, which the latter read with great relish. Books that unmasked fissures along economic and class lines provided him with rare intimate insights into the dominant political processes. These books radicalized Jayaprakash. He went through almost all the writings of Marx, Engels, Lenin, Trotsky and Plekhanov available in English. He was addicted to the *Daily Worker*, a newsletter that carried articles of Marxist scholars like John Spivak, Davis Karr, Peter Fryer, and the politically charged songs of Woody Guthrie.

With the help of Landy, who translated some of Marx's writings in German and the vast corpus of work of Marxist revolutionaries like Karl Liebknecht, Rosa Luxemburg and theoretician Karl Kautsky for his friends, Jayaprakash became familiar with those writings not available in English at the time, in the process acquiring a dynamic perspective of class and class consciousness. He also read the writings of M.N. Roy, an important member of the Communist International and frequently quoted from Roy's *The Aftermath of Non-Cooperation* and *India in Transition*.

Jayaprakash became a member of the communist cell at the university and participated in protests and public meetings. He also came in contact with young American students of northern and central European origin who regarded the Soviet Union as a powerful citadel and testing ground of Marxism. Even though America's total wealth more than doubled between 1920 and 1929, the racial and economic inequality in contemporary American society made the Soviet experiment in socialism the focal point of their hopes for a future based on social justice. Looking back at that period several years later, Jayaprakash wrote, 'Strangely enough, it was in the land of resilient and successful capitalism . . . that I became a convert to Marxism, or more precisely, to Soviet communism as it was then.'[9]

Jayaprakash began dreaming of a socialist revolution in India, comparable to the events of October 1917 in Russia. 'The Marxian science of revolution seemed to offer a surer and quicker road to it than Gandhiji's technique of civil disobedience and non-cooperation,' he recalled later, adding that, 'the thrilling success of the great Lenin, accounts of which we consumed with unsaturated hunger, seemed to establish beyond doubt the supremacy of the Marxian way to revolution.'[10]

The Russian revolution resonated with Jayaprakash due to the analytical insights it offered for radicalizing the Indian national movement to overturn colonial rule and create a new order, free of inequality. He was gripped by what Marx and Engels wrote in *The Communist Manifesto*, 'What the bourgeoisie therefore produces above all, are its own grave diggers.' Recalling those heady days, he wrote, 'Marxism provided another beacon of light for me: equality and brotherhood. Freedom was not enough. It must mean freedom for all—even the lowliest—and this freedom must include freedom from exploitation, from hunger, from poverty . . . At that time, I was not very certain about Gandhiji's stand on the vital question of equality which captivated me as much as the ideal of freedom. As a matter of fact, Roy's writings of those days (though Roy too later travelled far from those positions) persuaded me to believe that Gandhiji was against the social revolution and would, in a moment of crisis, hasten to uphold the system of exploitation and inequality. I did not understand then that Gandhiji had his own conception of the social revolution and the means to achieve it.'[11]

This new-found interest in social revolution encouraged Jayaprakash to think in non-clichéd ways. He embraced atheism and felt that the study of society and social change was his real calling. The shift of his academic interest from science to sociology meant that he would have to spend more time on his undergraduate degree but that did not deflect him from his chosen path. At that time, Edward Alsworth Ross, one of the founders of melioristic sociology,[12] was teaching at the university. This was an added attraction. Jayaprakash combined his study of sociology with courses on bacteriology and calculus.

That Jayaprakash was radicalized was evident. The crème de la crème of the Communist Party of America tried to draw him into their circle. He also made a mark on Manuel Gomez, of Mexican origin, who was in charge of the oriental wing of the Communist Party of America. Gomez directed Jayaprakash to complete his training in Marxist thought and revolutionary action at the Moscow Institute of Oriental Studies, telling him not to bother about his living expenses in Moscow. Once Jayaprakash reached there, the Soviet authorities would take care of the entire gamut of his needs.

Caught in the heady, unsettling dream of studying in Russia, Jayaprakash sought money for his travel from his father, who was aghast at the idea. He wrote to him immediately, advising him to complete his studies and return home without getting involved in the Russian adventure. Fearing unpleasant altercations with his father, Jayaprakash sought the intervention of Rajendra Prasad. Prasad responded by listing the difficulties he would have to face if he went to Moscow. He was of the view that since Jayaprakash's objective in life was national service, the proper place for him to live and work was India. Moreover, a Moscow sojourn could lead to his being barred from returning to India.

Rajendra Prasad's letter was like a kick in the gut. In the interregnum that followed, Jayaprakash moved to Chicago to look for a job. The year 1926 was drawing to a close and a severe economic recession was casting its shadow on the labour markets. There were no soup kitchens or breadlines yet, but certainly a sharp decrease in job opportunities. Jayaprakash lived in spartan conditions and had to trudge through the snow-covered streets of Chicago, for days, in search of employment. Employment eluded him; even in places with vacancies, he was told that no coloured people were wanted. Unable to clothe or feed himself adequately, he subsisted on a diet of rice and canned beans, washed down with a cup of coffee. Given his poor diet, his resilience was severely limited. One day, when he did not have even five cents in his pocket, he caught a severe chill that developed into a life-threatening pneumonia. Hospitalized for several weeks, he had to deal with a bad case of sepsis after a botched tonsillitis operation. He remained bedridden for about five months. An Indian expatriate, Chandra Singh, and some of his Indian friends tried to help him claw his way back to health. His illness also triggered a huge financial crisis: he incurred a debt of $900 and his father was forced to mortgage a portion of his land to bail him out.

Jayaprakash's close friend Abram Landy, meanwhile, managed to get a teaching assignment at the University of Ohio and persuaded him to move there and share his apartment. It was at Ohio State University that Jayaprakash finally got his undergraduate degree in 1928. His good performance earned him a fellowship of $30 per month for his master's programme. In addition, he earned a monthly salary of $80 as a graduate assistant in sociology, liberating him from the travails of manual labour and finally exposing him to an engaging cornucopia of museums and cinema theatres.

With the arrival of sound in 1927, cinema was coming of age. Jayaprakash enjoyed the melodrama and romance of Hollywood films. Actresses like Mary Pickford and Greta Garbo set his heart aflutter. American theatre, too, was coming of age. Jayaprakash enjoyed the social realism of Eugene O' Neill's plays and took his American friends to see Sudraka's *Mrichchakatika*, staged by a group of Bengali students. Fitzgerald had dubbed the American post-war years as 'the Jazz Age', and Jayaprakash too made the most of it by listening to jazz bands and going to the dance floor to learn the Charleston and the flea hop.

Tennis was trendy and he learnt to play it. Known for his radical views and laconic charm, he was a beau idéal. Many young girls were drawn to him.

The following year, Jayaprakash completed the requirements for his degree. His thesis, with 'cultural variation' as its theme, was discussed, analysed and adjudged the best essay of the year by the faculty of the university. Jayaprakash's idealism and vision for mankind's future, as well as his deep interest in the roots of social processes and social change, were clearly noticeable in his essay. He wrote with the certitude of an op-ed polemicist, concluding that 'the primary function of the sociologist is the study of social or cultural change'. Without it, one may be predisposed to become a 'social quack' but never a social scientist.[13]

Following his excellent performance, Jayaprakash planned to work for a doctoral degree in sociology. His destiny, however, willed otherwise. His mother fell seriously ill and sent word that she wished to see him. Now, nothing was more important for him than returning home to her. Cash-strapped as usual, he hitch-hiked from Chicago to New York, reaching London with the help of a friend in September 1929. With the Wall Street crash of October 1929 barely a month away, there was heavy unemployment in the city, foreclosing any chances of finding a job that would fund his trip back home. The money that his father eventually sent took a few weeks to arrive. Jayaprakash lived with Indian acquaintances at Gower Street in Bloomsbury, surviving on bread and margarine.

Jayaprakash's time in London helped him look beyond the city's clichés. He observed everyday life walking along the Thames embankment, Trafalgar Square, the London Bridge, Piccadilly Circus, Soho and other places. He went to Oxford to meet Dr S. Radhakrishnan, who held the coveted position of Spalding Professor of Eastern Religion and Ethics. He also tried to seek out Rajani Palme Dutt, one of the founder members of the Communist Party of Great Britain, at the party office. Dutt was in Brussels, but he managed to meet Dutt's elder brother Clemens who introduced him to several young communists. When Clemens asked him about his plan, he answered with consummate clarity: 'I will join the Congress and try to radicalize it. This is what Lenin too advocated in the Second Congress of the

Communist International when he said that communist parties should not isolate themselves from revolutionary liberation movements in colonies, even if the movements were being run by bourgeois leaders.'[14]

When the money from India finally arrived, Jayaprakash boarded the *Orient Lines*, sailing to Australia. He disembarked at Colombo, took a train to Trincomalee Port from where he boarded a ship to Dhanushkodi. From Dhanushkodi, a train brought him to Madras and then to Calcutta. He reached Patna only by the end of November 1929 and from there went to his village Sitabdiara, dressed in a dhoti-kurta borrowed from a friend.

Although Jayaprakash could not embark on his doctoral degree, the seven years spent in the United States were seminal in shaping him. The testimonials from his teachers were special.[15] Professor A.B. Wolfe, who taught courses on the history of economic thought and the economics of population, wrote that Jayaprakash was 'a young man of more than ordinary independence and maturity of thought'. The professor added: 'He shows distinctly an inquiring turn of mind and a critical capacity, rare even in the better class of graduate students.' Professor F.E. Dumley of the Department of Sociology affirmed that, intellectually, Jayaprakash ranked 'as high as or higher than any student I have ever had. He is a careful and critical thinker and a searcher after truth; of course, he is an avid reader. He is, in every sense, a scholar in the making.'

Professor Albert P. Weiss wrote that in his course on theoretical psychology, Jayaprakash was 'one of the brightest students' he had ever had. Professor Richard Steinmetz testified, 'Perhaps Mr. J.P. Narayan's most remarkable trait, to one living in a materialistic civilization, is his idealism. It infuses his daily life as well as his world outlook. It has been my experience in living with him to be surprised again and again by little unexpected acts of unselfishness.'

Most of Jayaprakash's associates were also smitten by the handsome, elegant young man with a quiet humour who kept track of exciting new developments in politics, literature and philosophy, especially the writings of Anatole France, Henrik Ibsen, Maxim Gorky, Bertrand Russell and George Bernard Shaw. He also read contemporary fiction: books by Ernest Hemingway, Virginia Woolf, Gertrude Stein,

T.S. Eliot, F. Scott Fitzgerald, Theodore Dreiser, many of whom lived as expatriates in Paris. And, of course, he devoured every book on Marxism that he could get his hands on, whether borrowed or bought second-hand with dog-eared, battered covers. Showing a polite reticence in accepting a cigarette while engaging with friends, the only time he smoked was at a farewell party held in his honour in New York on the eve of his departure, away from the febrile campus atmosphere.

2

Evolution of Political Life

Jayaprakash returned from America at a critical moment in Indian history. Though Gandhi was still a dominant force in Indian politics, revolutionaries like Bhagat Singh, Chandra Shekhar Azad, Ashfaqulla Khan and Surya Sen were radicalizing the movement through their subversive, powerful acts of heroism and sacrifice. Notions of revolution were stirring in the minds of even the politically quiescent young men and women. Peasants and industrial workers were showing signs of assertiveness by forming a political party in 1927 and using it as a platform to fight for their rights.

This new spirit was epitomized by the events that transpired during the 1927 Congress session held in Madras. Jawaharlal Nehru had recently returned from a long sojourn across Western Europe and Russia. During his travels, he attended the International Congress against Colonial Oppression and Imperialism at Brussels, where he was appointed honorary president of the Marxist-Leninist 'League against Imperialism'. The grounding in Marxism received at Brussels was consonant with his admiration for Lenin, who perhaps had the strongest impact on an entire generation of radicals and revolutionaries. Viewing imperialism as the highest stage of capitalism, Nehru was convinced that if imperialism had to go, so must capitalism. Radicalized by the European tradition, he moved for the passage of the historic Purna Swaraj (complete independence) resolution.[1] Absent from the Madras session, Gandhi was miffed at the 'hastily conceived' and 'thoughtlessly passed' resolution. The spectre of dominion status loomed large within the Congress. As its unapologetic defender, Gandhi warned Nehru that he was proceeding too fast.[2]

Although Nehru was upset by Gandhi's reproach, he continued unabated with his radical agenda. Nehru joined the movement for a nationwide boycott of the Indian Statutory Commission under Sir John Simon's chairmanship. The Simon Commission was appointed to consider whether India was ready for another instalment of constitutional reforms. Its presence was considered offensive by all shades of Indian nationalists because of its solely British membership. Wherever the commission went, it was greeted by strident cries of 'Simon, Go Back'. The government hit back with repressive measures. At Lahore, Lala Lajpat Rai, a former president of the Congress, was severely beaten when the police lathicharged a demonstration led by him.

Nehru braved police batons while leading a similar demonstration in Lucknow. His charisma, charm and revolutionary verve spurred the younger leadership of the Congress to continue to dream of complete independence and the inclusion of economic issues in its policies and programmes. Their time came when Gandhi ensured that Nehru was elected to preside over the Congress session at Lahore, despite serious opposition.

Nehru made the most of this extraordinary opportunity. His opening address as president of the Congress, in a makeshift city of tents on the bank of the Ravi in Lahore in December 1929, set the tone for a springtime of hope and optimism. The 'Purna Swaraj' declaration was promulgated to ebullient cries of 'long live the revolution' and unfurling of the flag of independence. Gandhi, who had been advocating caution, was forced to capitulate to the demand for complete independence. 26 January was declared as Independence Day. The stage seemed set for launching the Civil Disobedience Movement.

This was the contextual milieu surrounding Jayaprakash's arrival in India. He and Prabhavati went to Wardha to meet Gandhi. Gandhi showered him with love and showed an enormous interest in his ideological positions. Their differences set aside, Jayaprakash allowed himself to be drawn into the maelstrom of the Gandhian struggle for freedom. Prabhavati was already immersed in the constructive side of Gandhian politics that included a relentless crusade for eradication of untouchability, crusade for communal harmony and for promotion of khadi and self-sustaining village industries, national education and gender equity. She lived in Gandhi's ashram at Sabarmati, a world away from the comfort and largesse of deep-seated privilege that she was used to.

Prabhavati took to ashram life like a fish to water, endearing herself to all its inmates. She spent hours on ashram chores—including tasks normally considered abhorrent, like cleaning toilets.[3] Gandhi took a special interest in her education. She was taught Sanskrit and Gujarati. At Jayaprakash's specific suggestion, a working knowledge of English was imparted to her. She read and recited the Gita and the Ramayana, Gandhi's favourite texts. She was also encouraged to learn spinning, cooking, washing and cleaning.

Gandhi encouraged Prabhavati to maintain a regular diary and follow a fixed daily schedule that involved waking up before dawn at 4 a.m. for morning prayers, a ritual which was repeated before dusk at 5 p.m. Reminiscing about her time at the ashram for the oral history project of the Nehru Memorial Museum and Library (NMML), Prabhavati said, 'Once there was a pile of utensils waiting to be washed. I saw Gandhiji washing them. I ran to take over the chore, but he yelled at me. He had asked me to recite the Gita. He said: "Do the work that has been assigned to you. Why have you come here?"'[4] Slowly her mind too rejected the division between high and low. She saw deeper insights running through a supposedly banal routine and had no problems with the ashram's code of rules and observances. This included maintaining celibacy.

The bond between Gandhi and Prabhavati deepened. Jayaprakash's long absences, made worse by infrequent correspondence, had made her somewhat forlorn and low-spirited. Gandhi pulled her out of her wallowing loneliness and played the role of a doting father. We get glimpses of their closeness in letters exchanged when he was away on tour, or when she was away from the ashram. Some of her anguish at parting with Gandhi found its way into her letters. Gandhi seemed to find a way through even her unspoken words and took special care to calm her on such occasions: 'I can understand your misery . . . Physical separation will, however, always be there. Shake off anxiety and be firm and devoted to your duty. Keep writing to me.'[5] A few days later, he wrote again: 'Work as much as you wish to but do not let it tell on your health. Never grieve over separation. We will always be confronted with . . . separation from loved ones.'[6]

Replying to Prabhavati's grouse that he was not writing frequently enough, Gandhi wrote back playfully: 'Do you expect a letter from me by every post? What a girl! Well, I shall try to write.'[7] Next day, he wrote to her again: 'Do not take my absence to heart. Some day this body is bound to leave forever. Why be distressed over separation from it? We should find happiness in devotion to a cause for which our death would have a meaning.'[8] In another letter he says, 'I tore off your letter soon after reading it, but could not understand why you asked me to destroy it. There was nothing personal in it.'[9]

By now, like other women in the ashram, Prabhavati was obsessively drawn to Gandhi. When he left for a tour of Bengal and Burma in March 1929, she was disconsolate. Gandhi wrote a mildly admonishing letter to her after reaching Calcutta in early March 1929: 'Your nervousness caused me pain. You have to get rid of it. I can get solid work out of you only when I can make you live anywhere by yourself.'[10] Four days later, he wrote from Rangoon: 'You must be well by now. I want to be free from anxiety on your account. That can only be when you become brave and self-reliant.'[11] On another occasion, Gandhi was forced to accede to Prabhavati's wish not to be left behind at the ashram while he was moving from place to place. She treasured their shared time, content with the strictly rationed slice forked out for her every day during his 'charkha' sessions.

That even Gandhi could not easily reconcile with Prabhavati's periods of absence (such as when she went to visit her parents or in-laws) is evident from his letters: 'In my view now you are wasting time there. Ba (Kasturba) says, "Won't Prabha (Prabhavati) come to me?" She repeatedly asks, "When is Prabha coming?" I have to reach Allahabad on the 19th. If you can manage then come with me from there.'[12] He seemed to be aware that his presence in her life far outweighed the connection she felt for Jayaprakash. 'Till you have absolutely recovered you should stay with me. Your health is related to your mind. If you are near me you are likely to feel good.'[13] At the same time, Gandhi also encouraged her to work on her relationship with Jayaprakash and make an honest effort to understand his political views. He kept track of Jayaprakash's letters to Prabhavati and worried if there was inordinate delay.

At peace with a monastic existence at the ashram, Prabhavati took the celibacy vow. It was an audacious decision, a trailblazing choice propelled by a Gandhian, womanist perspective, taken without consulting Jayaprakash. When questioned on this, she said that her decision to remain celibate was not impetuous. She had been inclined towards celibacy for a long time. While stigmatization of the erotic at the ashram may have strengthened her resolve, Gandhi did not encourage her to embrace it. If anything, he was extremely discomfited by the idea and advised caution, asking her to first discuss the issue with Jayaprakash. Prabhavati, however, was adamant. For her the vow was a fruition of her desire to dedicate her life to the nation, and since Jayaprakash too was dedicated to the same goal, she did not see him objecting vehemently. She did write to Jayaprakash. Even if Jayaprakash found her decision repugnant and her judgement flawed, he wrote back calmly saying that a delicate matter of this kind needed to be discussed threadbare and could not be resolved through letters.

Prabhavati's refusal to reconsider her decision was heart-wrenching for Jayaprakash, a dismantling of romantic dreams nurtured during his seven-year separation from his wife. Even though her vow was destined to make their life together a difficult tightrope walk, he did not for a moment blame Gandhi and was appalled at Gandhi's suggestion of a second marriage. He enveloped his sense of disquiet and emotional tumult in spells of silence. Undercurrents of tension continued to haunt Jayaprakash's relationship with Prabhavati for a long time. Prabhavati kept the integrity of her vow but Jayaprakash was certainly no celibate. Many women were drawn to him, some with devastating consequences.

Jayaprakash met Jawaharlal Nehru in Lahore during the Congress session and was as starry-eyed as other young people of his generation.[14] He described his meeting with Nehru as a case of 'love at first sight'.[15] The attraction was mutual, borne out of a spirit of kinship. Nehru had a modern outlook. His vision of socialism was romantic, undogmatic, deeply personal and even poetic. Jayaprakash and Nehru spent hours brainstorming socialist ideas and seemed to agree on most of its succinct tag lines. Specifically, they spoke about challenging existing power relations and were convinced that economic struggle was destined to form the core of the national movement.

At this point, Jayaprakash was eyeing a teaching assignment at the BHU to ease his father's financial problems.[16] Nehru weaned him away from this idea by asking him to take charge of the newly created department of labour research in the office of the All India Congress Committee at Allahabad on a monthly salary of Rs 150. This was an extraordinary position for a young man not yet twenty-eight. Jayaprakash always acknowledged Nehru's seminal role in launching his political career. Writing to Gandhi before setting off for Allahabad, Jayaprakash said, 'I have great respect for him (Nehru) and my ideas are to a great extent similar to his . . . I shall, therefore, derive great satisfaction if somehow I can be with him.'[17] When he moved into a makeshift accommodation with Prabhavati at Allahabad, Nehru, then in Naini Jail, wrote to his father asking him to hand over refurbished rooms reserved for him at the Swaraj Bhawan to Jayaprakash and Prabhavati. Fond of Prabhavati, Nehru treated her like a sister and showered on Jayaprakash the warm affection given to a younger brother.

A relationship of mutual trust also developed between Prabhavati and Nehru's wife, Kamala. When they were together, they managed to keep aside the warp and weft of their separate lives, letting their hair down in close companionship. They sustained their friendship during periods of separation by writing long, unremittingly poignant and candid letters. These were letters that did not provoke or exasperate, but helped them deal with the ambiguities of their lives and their tenuous relationships. 'I cannot express how happy I feel when I am with you and especially when I think of your poor health I feel I should never leave you,' wrote Prabhavati.[18] Beseeching Prabhavati to join her in Anand Bhawan for a few days when she was away at the Gandhi ashram, Kamala wrote in a similar vein: 'Please come and stay with me. We will be so happy together.'[19] In another letter from Calcutta, she asked Prabhavati to bring a bunch of cheap khadi saris from Khadi Bhandar in Patna for her daughter Indira.[20] Several letters were exchanged during Kamala's struggle with tuberculosis at Bhowali. The steady flow of letters stopped only with Kamala's death on 28 February 1936.

For some time his work with the department of labour research absorbed Jayaprakash completely. He wrote letters to the secretary, All India Trade Union Congress (AITUC)[21] and also to secretaries of the fifty-two affiliated unions of the AITUC for past copies of publication, reports, gazettes and bulletins to begin work on a Labour Year Book. He established contacts with the British Labour Party. He also tried to wean back trade unions that had drifted away from the Congress. And yet there were moments of disenchantment. He confessed to Gandhi: 'At times I doubt whether it is right for me to devote my time to research in the present state of my country. Well, let us see how long I can repress myself.'[22]

His only other distraction at this point was the visit of his sociology professor, Herbert Miller. He took a break from his labour commitments to take Professor Miller to Patna, Nalanda and the Kashi Vidyapeeth at Banaras. One of the scholars they met at the Vidyapeeth was Narendra Deva, a renowned Marxist historian and philosopher who would later become one of Jayaprakash's closest and dearest comrades-in-arms. Their last destination was Allahabad where Jayaprakash had arranged a meeting with Nehru at Anand Bhawan. Recording an interesting anecdote related to this meeting for NMML's oral history project, Jayaprakash recalled, 'We were sitting in a large room overlooking Nehru's library and office which were crammed to the ceilings with books. Glancing at them Miller asked, "Living in this setting, is working for Socialism easy?" Nehru replied with a smile, "It actually increases the work efficiency." Professor Miller was extremely amused at this reply.'[23]

Even as the Civil Disobedience Movement was picking up momentum, Gandhi wrote to the viceroy, Lord Irwin, on 2 March 1930, offering to put off the impending movement if the government made certain concessions. These became famously known as Gandhi's 'eleven demands', a radical manifesto that called for, among other things, reduction by half of land revenue, military expenditure and salaries of civil servants; a protective tariff against foreign cloth; the discharge of all political prisoners; and abolition of the salt tax. Gandhi's eleven points were meant to secure legitimacy for the ensuing struggle. As expected, though much to the chagrin of those who expected a positive response, the viceroy remained impassive.

Gandhi launched the Civil Disobedience Movement and made defiance of the salt law the focal point for politicizing the masses. He was confident that a well-publicized protest against it would draw the widest possible popular support. Events proved him right. On 12 March 1930, he left Sabarmati Ashram on foot for Dandi, a village on the western coast of India, and broke the law by scooping up a lump of natural salt from the sea on 6 April. It was an epochal moment that received the unprecedented support of the European and American media. Contraband salt was manufactured at several places. Liquor and foreign fabric shops were picketed. Government institutions were boycotted. There were strikes and demonstrations.

The obstacles faced by the movement were formidable. Irwin promulgated several ordinances: the Bengal Ordinance to suppress dissent, the Press Ordinance to force nationalist papers to suspend publication, the Lahore Conspiracy Case Ordinance, the Prevention of Intimidation Ordinance, the Sholapur Martial Law Ordinance and Ordinance to Regulate Military Administration. Many Congress committees were declared unlawful. These acts of repression strengthened the nationwide spirit of dissent. Nehru's arrest on 4 April, while boarding a train at the Allahabad junction, followed by Gandhi's arrest on 4 May from his camp at Karachi, led to a further intensification of the agitation, bringing the total number of persons sentenced to various terms of imprisonment by January 1931 to nearly a lakh. This included eminent women leaders like Sarojini Naidu, Kamaladevi Chattopadhyay and Rukmini Lakshmipathi.

To his lasting regret, Jayaprakash could not take an active part in this struggle. While the movement was gathering momentum, his mother fell seriously ill, and it soon became clear that her end was near. Jayaprakash rushed from Allahabad to his village to be by her side. She died on 25 September 1930. Then, his father was paralysed and the entire responsibility of looking after the family and paying off the considerable debt incurred for his American sojourn fell upon Jayaprakash. He was torn between his commitment to the movement and the bevy of personal problems surrounding him. Not finding an easy solution, he finally wrote to Gandhi for advice. Gandhi told him to settle his family issues and asked Ghanshyamdas Birla, the millionaire industrialist, who was also his follower, to help Jayaprakash. Birla appointed him as his private secretary. Based in Calcutta, Jayaprakash helped the industrialist with his correspondence and some related work, but was not immune from the political storm raging in the country.

The Civil Disobedience Movement was suspended as a result of the Gandhi–Irwin Pact signed in March 1931. Congress workers arrested during the movement were released. The AICC office in Allahabad resumed a somewhat normal pace of work soon after. Jayaprakash quit his Calcutta job to return to Allahabad to take charge of the office. In addition to routine work, one of the first tasks before him was to document the history of the Civil Disobedience Movement. This history, described in the Annual Report of the Congress Working Committee, was never published. In the mutilated copy lying amongst the AICC papers at the NMML, there is a foreword signed by the three general secretaries of the Congress at that time: Syed Mahmud, Jairamdas Doulat Ram and Jawaharlal Nehru. They express their gratitude to Jayaprakash and Raghubir Sahai, who was also working in the AICC at that time. While Sahai collected the material for the report and assisted in its drafting, the bulk of the writing burden was shouldered by Jayaprakash.

While a major portion of the history of the Civil Disobedience Movement consists of factual information concerning the acts of resistance by Congress volunteers and the crackdown by the government, the prodigious text also underlines the significance of the movement. The following paragraph relating to the role of women serves as an example: 'The civil disobedience movement of 1930 worked many a miracle but there was no greater miracle than the part of the women in this campaign. How deeply it had affected the people and touched the mainsprings of Indian society was evidenced by the social revolution it brought about silently and without apparent effort. The shy and retiring women of India, unused to the rough and tumble of politics, came out of the shelter of their homes and insisted on being in the forefront of the struggle.'

The report gave details of the number of women arrested and convicted in five provinces: 200 in Bombay, 200 in Bengal, 221 in Delhi, 109 in Gujarat, 100 in Punjab, and estimated an overall figure of about 1500. The Muslim participation in the movement was significant, especially in Punjab, Bombay, Delhi and the North-West Frontier Province. The report mentions that many of the office-bearers of the Jamiat-ul-Ulema went to jail. The report also documented instances of police repression and terrorism.

The political situation remained tense even after the Gandhi–Irwin Pact. The government did not pay heed to the widespread demand for commutation of the death sentence handed to the young revolutionaries Bhagat Singh, Sukhdev and Rajguru for their role in the assassination of a police officer whose baton blows were suspected to have caused the death of Lala Lajpat Rai. They were executed on 23 March 1931, barely eighteen days after the signing of the pact. Even though the annual session of the Congress in Karachi at the end of March 1931 ratified the pact, there was strong resentment against the government in the rank and file of the party for the wanton disregard of Indian public opinion.

A majority of British officials were resentful of the importance given to the Congress by the viceroy, the negotiations with Gandhi on apparently equal terms. They were also bothered by the sight of Congressmen emerging from prison to a tumultuous welcome by the people. Winston Churchill thought that the government had gone too far in placating the Congress. Thus, it was not surprising that relations between Congressmen and government officials came under stress. At one stage, the Congress participation in the Round Table Conference in London looked uncertain. Although differences were somehow patched up and Gandhi sailed from Bombay on 29 August as the sole representative of the Congress to attend the conference, he returned from London empty-handed.

The political situation in India, meanwhile, continued to deteriorate. Congress leaders were picked up and jailed by the government one by one. The Congress Working Committee (CWC) was scheduled to meet in Bombay after Gandhi's arrival to take stock of the situation. Jayaprakash accompanied Nehru on a train from Allahabad for the CWC meet and strategically sat in a different compartment with all the crucial papers and documents. As anticipated, Nehru was arrested shortly after the train left Allahabad for violating the order restricting him from leaving the city; but Jayaprakash managed to reach Bombay undetected. Events moved swiftly towards another round of struggle. Immediately after landing in Bombay, Gandhi sent a telegram to the new viceroy, Lord Willingdon, seeking an interview to discuss the political situation but the request was declined. Acting under Gandhi's guidance, the CWC meeting of 1 January 1932 drew up a plan for another campaign of civil disobedience centred on boycott of foreign cloth, picketing of liquor shops and no-tax, no-revenue and no-rent campaigns all over the country. Gandhi was arrested on 4 January. People responded enthusiastically to the Congress call but the government struck hard. The police unleashed unbelievable brutality. Even women activists were not spared.

Kamala and Prabhavati were at the forefront of massive protests against shops selling foreign cloth and liquor. Defying the government ban, they led women's groups in selling khadi and contraband salt on the streets of Allahabad, from Civil Lines to Katra bazaar, unmindful of the midday sun. Motilal Nehru's strict instructions about not moving out to picket in the scorching heat of the summer months were regularly defied. They were rewriting the rules, scoffing at the suggestion of leaders like Krishna Kant Malaviya to take male escorts. Thousands of women took to the streets to protest. A page from Prabhavati's diary, sparse in description, is of the moment, inextricably personal and political: 'I went to the Congress office at 7:30. From there went to picketing to close down a government run school . . . went to Modern School at 1:30. Experienced lathi blows. Came home at 3. Spun khadi. Went for meeting at 6:30.'

Kamala and Prabhavati were arrested along with Nehru's mother, Swarup Rani, sisters Vijaya Lakshmi and Krishna, and hosts of other women who poured out of their homes, day after day, to defy government orders. Prabhavati was arrested on 3 February 1932, kept in Allahabad for a few days and then transferred to the Central Prison in Lucknow. Jayaprakash escaped arrest quite by chance. He arrived late at a meeting of Congress workers where the arrests were under way. Renewed civil disobedience, however, soon petered out under the weight of excessive repression.

If in such a situation, the Congress functioned with a modicum of normality, the credit goes in some measure to Jayaprakash. After the fateful meeting of the CWC, he returned to Allahabad and did whatever was possible to keep the Congress functional. Finding Allahabad unsafe for the work of maintaining the organization and keeping in touch with Congress workers, Jayaprakash moved to Bombay. Designated as acting general secretary of the Congress along with Lalji Mehrotra, who later became the mayor of Karachi, he worked under the guidance of the then acting president of the Congress, Sarojini Naidu, organizing countrywide boycotts and no-tax campaigns.

To ensure that the freedom movement remained alive in different parts of the country, Jayaprakash began work on building an extensive illegal underground network. His volunteers distributed printed literature and recruited supporters, creating innovative spaces for incubating nationalist political thought and action, amplifying voices that could not otherwise have made themselves heard. Helping him in this work was Uma Shankar Dikshit, who later occupied a high office within the Congress and the government. As a result of Jayaprakash's initiative, Congress circulars and brochures printed and copied on worn-out typewriters and cyclostyling machines began to be regularly ferried to different parts of India.

Almost all the circulars contained detailed instructions. For instance, listing out the programme to be followed on All India Prisoner's Day on 4 July 1932, the circular to all provincial Congress committees issued by Jayaprakash stated: 'The Congress committees should call an all-day strike in the cities and towns. In the afternoon they should organize processions. The processions should be accompanied with placards giving facts about jail atrocities, particularly about the ill treatment of women and boys and displaying protests against them. If possible, it is desirable that some sort of demonstration should be made in front of local jails. The day's programme should end with a public meeting.'[24]

It was due to Jayaprakash's effort that the *Congress Bulletin*, suppressed for long, began to appear at regular intervals.

Jayaprakash ensured continuity in Congress work by seeing that a backup team was ready to take the place of those put under arrest. He went around the country incognito in connection with organizational work. He even managed to arrange a clandestine meeting of the CWC in Banaras and teamed up with Narendra Deva, Sri Prakasa, Rambriksh Benipuri and Bisheswar Prasad Sinha to set up a Socialist Research Institute with the aim of propagating socialism through books, pamphlets, lectures and conclaves. The institute was founded on the conviction that Indian interests would be best served by bringing in socialism. Jayaprakash worked on an exhaustive syllabus to guide people interested in socialism. What he was doing was in keeping with his ideological moorings and represented a significant shift in the contours of Congress politics.

There were several warrants of arrest pending against Jayaprakash at different places. Ignoring these, he accompanied a British Labour Party delegation on its visit to Madras to study the government's repressive actions and to look into the charges of police brutality. On 7 September 1932, soon after he had seen off the delegation at the Madras railway station, he was arrested. The next day, on 8 September 1932, the *Free Press Journal* of Bombay splashed the news under the headline 'Congress Brain Arrested'. Jayaprakash was taken secretly to the Arthur Road Jail in Bombay, sentenced to one year's imprisonment and sent to the Nasik Central Jail.

Nasik Jail marked a turning point in Jayaprakash's political life. A group of educated, progressive, young Congressmen who dreamt of a socialist revolution were lodged here: Achyut Patwardhan, Minoo Masani, Asoka Mehta, N.G. Gorey, Charles Mascarenhas, C.K. Narayanswamy and M.L. Dantwala. The other political inmates like Morarji Desai, Shankarrao Deo, the Kumarappa brothers and K.G. Mashruwala largely kept away from this revolutionary fringe group. Confined in a single cell from 6 p.m. to 6 a.m., political prisoners were permitted to hang out together in the B-class prison yard during the day. This is where they debated, exercised and read. Deeply nostalgic about the time spent in Nasik, Jayaprakash reminisces, while writing to Minoo Masani several years later from his cell in the Central Prison, Agra, 'The Nasik days were the happiest days I have yet spent in prison, and I cherish dearly the friendships I made there.'[25]

The doctrinal differences on the need to develop a radical socialist anti-imperialist struggle were resolved through debates and discussions. The London School of Economics (LSE)-educated Masani often wrestled with Jayaprakash over the question of democracy versus dictatorship. In Masani's words: 'I was a staunch democrat of the British Labour Party and had little sympathy with communist methodology or technique. Jayaprakash on the other hand was a staunch believer in the dictatorship of the proletariat, whatever that may mean. Marxism was the bedrock of his socialist faith.'[26]

The group evolved a consensus on the need for progressive socialization of the means of production, distribution and exchange. Looking at Gandhi's constructive programme with a measure of hostility and ridicule, they agreed on the need for class struggle and the revolutionary upsurge of the toiling masses. It was apparent to them that the socialist movement could not continue under the leadership of the blithely pro-Moscow Communist Party whose politics was shaped by Russian foreign policy. Many of the communists were in prison, facing trial at Meerut. However, a majority of them had dissociated themselves from the mainstream of national struggle and had denounced it as being waged in the interest of the bourgeoisie.

The warm sense of shared ideas and dreams of this small, radical group of friends who were coming of age politically, resulted in plans for the formation of a socialist party. The party would function within the broad framework of the nationalist movement and keep it on the path of struggle, away from the pernicious hold of constitutionalism, towards which the movement seemed to be drifting.

Their primary concern was to radicalize the Congress and develop it into a real anti-imperialist organization. Their firebrand ideas, shared with other like-minded young leaders, notably, Narendra Deva, Yusuf Meherally, Purshottam Trikamdas, Ram Manohar Lohia, Dr Sampurnanand, Kamaladevi Chattopadhyay, Sri Prakasa, Dr K.B. Menon and Ganga Sharan Sinha led to the foundation of the Congress

Socialist Party in 1934, in which Jayaprakash played a leading role from the very beginning. In the evocative words of Yusuf Meherally, 'Jayaprakash Narayan came out of prison with an idea, a purpose and a vision. And out of that was born the Congress Socialist Party.'[27]

3

The Congress Socialist Years

The aftermath of the Civil Disobedience Movement led to apoplectic anguish in a section of Congress workers, dissatisfied as they were with Congress methods. Cynical and hard-bitten, they believed that a socialist orientation of the national movement was a necessity. For them, socialism was no longer an abstract philosophy but a potent method of political engagement that could transform reality, just as Lenin's Bolshevik uprising had overturned centuries of feudalism in Russia. Some of them joined the Communist Party of India, founded in 1925. Many others, who were not wholly converted to Marxism, were drawn to socialist thoughts, untainted at this point with news of Stalinist gulags and purges. They pinned their hopes on Nehru, not without reason.

A letter written by Jawaharlal Nehru to Minoo Masani, who was then engaged in organizing a group of socialist Congressmen in Bombay in December 1933, was much more than a subtle endorsement of left-wing politics within the Congress: 'I would welcome the formation of Socialist groups in the Congress to influence the ideology of the Congress and the country. As you are aware, I have been laying stress on the Socialist idea very much in my recent speeches and writings. I believe that the time has come when the country should face this issue and come to grips with the real economic problems which ultimately matter. All over the world today, people are being forced to think in terms of economic and social change and we, in India, cannot afford to remain in the backwater of pure politics. The time has undoubtedly come now when we must think more clearly and develop a scientific ideology. This is, so far as I am concerned, one of socialism and I would, therefore, gladly welcome the formation of groups to spread this ideology.'[1]

Nehru played a major role in moving the Karachi Resolution on Fundamental Rights and Economic Policy. Dubbed as the first socialist charter, the resolution advocated nationalization of key industries and mineral resources. It also stated: 'In order to end the exploitation of the masses, political freedom must include real economic freedom of the starving millions.'[2] Much to the chagrin of the budding group of socialists, the resolution remained silent on issues related to rural indebtedness and elimination of landlordism, even as it spelt a dramatic departure from the sterile dogma that had for years dogged the Congress.

Socialist-minded young Congressmen in Bihar founded the Bihar Socialist Party in July 1931 under the leadership of stalwarts like Rambriksh Benipuri, Phulan Verma, Basawan Singh, Yogendra Shukla, Abdul Bari, Ganga Sharan Sinha and Ambika Sinha. Jayaprakash was closely associated with the party since its inception and was designated its secretary after his release from prison in 1933. He played an important role in the formulation of its objectives and rules. Although he was an ardent Marxist, he was appalled to see the communist stand on the nationalist movement and was convinced that so long as India remained under foreign rule, the priority had to be a united fight for freedom. It was laid down in the rules of the Bihar Socialist Party that only those who were members of the Congress could become members of the party. Jayaprakash also reached out to other socialist groups in the country, including the Punjab Socialist Party.

The Punjab Socialist Party was an avant-garde socialist group that did not believe in armchair socialism but began to mobilize workers and peasants with fervour and determination. A prominent example was Benipuri, who actively spearheaded a movement for the abolition of the zamindari system in Bihar, a source of exploitation of the peasantry. The fiery, inspired speeches and writings of Nehru after his visit to the Soviet Union in 1927 were not yet unhitched from memory. When news came that the All India Congress Committee was going to hold its next session in Patna in May 1934, Jayaprakash and his socialist associates sought to address the existential crisis facing the national movement by weaning the anti-imperialist elements in the Congress away from its bourgeois leadership. With this end in view, they summoned a conference of their own, of socialist-minded Congressmen from all over India to also convene at Patna.

The first All India Conference of Socialists met under the chairmanship of Narendra Deva at the Anjuman Islamia Hall in Patna on 17 May 1934, a day before the scheduled meeting of the AICC. An epochal meet, it was attended by a hundred delegates from five provinces—Bihar, United Provinces, Kerala, Madras and Bengal— who announced their disenchantment with the party programme being promoted by a section of the top right-wing leaders of the Congress. Young radicals present at the conference attacked the proposal for council entry and protested that this ran counter to the 1929 Lahore Resolution, which had called for boycotting the legislatures, demanding nothing less than complete independence. They also charged that 'the nationalist movement under the leadership of Gandhi and the old guard was drifting inevitably towards constitutionalism and accommodation with the British'.[3]

Cognisant of the deepening world economic crisis and the rise and growth of fascism in Europe, the socialists declared that the historical moment for establishing an organization of Marxian socialists in the Congress had arrived. With that end in view, a drafting committee for preparing the programme and constitution of the proposed All India Congress Socialist Party was set up with Narendra Deva as president and Jayaprakash as secretary. The committee was cautious about not placing a full-blown socialist manifesto before the Congress, for fear of alienating its conservative sections. It also decided against obstructing Gandhi's constructive programme.

The draft proposal of the socialist programme was sent to the AICC for approval. The Congress welcomed the formation of a group that represented a different school of thought. However, during a meeting in June 1934, the Congress Working Committee observed that it was necessary, in view of loose talk about confiscation of property and the necessity of class war, to remind Congressmen of the resolution adopted by the Congress session in Karachi in March 1931. The resolution laid down principles that were diametrically opposed to confiscation of private property without just cause or compensation. It also provided that confiscation and class war were contrary to the Congress creed of non-violence.

Nehru, then in jail, was visibly annoyed by the Congress Working Committee's resolution. He noted in his diary: 'To hell with the CWC passing a pious and fatuous resolution on a subject it does not understand or perhaps understands too well.'[4] He felt that the Congress was getting aggressively anti-socialist. Aghast at the tirade against socialists, Narendra Deva, Sampurnanand, Sriprakasa and Jayaprakash issued a strong rejoinder from Banaras on 22 June 1934. The rejoinder stated that the Congress Working Committee's resolution came to them as a painful surprise and they were not prepared for the deliberate offensive. 'The resolution of the Working Committee,' they said, 'is shocking beyond words. It shows how reactionary the present leadership of the Congress has become. For us Socialists it can mean only one thing— the redoubling of our efforts to overthrow that leadership.'[5]

This rejoinder upset Sardar Patel who had not been able to stomach the Congress's leftward swing. He accused the Congress socialists of trying to create a split in the party.[6] In another rejoinder issued on 18 July 1934, Jayaprakash remarked that Patel was labouring under certain misapprehensions and that the socialists were not interested in causing a split. In fact, he added, to cause a split or not was in the hands of the Congress leaders themselves.[7] If the latter persisted in their view that the socialist programme was opposed to the creed of the Congress, it would mean only one thing: the socialists must either give up their programme or leave the Congress.

Alarmed at the continued political in-fighting, Nehru, then just out of prison, wrote a letter to Gandhi on 13 August 1934, expressing his anguish at recent developments: 'I feel that the time is overdue for the Congress to think clearly on social and economic issues but I recognize that education on these issues takes time and the Congress, as a whole, may not be able to go as far at present as I would like it to go. But it appears that whether the working committee knows anything about the subject or not, it is perfectly willing to denounce and to excommunicate people who happen to have made a special study of the subject and hold certain views. No attempt is made to understand those views, which are held by a very large number of the ablest and most self-sacrificing people in the world. Those views may be right or wrong but they deserve at least some understanding before the working committee sets out to denounce them.'[8]

Gandhi replied from Wardha, almost as soon as he received Nehru's letter, 'I understand your deep sorrow. You were quite right in giving full and free expression to your feelings . . . I have the same passion . . . for the common good . . . I must take full responsibility for the resolutions and the whole conception surrounding them . . . of course, here comes in the difference of our emphasis on the methods or the means which to me are just as important as the goal . . . I have looked up the dictionary meaning of socialism. It takes me no further than where I was before.'[9] Gandhi, however, realized that India's cadre of socialists, consisting of some of the best and brightest educated minds, had the potential to wean Nehru away from the party. Perhaps a little impetuously, he decided that the best way to keep Nehru in the Congress was to step down himself. 'My presence more and more estranges the intelligentsia from the Congress,' he wrote self-effacingly in his letter of resignation.[10]

It was an interesting phase of the national movement with the right and the left ideologies on a collision course. There was a consistent 25 to 33 per cent support for CSP and other left groups within the Congress. Jayaprakash's was a no-frills existence: socialism was at the centre of his life. But he was much more than a brilliant ideologue and political analyst. He worked at all hours of the day and night to strengthen the provincial wings of the party. His efforts triggered an avalanche of support. There was emotional hunger for a new politics and hundreds of young supporters were mobilized as part of a potentially transformative movement. Rarely demagogic, Jayaprakash's speeches were delivered with the verve and passion of a trained orator. The force of his powerful oratory, combined with his revolutionary aura, won over the youth.

Attributing the moulding of his political development in part to Jayaprakash's fiery speeches in Kerala, E.M.S. Namboodiripad writes,

'The speeches he delivered during that visit and the informal discussions
he held underlined the importance of organizing the trade unions
and the kisan sabhas without which no determined struggle could be
waged for independence, nor could the compromising policies of the
Congress leadership be fought. He sought to generalize the experience
of the strikes and hartals which took place during the civil disobedience
movement and pointed out how these forms of militant mass action
helped in paralyzing the administration. Improving on this experience
and developing the united strength of the working class, he pointed out,
was the method through which the mighty British rule could be broken.
We saw in this the real alternative to the Satyagraha, parliamentary and
terroristic methods with which we were so far familiar.' Namboodiripad
goes on to add that the path shown by Jayaprakash was so attractive to
young Congressmen and women that thousands of them plumbed for
it in a few months.[11]

The final launch of the All India Congress Socialist Party with
Jayaprakash as its general secretary took place at a conference of
thirteen provincial wings of the CSP held in Bombay on 21–22
October 1934. Congress flags and portraits of Marx and Lenin were
equally visible at the conference. This marked the formal emergence
of Jayaprakash as an all-India leader at the age of thirty-two, a position
which he held for many years, bringing to the table remarkable gravitas,
passion and commitment. Minoo Masani, Mohanlal Gautam, N.G.
Gorey and E.M.S. Namboodiripad were elected joint secretaries. The
elected members of the executive committee were Narendra Deva,
Sampurnanand, Kamaladevi Chattopadhyay, Purushottam Trikamdas,
P.Y. Deshpande, Ram Manohar Lohia, S.M. Joshi, Amarendra Prasad
Mitra, Charles Mascarenhas, Nabakrushna Choudhuri and Achyut
Patwardhan. Besides them, five persons were elected as substitute
members, namely, Yusuf J. Meherally, Sarat Batliwala, Rohit Mehta,
Faridul Haq Ansari and Rambriksh Benipuri. They were to take the
place of absent members by rotation.

The constitution of the Congress Socialist Party, as adopted by the
Bombay Conference, provided that the objective of the party would be
the achievement of complete independence. The party's membership
would be open to members of the Congress who held membership of

an affiliated provincial Congress Socialist Party, as long as they were not members of any communal organization or of any other political organization whose objectives and programmes ran contrary to that of the CSP. A clause allowed for the collective affiliation of trade unions. Immediately after its formation, the party entered into an agreement with the All India Trade Union Congress, pledging to make it the central organization of Indian labour.

The CSP took a strong stand against moves made by the Congress right-wing to take the Congress back to the path of constitutional agitation followed during the pre-Gandhian era. It held that such attempts ran counter to the creed of the party and to the fundamental principles and policies it had been following since 1920. The CSP further asserted that parliamentary activities conducted by the Congress must be based on revolutionary use of the legislature to achieve complete independence and end the economic and political exploitation of the masses. CSP members participated in labour strikes in a number of places, leading to the Ahmedabad textile workers strike, the Calicut tile and textile workers strike, the British-India steam navigation company workers strike, and the Berhampur and Jalgaon textile workers strike. Jayaprakash's efforts to bring about left unity, meanwhile continued to remain unattainable. The Communist Party of India labelled CSP a bourgeois façade. The Royists extended support to the CSP initially but soon enough M.N. Roy was found directing his followers to join CSP with the objective of splitting it and absorbing the real 'proletarian elements'.[12]

Immediately after the conference, Jayaprakash took up the work of organizing provincial parties. A central office opened at Banaras. Provincial parties were formed in Andhra, Assam, Bengal, the Central Provinces and Berar, Bombay, Delhi, Gujarat, Kerala, the United Provinces, and Utkal. A section of the press was extremely critical of these developments. The Hindustan Times called CSP a party of bootleggers. The Pioneer insinuated that the party was securing funds from Russia. Calling it a most vicious and mendacious propaganda, Jayaprakash said, 'Russia is undeniably a great inspiration to us, as it is to all the exploited people, but it is mischievous to suggest that we have any such connection with it as per the Pioneer's insinuation.'[13]

The most comprehensive exposition of Jayaprakash's ideological position is to be found in his book *Why Socialism?*, published by the CSP in January 1936. With that, he emerged as the leading theoretician of his party, with a strong, uncompromising vision of socialism and its applicability to Indian conditions. Writing about the significance of this book, E.M.S. Namboodiripad said, 'Among the voluminous material on the birth and development of the Congress Socialist Party, a prominent place should be given to a book written by Jayaprakash Narayan under the title, *Why Socialism?*—that opened the eyes of a large number of young Congressmen and women who were groping towards a new path since they had become frustrated with the utter futility of the programmes and practices adopted by the right-wing leaders of the Indian National Congress. Striking a personal note, I may state that *Why Socialism?* showed us, the young Congressmen of Kerala, that the path mapped out by Socialism was superior to Gandhism, the parliamentary path as well as individual terrorism—three ideological approaches which were then contending for ascendancy in the Congress. *Why Socialism?* therefore became the textbook through which we imbibed the elements of the new ideology.'

The first chapter called 'The Foundation of Socialism' was an elucidation of socialism from a Marxist perspective that ended with a call to abolish the root cause of inequality: the private ownership of the means of production. In the next chapter titled 'What the Congress Socialist Party Stands For', Jayaprakash strongly refuted the contention of opponents of socialism that the latter would not succeed in India because its traditions were different from the European countries where socialism originated. He asserted that if there was a socialist party in power, it could foment socialism in any part of the world.

Distilled to its essence, *Why Socialism?* stood for transfer of power to the producing masses; state-controlled development of the economy, progressive socialization of all means of production, distribution and exchange; organization of cooperatives for production, distribution and availability of credit in the unorganized sectors of the economy; elimination of princes, landlords and all other classes of exploiters with zero compensation; redistribution of land to peasants; encouragement and promotion of cooperative and collective farming by the state;

liquidation of debts owed by peasants and workers; recognition by the state of the right to work; adult franchise on a functional basis; zero tolerance of discrimination between different religions or castes and community by the state and complete gender equity.

The third chapter of his book critiqued the alternatives to socialism; it included a polemic against Gandhism. Jayaprakash deemed it a 'dangerous doctrine', a compound of 'timid economic analysis, good intentions and ineffective moralizing' that was deceiving the masses and encouraging the upper classes to continue their domination.[14] He found nothing new or peculiarly Indian in what Gandhi said and felt—which a large number of Western writers had zeroed-in on—the same arguments that class struggle was anathema, capital and labour were interdependent and necessary for each other and revolution was wasteful. In Jayaprakash's words, 'These are the commonest ideas of the West preached by smug bourgeois professors, thinkers and churchmen.'[15]

In the fourth and last chapter, titled 'Methods and Techniques', he argued that the need of the hour was to organize the masses—both the peasantry and labour—and make them politically conscious. The best way to achieve such an outcome was to strengthen their class organizations and instil political consciousness. This was the main task for socialists.[16]

The ideas propounded in *Why Socialism?* were duly reflected in the ideological line adopted by the Congress Socialist Party. The thesis of the party, drafted by Jayaprakash and adopted by its second conference held at Meerut in January 1936, described CSP as 'an organized body of Marxist Socialists'. It went on to declare that their task involved the weaning away of anti-imperialist forces in Congress from the existing bourgeois leadership to bring them into the fold of revolutionary socialism. The thesis adopted by the third annual conference of the party at Faizpur in December 1936 was an ambitious extension of the Meerut thesis and spoke of developing and broadening the Congress to transform it into a powerful anti-imperialist force.[17]

The appropriately named political journal *Congress Socialist* worked as the party's mouthpiece and a powerful instrument of political propaganda with Lohia and later Asoka Mehta as its editors.

The Jayaprakash Papers at the Nehru Memorial Museum and Library contain several appeals to party workers and provincial executive members to write for the journal and expand its membership. Appealing for support, Jayaprakash wrote: 'No member of the party is free from responsibility towards *Congress Socialist*.'[18] A lecture series was initiated on subjects like development of socialist thought, development of capitalism and imperialism, fascism and the decay of capitalism and the anti-imperialist struggle in India. Jayaprakash also set up socialist study circles and camps built around shared political interests. The first of these was held from 15 May 1937 for two weeks at Almora with Yusuf Meherally as the convener.[19] A socialist book club was instituted with Subhas Bose, Narendra Deva, Minoo Masani, P.C. Joshi, Lohia, Mulk Raj Anand and Z.A. Ahmed as founder members. His efforts to enlist Nehru as one of the members did not bear fruit, although Nehru funded the *Congress Socialist* as often as he could.

Not all the leaders of the CSP were committed to Marxism with the same fervour as Jayaprakash. Minoo Masani and Ashok Mehta were inspired by Fabian socialism, Sampurnanand by Vedantic socialism, and others like Achyut Patwardhan were influenced largely by Gandhi's teachings. Ruminating about their halcyon socialist days, Minoo Masani wrote, 'The important issue about the character of the Congress Socialist Party—whether or not it was a Marxist party—and the question of its relations with the Communist Party . . . were discussed in private sessions of the Executive Committee . . . After considerable resistance on the part of Yusuf Meherally, myself and others, Jayaprakash managed to persuade the executive to agree that ours was a Marxist party.'[20] Jayaprakash sent Masani to Moscow in 1935 to discuss the question of an alliance between the CPI and CSP. When Masani reached Moscow, he found himself dealing with British communists led by Harry Pollitt, Ben Bradley and R. Palme Dutt. His suggestion that the CPI dissolve itself in order to create a united Socialist Party was stonewalled.

Nehru was elected president of the Congress in 1936 and re-elected in 1937 for a second term. Even though the socialists were aware that he did not command the support of a majority of senior Congress leaders, they nonetheless felt that with his radical socialist agenda he could act as an effective barrier against right-wing forces. Together, they could outmanoeuvre the right leadership. Jayaprakash also tactically softened his own stand to reassure the conservative segments in Congress that their party was not going to be overrun by socialists. It was not the CSP's 'purpose', he said, 'to convert the whole Congress into a full-fledged Socialist party. All we seek to do is to change the content and policy of that organization so that it comes truly to represent the masses, having the object of emancipating them both from the foreign power and the native system of exploitation.'[21]

Writing in an essay for *Congress Socialist*, Jayaprakash tried to silence discordant voices within the Congress by reiterating, 'Our policy is dictated by the simple consideration that an organization whose task it is to unite all genuinely anti-imperialism classes on one front against imperialism, needs not Socialism but a broad anti-imperialist programme.'[22] And then again in a speech delivered at the April 1938 CSP conference in Lahore, he said, 'There is no quarrel between the Socialists and the Congress over the red flag and the tricolor. Those who stand under the red flag to fight the battle of the poor kisans and the oppressed mazdoors take pride in standing under the national flag of India to fight the battle of her freedom.'[23]

In April 1936, at the Congress session held at Lucknow, a resolution was passed rejecting the Government of India Act of 1935. Jayaprakash made no bones about the fact that he was appalled that the Act ignored a one-man, one-vote democracy and provided for limited devolution of power. The enfranchised population of 34 million was permitted to vote because of its property ownership or educational qualification. Provincial governments had the right to veto all legislation. Nehru joined Jayaprakash in strongly condemning the Act. He agreed that the Act was deliberately designed to strengthen vested and reactionary elements. Nehru further felt that the acceptance of office under the Act would be a retrograde step that could lead to the disintegration of the Congress.[24] Even though the Congress condemned the 1935 act, it decided to participate in elections in the provincial legislatures which took place in 1937 and in its election manifesto asked for the convening of a Constituent Assembly.

In his interaction with the press, Jayaprakash observed, 'Disappointing though the Lucknow Congress has been, it bears the stamp of the personality of its President. Resolutions on war, mass contact agrarian programme, civil liberties all owe their origin to the President and, if I may point out, to our Party. Even in their mutilated form, they represent a very appreciable advance.'[25] Nehru's stand was clearly articulated in his presidential address where he stated that the key to the solution of the world's problems, and of India's problems, lay in socialism: 'That (socialism) involves vast and revolutionary changes in our political and social structure, the ending of vested interests in land and industry, as well as the feudal and autocratic Indian states system . . . the ending of private property, except in a restricted sense, and the replacement of the present profit system by a higher ideal of cooperative desires . . . Socialism is thus for me not merely an economic doctrine which I favour: it is a vital creed which I hold with all my head and heart.'[26]

The formation of the All India Kisan Sabha which, by 1939, had 8,00,000 members, was also a significant step in the socialist direction.[27] Nehru became the centre of radical aspirations. Clinging to a rose-tinted view of Nehru's ideological support, the socialists believed that underlying historical forces would work in their favour.

In a strategic swerve from its rigid opposition to the contesting of elections, the CSP took the less doctrinaire position of opposing the formation of ministries. Several socialists, including prominent leaders and ideologues like Narendra Deva, were put up as candidates. Jayaprakash plunged into campaigning. His admiration for Nehru during the days of campaigning in Bihar is apparent from these words, 'It began in right earnest after the visit of the stormy Pandit Nehru. He shook up the whole province as nothing else had done in the recent past. It was as if a giant had come forth who picked up the sleeping province in his hands, and gave it a mighty shake-up that brought it to life and consciousness. The response and enthusiasm of the people have been a revelation to us. And such touching faith in the Congress. The Congress is their hope . . . it will relieve them of their distress. This march of the hungry peasant to the polling booth is prelude to the march to the battle-field.'[28]

Soon after the Lucknow session of the Congress in April 1936, at Gandhi's behest and with Nehru's support, Jayaprakash was nominated as a member of the fifteen-member Congress Working Committee along with Narendra Deva and Achyut Patwardhan. It was a singular honour, given that Jayaprakash was only thirty-four at the time. He had to resign after a few months, as he was not a member of the All India Congress Committee, an essential requirement. However, his stature in the Congress continued to grow. At the party's Tripuri session three years later, he was entrusted with the task of drafting one of its main resolutions on 'The National Demand'.

Nehru's critics within the party, fearing that 'socialist fringe ideas' would be pushed into the mainstream, complained that he was trying to constitute a socialist working committee. In a joint letter addressed to Nehru, Patel, C. Rajagopalachari, Rajendra Prasad, J.B. Kripalani, Jairamdas Daulatram, Jamnalal Bajaj and other right-wing elements within the party threatened that in the situation created by him, they would not shoulder the responsibility of organizing and fighting elections. Gandhi had to intervene to restore peace. Combative and confident, Congress ended up doing very well, gaining a clear majority in six out of eleven provinces and emerging as the single largest party in another three.

The Congress's success at the polls rendered the CSP's opposition to accepting office—supported by other leaders like Vijay Lakshmi Pandit, Sarat Chandra Bose and Rafi Ahmed Kidwai—inconsequential. When the anti-ministry imperative came up for final discussion, a resolution moved by Rajendra Prasad and Patel on the conditional formation of ministries was accepted. Jayaprakash's amendment against this move was defeated. Subsequently, Congress ministries were formed in seven provinces that included Bombay, Madras, the United Provinces, Bihar, the Central Provinces, Orissa and the North-West Frontier Province.

Jayaprakash continued to work on the same programme he had been working on since the foundation of the CSP—organizing peasants and workers and bridging the gap between grassroots social movements and party-led moves to end inequality. 'Our swaraj must mean swaraj for the poor. Over and above political democracy, swaraj must mean economic democracy. For this purpose, the capitalist oligarchy has to be destroyed and economic power transferred to the people in general. It will take some time after the establishment of swaraj to establish Socialism. But the balance of power must immediately pass into the hands of the people so that it can work for the people and develop agriculture and industry.'[29]

The practice of holding annual Congress sessions in rural areas, beginning with the 1937 Faizpur session in Jalgaon district of Maharashtra, was welcomed by Jayaprakash. And though his effort to extract an advance commitment from the Congress leadership to refrain from accepting office under the 1935 Act failed, he observed, 'The Faizpur Congress was a success in many ways. First, it was a great success as the first village Congress. The lakhs of peasants who flocked to it gave it a meaning and a content which were new in the history of the Congress . . . It was after two years that Gandhiji made his appearance on the Congress rostrum. The President (Jawaharlal Nehru) of the Congress had just finished his inspiring address. As Gandhiji climbed up and his small figure came into view, there was a spontaneous sensation of joy and enthusiasm in that vast sea of humanity.'[30]

The role of the Faizpur Congress in putting together a framework for a joint national front against imperialism was significant. The Faizpur resolution, incorporated into the Congress election manifesto, transformed elections into a massive demonstration of national solidarity against imperialism. The resolution focused heavily on agrarian reforms and subsequently became a part of the Congress election manifesto in 1937. This was seen as a victory for the CSP and the All India Kisan Sabha, despite the dropping of two vital demands: abolition of zamindari and redistribution of land. The socialists had to be content with the introduction of agriculture income tax, end of levies on farm labourers, introduction of cooperative farming, securing of living wages for agricultural labourers and recognition of peasant unions.

Following the Faizpur Resolution, the socialists began agitating for transformative agrarian reforms, leading to ugly clashes with Congress committees dominated by landed interests and vitriolic attacks by a section of the press. Jayaprakash faced strong personal attacks from the editor of *Searchlight*, a prominent pro-Congress daily published in Patna that suggested that the peasant movement was packed with unpatriotic subversives. In a strongly worded rejoinder to Rajendra Prasad's statement published in *Searchlight* on 7 January 1938 regarding the Kisan Sabha in Bihar, Jayaprakash wrote, 'In this charge-sheet Rajendra Babu mentions the peasant rallies that were held at Patna. It passes my comprehension how they have been found to be objectionable. To me, they are the two high peaks of our movement. These peasant mobilizations were held not because we had no faith in the Congress ministry, but because we wanted to utilize the freer atmosphere created to raise the agitation to a higher level (that agitation, be it remembered, is the motive force to the national movement itself) to link up mass agitation with the work done in the legislature.'[31]

Jayaprakash mocked Rajendra Prasad for alleging that slogans like *malguzari loge kaise, danda hamara zindabad*[32] were being widely used: 'It is exasperating to find a person like Rajendra Babu seriously making such a charge. Surely, we must credit the masses with some sense of humour and inventiveness. We have not forgotten how during the last Assembly elections all kinds of slogans, songs and caricatures were heard. They were all creations of the newly awakened mass mind. They were crude and rough-hewn, often far removed from Congress ideals and standards. However, they were, just the same, products of a great phase of our movement.'[33]

Taking a cue from Bihar, zamindars in other provinces took recourse against repressive measures. Tenants were ejected from their age-old holdings, agrarian riots were provoked and the agrarian bills whittled down. In a letter written to Nehru, Jayaprakash voiced his apprehension about a burgeoning ideological strain that was transforming the Congress 'from a democratic organization of millions of down-trodden people into a handmaid of Indian vested interests'.[34] He alleged that a vulgarization of Gandhism made this transition easy and also gave Congress the requisite demagogic armour.

Jayaprakash also flagged the issue of violation of civil liberties by Congress ministries and noted with dismay the 'spirit of tardiness' in releasing non-Congress political prisoners, in legalizing non-Congress organizations and in refunding the securities forfeited by non-Congress journals.[35] By far the most abysmal record was that of the Madras ministry headed by Rajagopalachari. While releasing socialist workers arrested by the previous non-Congress government, it declared that it would take all necessary steps against the propagation of ideas of class hatred and the use of organized or unorganized violence. Socialists like Batliwala were arrested on charges of sedition. A vigorous campaign to eliminate left influence was launched in Andhra Pradesh as well.

Jayaprakash was incensed. It was evident that every effort was being made to smother socialism. With a punctilious strategy drawn out before the next Congress session at Haripura, he pledged that he would make Congress responsive to the needs of the awakened masses.[36] The CSP mounted an attack on right-wing leaders for continuing acts of repression, especially against labour and peasant struggle. They also denounced the policy of non-intervention in states, the gagging order on labour leaders in Cawnpur, the unceasing assault on Kisan Sabhas, and the overall proclivity to compromise with capitalists and landlords on peasant and labour legislations.

Socialists welcomed the 1938 Haripura session of the Congress held under the presidency of Subhas Chandra Bose at a village near Bardoli. Over 2,00,000 people from every province and district in British India and many Indian states attended the session. Jayaprakash described the event in a poetic voice: 'The deserted banks of the Tapti were alight for a few momentous days. The banks must already be once again enveloped in darkness. But the rays of light that went forth from there will penetrate every home in India and shine upon our path till we gather again a year hence to light another lamp on our darkened road.'[37] What he probably did not anticipate was that Haripura would turn into a morbid theatre of clashes between the right and left.[38]

Differences within the Congress had widened since its acceptance of office. These differences were exacerbated when the UP and Bihar Congress ministries resigned over the governor's refusal to release political prisoners. In an absolutely bizarre blame game, the socialists were held responsible for discrediting Congress ministries and engineering their collapse. The rhetoric used by leaders like Patel was openly confrontational. Writing on the lessons of Haripura, Jayaprakash said, 'Haripura's chief contribution to my mind would be in the direction of opening a new chapter in the relations between the right and left wings of the Congress . . . Sardar Vallabhbhai's attack, Mr. Jairamdas's and Mr. Bhulabhai's remarks about left and right, Mr. Kripalani's veiled threats, all pointed to a much deeper estrangement than was expected and signalled a bitter and determined fight that is bound to prove ruinous for the Congress. In the words of Professor (Harold) Lasky, by insisting too much and too often on the wings, we run the risk of forgetting the flight of the bird.'[39]

A subtle but noticeable change emerged in Jayaprakash's hostility to the issue of accepting office and to Gandhi's leadership during the Haripura Congress. The shift in attitude was evident when Patel's vicious tirade elicited a calm, introspective response. Jayaprakash felt that socialists were, at times, hypercritical of the Congress ministries, undermining their achievements. He began to see the Congress resolutions and manifestoes as more left than right, thus creating the possibility for both the groups to abandon their differences and work together.

The clash of the right and left continued, however, at the next important AICC meeting held at Delhi in September 1938. A resolution condemning the left-wing's preoccupation with mass organization and struggle that catalysed violence led to the walkout of a section of the left wing from the meeting. Not present at the meeting, Gandhi nonetheless condemned the walkout and admonished left-wingers saying that democratic norms entailed the 'graceful' acceptance of majority view. The socialists responded by pointing out that the 'majority' in the resolution under dispute was nominal: of the 155 or 160 members present that day, about fifty walked out and twenty-five voted against the resolution.[40] In the debate on the resolution, the socialists emphatically stated that they were not advocates of violence.

The 1939 Congress session held at Tripuri once again brought the right–left divide into focus. The drama unfolded with an acute leadership crisis triggered by the re-election of Subhas Chandra Bose as president for a second term, against the wishes of Gandhi and other senior leaders who had wanted Pattabhi Sitaramayya for that position.[41] Bose's victory in the election was seen as the triumph of the radical wing of the Congress. Infuriated old leaders retaliated by moving a resolution to express faith in Gandhi's leadership. This resolution was eponymously known as the Pant Resolution, as it was moved by Govind Ballabh Pant, head of the Congress ministry in UP at the time.

As the CSP had a sizeable number of delegates at the Congress session, its stand on the resolution was extremely critical. Jayaprakash moved an amendment to the Pant Resolution in a bid to soften the blow to Bose, but it was defeated. Instead of taking a further stand against the resolution, as was expected of Jayaprakash, he announced his group's neutrality towards it, thereby facilitating its passage by a massive majority. This eventually led to Bose's resignation from the presidency. Jayaprakash was criticized by many for his stand, but he justified his position of neutrality on the ground that Gandhi's continued leadership of the Congress was, at that stage, invaluable. 'Mahatma Gandhi is making history. He is a stupendous force of history. We must march with history,' he said, responding to Gandhi's rather provocative article titled 'The Dissentients' published in *Harijan*. The text of the response published in the *National Herald, Searchlight* and *Amrita Bazar Patrika* on 26 January 1940 went on to say, 'We a handful of Socialists cannot fight alone and win Swaraj. The whole Congress must fight and the Congress can fight today only under the leadership of Gandhiji. And Gandhiji imposes conditions for his leadership. We accept these conditions unreservedly. These conditions however cannot be a change of faith.'[42]

The matter, however, remained mired in controversy in leftist political circles and in the press. Jayaprakash's contention, that he did not support the resolution because he was unable to accept its ideological implications, did not pass muster. He repeatedly faced the accusation that he had surrendered to Gandhi and that his ostensible neutrality was another name for 'tailism to Gandhism'.[43] But Jayaprakash remained unaffected by the vitriol, and was able to push a seminal resolution on the 'National Demand': a decisive step towards self-determination.

Paradoxically, Tripuri was also an occasion for celebration for the Congress old guard, as it was the first step in purging the party of 'undesirables' that included the Bose faction, the communists and the Congress socialists. Their efforts to weed out 'left elements' could also be seen in the run-up to the Tripuri Congress. P. Sundarayya, a communist in charge of the Andhra CSP, was debarred from standing in the election of delegates to the Congress. More than 35,000 members with left affiliation were disqualified in West Krishna district alone.[44] The move to put together a Left Coordination Committee with Bose's Forward Bloc, Roy's Radical League, Kisan Sabha leaders, the CSP and the CPI failed to take off in a meaningful way. The right offensive, on the other hand, continued unabated, taking an apocalyptic form at the AICC meeting in Bombay in June 1939 with the passing of a resolution banning any form of Satyagraha without prior permission of the provincial Congress committees. The communists hoped against hope that a united left would be able to mobilize the masses openly against this astoundingly retrograde resolution.

Another issue that preoccupied Jayaprakash was the Congress position on World War II, which had broken out on 1 September 1939 as a result of the invasion of Poland by Germany. In a terse statement, he asserted that the Congress had no option but to oppose, with all the strength at its disposal, the use of Indian resources, men and money by Britain in a war which was clearly being fought to safeguard the latter's imperialistic possessions. Giving a call for resistance, he accused Britain of committing aggression against India by ignoring repeated declarations of the Congress that it would not tolerate India being dragged into the war. 'What answer can there be to this British aggression against India than the most determined resistance?' Jayaprakash observed. 'If we have any self-respect and if we maintain our objective of complete independence, we cannot possibly do less. Resistance in such circumstances is not opportunism but a political and moral necessity . . .'[45] The Congress at this stage ruled out cooperation with the British war efforts, wary of Britain which 'like a leech was sticking to its empire'.[46] The CPI, too, focused on the fascist and imperialist character of the war, choosing to oppose it. The Hindu Mahasabha and the Muslim League offered cooperation to the government in its war efforts.

Jayaprakash continued to be consumed by the idea of left unity. It was due to his unbroken belief that all Marxists needed to work together to usher in socialism that the CSP opted for unity with the communists. The communists on their part had received a new directive from the Comintern. The Congress was no longer to be boycotted and destroyed but supported as an anti-imperialist national front. This was a volte-face from its earlier stand on Gandhi and the Congress when it had attacked the bourgeoisie nationalism of the Congress and called Gandhi a lackey of Indian capitalists. The Dutt–Bradley thesis endorsed the role of the Congress as a mass organization of many diverse elements seeking national liberation.[47] It helped CPI shed its sectarianism by underscoring the need for left unity. This thesis was officially approved by the politburo of the CPI, an unexpected development that delighted Jayaprakash.

Dreaming of a cohesive anti-imperialist united front, Jayaprakash moved a resolution at the socialist conference at Meerut in January 1936 for the acceptance of CPI members into the CSP on individual basis. Members of the CPI were not only able to occupy important positions in the CSP but also to enter the Congress via the CSP after an agreement with P.C. Joshi, the general secretary of the CPI. E.M.S. Namboodiripad and Sajjad Zaheer were nominated joint secretaries of the CSP at the national level. P. Sundarayya took charge of the CSP in Andhra, Namboodiripad led the Malabar unit and A.K. Gopalan and P. Ramamurthi, the unit in Madras. It was agreed that both parties would recognize each other as bona fide socialist parties and would cooperate, with a view to eventual merger.

The agreement played an important role in the unification of trade union movements and strengthening of the peasant and student movements despite the strong apprehensions of Ram Manohar Lohia, Minoo Masani, Asoka Mehta and Achyut Patwardhan that efforts at unity were eventually doomed to fail. Numerous associations, study circles and forums were formed to sustain the spirit of the united socialist movement. The most significant amongst these was the Indian Progressive Writers Association led by Munshi Premchand, Josh Malihabadi, Maulana Abdul Haq, Mulk Raj Anand and Sajjad Zaheer. Nehru's advocacy of a united front, his appointment of communists like Z.A. Ahmed and M. Ashraf to important positions in the office of the AICC also created much more than a sliver of hope.

For a while, unity seemed to work as both the CSP and the CPI operated in unison on economic and social policy issues. A joint appeal for legalizing the CPI was issued by Jayaprakash and P.C. Joshi.[48]

The appeal recognized the role of the party in bringing the rich global heritage of revolutionary movements into the national movement. This was followed by a joint statement on May Day, 1939: 'The Tripuri resolution gave the slogan for nationwide struggle against imperialism and for the enforcement of National Demand for Independence. To implement that resolution, we require all round unity—above all Socialist-Communist Unity—the bedrock of Left unity and the main lever of the United National Front.'[49]

Once the door to the communists opened, they penetrated freely into the rather amorphous mélange of socialist ranks. Jayaprakash was greeted with cries of 'Indian Lenin' wherever he went. He certainly was on a high and his ensuing naivety in refusing to read the writing on the wall surprised even his closest followers. There were attacks and counterattacks from both sides. CSP leaders like Minoo Masani, who were bitter critics of the communists, sent shockwaves by circulating secret documents of the CPI amongst members of the national executive of the CSP. The documents described the CPI as the only genuine socialist party and detailed the considerable influence exercised by it. Seen as treasonous, these documents sparked frenzied reactions. The secret journal published by the CPI was also regarded with great suspicion. And then, sure enough, in a letter dated 5 September 1939, the general secretary of the CPI, P.C. Joshi, accused Jayaprakash of pandering to left nationalism and of being unable to unify the forces of struggle, or put up a successful resistance to right disruption.[50]

Following that, in his mimeographed 'War Circular 2' of 31 December 1939, addressed to all party units and members, Jayaprakash ruefully confessed that 'owing to our anxiety for unity we have admitted a number of Communists (when I use the term Communist I mean members of CPI) into our party and they are openly . . . doing their best to undermine the CSP . . . The present policy of the Communists negates the whole basis and even objective of unity. It is grounded on their exaggerated estimation of their ability to crush CSP. Their leaders have openly boasted of crushing CSP.'[51] In a rather severe indictment of the CPI, he added that it had completely torn off its mask and stood as the sworn enemy of the CSP and every other progressive organization with which it had worked before. Sharp differences arose on the war issue, undermining all efforts at unity.

Their brief relationship caught in a death spiral, the CPI, in turn, began accusing the CSP of betraying socialism and pursuing a policy of opportunism and disruption 'ending in the camp of Trotskyite traitors'.[52] By March 1940, it became clear that any further delay in expelling the communists from the party would severely impact the CSP. At Ramgarh, the national executive of the CSP did just that. But by then, most of the state, district and local units of the CSP in the southern states had already drifted to the CPI. It was the same story in nearly all the labour organizations. The CSP faced a bewildering new landscape and, in Madhu Limaye's words, was 'all but finished'.[53]

On a warpath, the communists charged the Gandhian leadership with bankruptcy and hypocrisy, accusing it of sabotaging the national struggle. They continued to attack radical left allies within the Congress. Even Nehru was not spared. Nehru's role, they said, was to bark at the communists and hang revolutionary draping around the working committee resolutions. They also published a new statement of policy titled 'Proletarian Path'. Its demands included the revolutionary use of the war crisis to cripple major industries, followed by armed insurrection. They began by immobilizing the textile mills in Bombay by dramatically co-opting 1,50,000 mill workers. The official response was no less dramatic. Most of the communist leaders were detained under the Defence of India Act. By February 1941, nearly 480 communists or communist supporters were arrested.

Jayaprakash's quest for Marxist unity had clearly failed and he accepted full responsibility for it. But what is more significant from the point of view of the evolution of his political thought is that this experience created in him a deep aversion for communists. The Moscow trials against the Trotskyites and several top officials of the Red Army reinforced his doubts about the soundness of the Soviet experience. The politburo's swerve of opinion on the war issue also shocked him. When Germany invaded Russia on 22 June 1941, the imperialist war metamorphosed almost overnight into a people's war. If there was some initial resistance against this line, it was largely overcome by mid-1942.

After years of charting out a political line that was diametrically opposed to Gandhi's, after debating, arguing and disagreeing with him, it was evident that Jayaprakash was adapting to the ideological shock of separating from communism by drawing closer to Gandhi. Taking his belief in Marxism out of its rigid, doctrinal orthodoxy, he conceded at this point that the effective leadership of Congress could only be in the hands of Gandhi and it would be suicidal to fight him. His dream of a red dawn was put on a the backburner.

4

The Making of a National Hero

Jayaprakash continued to play an important role in national politics and emerged as the poster boy of democratic, radical dissent. He was lionized for a brand of politics that was free of compromises. A hero to hundreds of young Indians, he was mobbed by adoring crowds whenever he went to mobilize public opinion against Britain's war strategy. He continued to work for the development of peasant and labour mass movements, taking pride in the successful strikes led by the CSP in Bihar.

The official British response to the disruption of its war efforts and strikes in industrial centres was to arrest leaders. Labour leaders like S.A. Dange, B.T. Ranadive, S. Mirajkar, A.S.K. Iyengar and S.P. Parulekar were arrested in Bombay. The arrests spread to other parts of the country to include prominent leaders like Sajjad Zaheer, S.V. Ghate, N.G. Ranga, Rahul Sankrityayana and Sahajanand Saraswati. Jayaprakash was arrested from the Jamshedpur residence of one of his friends on 7 March 1940, incriminated by his rigid stance on the issue of war and a public appeal to Tata Iron and Steel Company (TISCO) workers to strike.

Pleading guilty to the charges levelled against him by the government prosecutor, Jayaprakash passionately proclaimed, 'I have been charged with trying to impede the production of munitions and other supplies essential to the efficient prosecution of the war, and with trying to influence the conduct and attitude of the public in a manner prejudicial to the defence of British India and the efficient prosecution of the war. I plead guilty to these charges . . . As far as the charge of endangering the defence of British India, I think the irony of it cannot be lost upon us. A slave has no obligation to defend his slavery. His only obligation is to destroy his bondage. I hope we shall know how to defend ourselves when we have achieved our freedom.'[1]

The news of Jayaprakash's arrest and his defiance during his trial turned him into a symbol of resistance. He was regarded as a man who always put his beliefs before political expediency. Despite their ideological differences, Gandhi spoke in support of Jayaprakash. 'He is no ordinary worker. He is an authority on Socialism. It may be said that what he does not know of Western socialism, nobody else in India does. He is a fine fighter. He has forsaken all for the sake of the deliverance of his country . . . His industry is tireless. His capacity for suffering is not to be excelled. Is this arrest a prearranged plan, or is it a blunder committed by an overzealous officer? If it is the latter, it should be set right.'[2] Nehru also emphasized the significance of Jayaprakash's arrest, stating that the latter was a dear and valued comrade and that this action against him indicated the determination of the government to declare war on the Congress.[3]

Jayaprakash was sentenced to a term of nine months at the Hazaribagh Central Jail. Amidst the national tumult, the atmosphere in the prison was relatively calm and he did not allow his spirit to falter. His stock of books was constantly replenished by friends. He found bliss in reading for many hours straight. He devoured *The Grapes of Wrath*, books on China and Japan, P.G. Wodehouse, complaining occasionally about the lack of periodicals like the *New Leader* and *Labour Action* due to 'stupid' censorship. In a letter addressed to his close friend Minoo Masani, he sounded almost ebullient. 'I have to thank you . . . for the excellent books . . . *The Grapes of Wrath* is an astounding thing. Such vividness combined with such scientific probity. Wodehouse, of course, never fails to cheer up the gloomiest hours. I had a hearty laugh all through and read it all at a stretch.'[4] He was idolized by fellow inmates and gave classes on socialism to them. He also found time to comment on contemporary political developments through articles in select newspapers, writing under the pseudonym 'A Congress Socialist', a catch-all sobriquet for like-minded young socialists.

By this time, Jayaprakash was clearly moving towards a radical path of struggle. He felt that the Congress leadership was concentrated in the hands of a coterie that was anti-labour, anti-peasant and completely bourgeois in orientation. He planned to begin work on forming a new revolutionary party based on Marxism–Leninism. The new party was to be independent of other political organizations. It was envisaged as an underground network of revolutionaries, an organization carrying out illegal activities. With this context in mind, he wrote, 'We need mass organs of struggle and for seizure of power. I see these in the kisan and mazdoor sabhas chiefly. These will have to be united in a mighty union of peasants' and workers' unions (Congress of Peasants' and Workers' Soviets). The formation of this union should be one of our objectives in the immediate future.'[5] He also unremittingly listed the flaws of the Muslim League and its failure to participate in the freedom struggle. Jinnah, he felt, was a traitor and a conceited historical fool for all his Führer-like attitudes.

Jayaprakash welcomed the decision of the Congress to launch a civil disobedience movement in its fifty-third session at Ramgarh in March 1940. Concomitantly, however, he debunked efforts of its leaders like C. Rajagopalachari to persuade the AICC to adopt a resolution for cooperation in the war. He also critiqued Viceroy Lord Linlithgow's proposal for dominion status of the Westminster variety. The proposal was hailed by the Congress president, Rajendra Prasad, as the clearest of all declarations hitherto made.[6] Crusading strongly against this stand, Jayaprakash addressed a letter to Nehru on 20 July 1940. 'Dear Bhai, you can imagine how recent events have grieved and hurt us. Rajaji has stabbed us in the back. All of us here expect you and beseech you to lead the opposition in the A.I.C.C. and the country. You should resign your seat in the Committee. After a settlement, that is. If it comes about, you must leave the Congress and form another political organisation to fulfil the remaining part of the political task and the main part of the social task of the Indian revolution. Will you do it?'[7]

When Nehru failed to respond, Jayaprakash sent a secret undated letter to Subhas Bose through a special messenger. Spelling out his central contention, he wrote, 'To my mind our basic task today is to chalk out a line of action that is fundamentally independent of the Congress . . . There is not an iota of doubt left that civil disobedience if started would be for no greater purpose than that of forcing concessions out of imperialism . . . Our work henceforth must proceed on the opposite assumption entirely: that the Congress is no longer the main basis for political action. We must explain the character of the present Congress leadership in plain terms to the masses (negative). We must build-up their own instruments of struggle and teach them to depend solely upon those.'[8]

Bose had other plans. He was preparing for his escape from India. There was no response from his side either. The closing months of 1940 were crammed with war-related narratives. The viceroy's offer to set up a War Advisory Council and expand his own Executive Council to include the princely states 'and other interests in the national life of India'[9] could not address the soaring expectations of the people. The launch of the individual civil disobedience movement proposed by Gandhi seemed like a historical inevitability.

After his prison term was over, towards the end of 1940, Jayaprakash was arrested again, in early 1941 in Bombay. He was kept for a short spell in the Arthur Road prison and then, without trial, in the barracks of a notorious camp jail at Deoli, 80 miles from Ajmer, set up to house hardened political prisoners. The prisoners were largely communists, Congress socialists, revolutionaries from Bhagat Singh's Hindustan Socialist Republican Association, Royists, Labour Party comrades, members of the Forward Bloc, the Revolutionary Socialist Party and people like Hakim Khan, a close associate of Abdul Ghaffar Khan.[10] Jayaprakash saw Deoli as a great opportunity for mobilizing support for the armed struggle that he was dreaming of. He strongly critiqued political associates who were critical of socialism: 'No one has a right to be disillusioned with Socialism or Communism because of disillusionment with the Stalin regime . . . It would be the same thing as being disillusioned with Gandhism after the Congress ministries. I have no doubt that if the Gandhian State came into being the Stalins of Gandhism in spite of their best intentions would make of it no better mess than Lenin's successor has done with the Soviet State. But no one, on that account, should have the right to be disillusioned with

Gandhism itself.'[11] He tried to put protocols related to underground work in place by directing old associates like Basawan Singh to go underground and begin the process of recruitment and publicity.

The prisoners in Deoli lived in barracks segregated into two camps. After a while, the detention authorities loosened up slightly and allowed members of both the camps to associate in the common playground in the morning and evening. These periods of recreation were enough for Jayaprakash to persuade organizations like the Revolutionary Socialist Party to come into the CSP fold. His 'classes' on Marxism were very popular, drawing the attention of a junior officer who agreed to smuggle letters out from the camp. In a note to a close friend, Jayaprakash complained that there were no Marxist books available at the camp. 'Please send one copy of each from the books of Marx, Engels, Lenin . . . These books are necessary for the class work here.'[12]

His friends continued to send Jayaprakash books that helped in a 'little intellectual spring-cleaning'. He enjoyed books with Marxian moorings such as Lucien Laurat's *Marxism and Democracy* and Arthur Koestler's *Darkness at Noon*, one of the most celebrated political novels of the twentieth century, an indictment of Stalin's purges in 1938. What possibly engaged him was Koestler's quasi-Marxist rumination on history and destiny. He also used his time in debates about India's position on the war with communist leaders like S.A. Dange, Muzaffar Ahmed, S.S. Mirajkar, Ajoy Ghosh and B.T. Ranadive.

One of the most trenchant critiques of Jayaprakash's politics came from his wife Prabhavati. In the 1930s, they lived together for short spells—at Swaraj Bhawan in Allahabad and a tiny house jointly rented with his socialist friend Ganga Sharan Sinha in Kadamkuan, Patna. It was a penniless, hand-to-mouth situation, with Gandhi bailing them out frequently with small grants. Jayaprakash's associates during that period recall how he was often forced to travel ticketless. He was preoccupied with eighteen hours of political work daily, week after week, leading Gandhi to remark that Jayaprakash seemed more married to socialism than Prabhavati. His agnosticism troubled her, as did his political beliefs. She spent hours bent over her spinning wheel, upset when Jayaprakash questioned the role of khadi and charkha in resuscitating the villages of India, or in removing the grinding poverty of the masses. She fired off several letters to Gandhi expressing a nagging scepticism about their life together. Punctilious in answering her letters, Gandhi chafed against her scepticism, encouraging her to spend time with Jayaprakash, sometimes using levity to deal with her low spirits.

By 1940, their relationship looked stronger. Jayaprakash kept Prabhavati free from any burden of expectation, sublimating his desire for physical intimacy. On her part, she seemed ready to embrace his complexity and his unusual commitments. Remembering her reaction to the news of Jayaprakash's arrest in March 1940, a socialist comrade said that when he broke the news, she was at Ramgarh to attend the fifty-third session of the Congress. Her concern and anxiety surprised everyone. She visited Jayaprakash as often as she could at the Hazaribagh jail and later at Deoli. Her frequent visits prompted her involvement in the clandestine smuggling of letters from jail, carried out with some amount of ingenuity under Jayaprakash's directions. 'Take a big old book with a thick binding, tear the binding off, place the letter there, get the book bound again and send it . . . If you get this letter, tell me tomorrow in the interview that, "You had a headache last night." This will be a hint for me of the delivery.'[13] To communicate that she had received a set of previous letters, she was told to use the following code: 'All are well at the house of Babuni, both at Murar and at Daltonganj.'[14]

The smuggling of letters stopped when an important bundle of correspondence was seized by the superintendent of the detention camp. Jayaprakash tried to slip it into Prabhavati's hands, under cover of handing her a sheet of paper with measurements for a new pair of slippers. Prabhavati flinched, drawing the attention of the jail officer. A scuffle between Jayaprakash and the officer followed. Eventually, the officer managed to raise an alarm. That, more or less, sealed the fate of the letters. Jayaprakash was roughed up and taken to the office of the superintendent who asked him whether he had any regrets. Characteristically, Jayaprakash's only regret was that he had failed and been caught.

The home ministry decided to publicize the text of Jayaprakash's letters, with the aim of tarnishing his image and driving a wedge between him and Congress leaders. On 18 October 1941, almost all the newspapers with the exception of *The Hindu* of Madras, *Hindustan Times* of Delhi and *Free Press* of Bombay published the full text of the letters. However, far from driving a wedge, the publication of the letters won him the admiration of the public. Even those who did not approve of his methods applauded Jayaprakash's courage and single-minded determination to see the country free as soon as possible. This mood was reflected in Gandhi's statement issued to the press on 21 October 1941. While calling upon the Congress to retain its faith in non-violence, he questioned the government's right to arrest Jayaprakash. 'Frankly, all nationalist forces, no matter by what name they are described, are at war with the Government. And, according to the accepted canons of war, the method adopted by Jayaprakash Narayan is perfectly legitimate . . . He has had his training in America for seven long years and is a student of the methods adopted by Western nations in their fight for freedom. To practise deception, to resort to secret methods and even to plot murder are all honourable and turn the perpetrators into national heroes. Are not Clive and Warren Hastings national heroes? If Jayaprakash Narayan was in the British Diplomatic services, and by secret diplomacy achieved something of importance, he would be covered with distinction.'[15]

On 16 October, the government issued a communiqué alleging that the CSP's plans to consolidate its position by winning over important members of terrorist organizations were seized from Jayaprakash while he was trying to smuggle them through his wife. Reacting strongly to this allegation, Gandhi wrote, 'The sensation with which the event has been disclosed to the Indian world is ill-conceived. The annotations in the communiqué are probably wholly unwarranted. When it is borne in mind that Jayaprakash Narayan is an untried detenu the annotations look very like hitting below the belt. The government should have shown Jayaprakash Narayan the document or documents seized, and published his answer if he had any to give.'[16]

The reference to Prabhavati in the communiqué clearly upset Gandhi. 'The way in which his poor wife has been dragged in is unfortunate. She knew nothing of the attempt, for it was frustrated before anything could reach her. I may inform the public that Prabhavati does not share Jayaprakash Narayan's view. She was put under my charge by her parents when she was not yet fifteen and while her husband Jayaprakash was still in America. She has wholly accepted my view of Indian politics and is one of my most faithful co-workers. As husband and wife, Jayaprakash Narayan and Prabhavati Devi are an ideal couple. Jayaprakash has never sought to impose his views on Prabhavati.'[17]

Gandhi also shot off a letter to Jayaprakash, the contents of which can be surmised from Jayaprakash's reply: 'I have seen one of the statements you have issued regarding those letters. It gave me much satisfaction; it only proves your greatness. I was surprised as well as pained to know about Prabhavati. Our relationship was never based on harmony of thoughts, then why should she be so disturbed over my ideas? You may kindly make her understand.'[18] Prabhavati's diary entries remain silent on this entire episode. Jayaprakash detached himself from personal issues to protest in support of long-standing demands of the prisoners at Deoli that included the disbandment of the camp prison and repatriation of prisoners to their home provinces. His protest was in the form of a hunger strike that continued for thirty-one days. Alarmed at the duration, Gandhi sent him a telegram saying, 'Strongly advise discontinuation of the hunger strike by you and others, public opinion being created for securing relief.'[19] Jayaprakash was placed in solitary confinement for his intransigence. He broke the strike only when the core issues were resolved. The jail was dismantled and its prisoners repatriated to their home provinces. Jayaprakash was sent to Hazaribagh Central Prison where another memorable chapter of his life began.

Incarcerated at Hazaribagh Central Jail, in a cell earlier occupied by Khan Abdul Ghaffar Khan, Jayaprakash grappled with powerful emotive ideas and dreams. The news of the Quit India Resolution being adopted by the AICC on 8 August 1942, the arrest of top Congress leaders, countrywide protests and their brutal suppression, strengthened his desire to break free. To an intrepid freedom fighter like him, it was galling to sit idle in prison while such a momentous struggle was going on in the country. Radicalized further during his long spell in prison and with a now-or-never spirit, he began dreaming of building a strong underground network of armed revolutionaries.

He was convinced that guerrilla warfare would work best in such a politically volatile environment.

Finally, taking advantage of the atmosphere of revelry on the night of Diwali, Jayaprakash managed to scale the 17-foot-high wall of the jail with the help of trusted comrades who made a human ladder. He then descended with the help of a rope made of knotted dhotis. Four of his associates distracted the guards by narrating amusing stories and anecdotes. It was a definitive moment on the night of 8 November 1942. For the next several days, Jayaprakash, coping with sciatica, and five of his closest associates from jail—Yogendra Shukla, Surya Narain Singh, Ramanand Misra, Gulab Chand Gupta and Shaligram Singh— braved rough conditions in harsh, hostile terrains. They subsisted on forest fruits and an occasional meal of puffed rice, sleeping on hard ground under the open sky without any cover in the cold November nights. Jayaprakash had to be carried part of the way before a bullock cart came to their rescue.

The group split a few days later. The first group proceeded to north Bihar. Jayaprakash was in the second group with Ramanand Misra and Shaligram Singh. They managed to cross over to Gaya and reach Sukhodeora, the village of a Congress associate. For some time, they enjoyed the comfort of a home. Equipped with a little money, clothes and comfortable walking shoes, and hiding under heaps of jute bags in bullock carts, they managed to reach Dehri-on-Sone undetected. They then took a train to Mughalsarai, crossed the Ganga by boat and reached Kashi. Jayaprakash used different disguises to travel to Delhi and Bombay, connecting with comrades like Achyut Patwardhan, addressing clandestine meetings and distributing bootlegged Marxist literature. The government offered Rs 5000 for information leading to Jayaprakash, an amount that was later raised to Rs 10,000.

Schooled in the Hegelian and Marxian tradition, with its roots in universal history and the dialectical method, Jayaprakash used his underground sojourn to write two extremely thought-provoking, acerbic letters to freedom fighters. Writing both as a polemicist and practising socialist, his letters lifted the lid on different nuances of the freedom movement. The emotive text of the letters ended with the most popular slogan of the period, 'Do or Die'. In his first letter, issued in February 1943, Jayaprakash exhorted the fighters for freedom not to be disheartened because of the apparent suppression of the 1942 movement. 'The history of all revolutions shows that a revolution is not an event. It is a phase, a social process. And during the evolution of a revolution, tides and ebbs are normal.'[20] The Indian revolution, he explained, was ebbing at that time not because of the superior physical force of the British, but two other reasons. First, there was no efficient organization that could function and effectively lead the forces that were unleashed by the August uprising. Second, after the first phase of the uprising was over, there was no cohesive plan to take it further.

'The failure was ours,' Jayaprakash admitted. 'We should have supplied them with a programme for the next phase. When this was not done, the revolts came to a standstill and the phase of the ebb began . . .'[21] The main task was to remove the shortcomings and prepare for the next phase. Boldly asserting that recourse to violence was unavoidable, he added a caveat, 'I have no hesitation in admitting that non-violence of the brave, if practiced on a sufficiently large scale, would make violence unnecessary, but where such non-violence is absent, I should not allow cowardice, clothed in shastric subtleties, to block the development of this revolution and lead to its failure . . . Throughout the world where men are fighting, dying and suffering today, the alchemist is at work, just as he is in India, where he has already let loose a mighty social upheaval.'[22]

In a second letter written in September the same year, Jayaprakash engaged with the issue of ends and means. While remaining convinced that the use of violence was necessary to carry on the struggle for freedom effectively, he felt that there was no point getting caught in a dilemma about the method to be adopted. 'Every fighter for freedom,' he wrote, 'is free to choose his own method', adding, 'those who believe in non-violence may harbour the fear that those who practice violence might compromise the position of Gandhiji. That fear is unfounded. Gandhiji's adherence to non-violence is so complete that not a hundred thousand Churchills and Amerys will be able to compromise him.'[23] Another issue to which Jayaprakash devoted considerable space in this letter was the efforts of leaders like C. Rajagopalachari, Bhulabhai Desai and K.M. Munshi to end the political deadlock. He felt that such actions would only harm India's interests and described those who were driving them as 'saboteurs of the freedom movement'.[24] A continuation of the political deadlock was essential. It showed that India remained unbeaten and that its indomitable spirit of resistance was still alive.

Critiquing communists who were denouncing Bose, Jayaprakash quipped, 'Those who are themselves quislings of Britain find it easiest to denounce him. But nationalist India knows him as a fervent patriot and as one who has always been in the forefront of his country's fight for freedom.'[25] At the same time, he took care to emphasize that India's freedom would not come as a gift from the Japanese, but would depend on the strength and resources of its citizens. India alone represented 'the aspirations of the disinherited and dispossessed of the earth. India's fight for freedom is at once anti-imperialist (and therefore also anti-fascist, for imperialism is the parent of fascism) and a drive to end the war through the intervention of the common man. Neither allied nor axis victory is our aim, nor do we pin our hope on either. We work for the defeat of imperialism and fascism both by the common people of the world and by our struggle, we show the way to the ending of the war and the liberation of the black, white and yellow.'[26]

His ideas came to fruition in a candid letter addressed to students that remains a touchstone text for newcomers to radical politics. Acknowledging the special role of students in the August uprising while seeking a renewed affirmation of their commitment to revolution, Jayaprakash wrote, 'In every field of preparation, we need your help. We have to work in the villages and industrial centres, on the railways and in the mines, in the army and the services. We have to publish and distribute our literature, maintain our contacts and communications, we have to raise and train a militia and bands of technical workers for sabotage and similar activities, and we have to continue our present clashes and skirmishes with the enemy. A network of organizations, working under a coordinated and central command, is being built up. Through our existing contacts with you, we shall attempt to reach you and to entrust different duties to each of you as may be prepared to enlist in the army of the revolution.'[27] Encouraging students to leave their colleges and universities, Jayaprakash reminded them of periods in a nation's life when the halting of individual development was a necessary imperative for national growth. Citing the example of students in China and Russia who marched to the battlefront and laid down their lives, he advised his youthful acolytes to resist listening to cowardly words and plunge into the 'whirlpool of national life'.[28] He also shot off a rousing appeal to American officers and soldiers present in India to extend their support to the Indian struggle for freedom.[29]

Jayaprakash's letters and the news of his audacious exploits gave him the status of a radical ideologue even before he set up a cadre of armed guerrilla revolutionaries called Azad Dasta in the terai jungles of southern Nepal. This group included a few of his old associates like Suraj Narain Singh, Gulab Chandra Gupta and Ramanandan Mishra. They were joined by several other activists, most notably, Kartik Prasad Singh, Anandi Prasad, Baidyanath Jha, Rameshwar and Nityanand Singh and Ram Manohar Lohia. Many of them were in their twenties, energized with the promise of a new type of politics. The Azad Dasta was stationed in Bakro ka Tapu, a forested area north of Jaleswar. It was from here that Jayaprakash hoped to launch a countrywide revolution. He set up a clandestine radio station to broadcast news from the underground, much like Usha Mehta's broadcasts on the Congress Radio and Subhas Bose's Berlin Radio transmissions. A blaze of revolutionary fervour spread across areas in Bihar like Purnia, Bhagalpur, Banka, Mongher, Muzaffarpur, Champaran, Shahabad and the Santhal Parganas.

Setting aside existing gender boundaries, Vijaya Patwardhan, the petite, sharp-featured, London-educated sister of Achyut Patwardhan also joined Jayaprakash's guerrilla warriors. Vijaya idolized and adored Jayaprakash from the time she met him at Achyut's underground hideout in Bombay. Just out of university, she delighted in being part of a radical and subversive movement. Recalling those heady days, several years later, she wrote, 'I was crazy about Jayaprakash . . . I wanted to be with him. Achyut dissuaded me from going to him, but I refused to listen. I joined him on 15th March 1943. We travelled to a few places together before reaching his hideout in the jungles of Nepal.'[30]

Assuming a new name and identity, Vijaya took over Jayaprakash's secretarial and other miscellaneous work with youthful verve. She also helped him comb the area to mobilize support, using different disguises to avoid detection and arrest. Their escapades were legendary, evocative of an erotic complicity that was tender and intimate. The camaraderie survived the tumult and turmoil of their stormy lives but ended when the police got wind of their secret location. She managed to escape to Calcutta but was eventually forced back to the family home in Pune. She was declared mentally unstable and given electric shocks to rid her of her obsessive love for Jayaprakash. Written out of his life, her own role in the revolutionary underground erased, or sidelined, she spent her entire life in solitude.[31]

The training hub for guerrilla warfare was established in the Suranga hills. The cadets were trained by Suraj Narain Singh and Sardar Nityanand Singh, a member of the Azad Hind Fauj. Their training encompassed learning how to blow up roads and bridges, disrupt railway signal cabins and telephonic communication, and attack factories, mines and docks. They were also trained in incendiarism, the burning of enemies' offices, stores, etc. Jayaprakash hoped that they would become leaders of mass insurrection.

The British authorities soon got wind of what was happening and began closing in. Intelligence Bureau reports of the Home Department took note of two highly 'pernicious' documents titled 'A.B.C. of Dislocation' and 'Instructions-Sabotage of Communication'. Both of them were attributed to Jayaprakash.[32] There were reports of trains being looted in Barauni and other junctions, and wagons of ammunition falling into guerrilla hands. An Intelligence Bureau report of the Bihar Special Branch alleged the formation of suicide squads and four guerrilla training centres.[33] The British applied pressure on the Government of Nepal to arrest Jayaprakash and members of his Dasta and deport them to India. The Nepalese authorities succeeded, in due course, in locating Jayaprakash and Lohia, arresting them along with four of their associates, including Kartik Prasad Singh and Baidyanath Jha, in May 1943.

Members of the Azad Dasta were lodged in a makeshift prison that went by the name of Bada Hakim ka Jail at Hanuman Nagar, near Janakpur. During his visit to the riverbank the next morning to wash himself, Jayaprakash spotted a boy known to him and asked him to convey the news of their arrest to other members of the Azad Dasta. In a dramatic move, a little before midnight, the prison was surrounded by Jayaprakash's men and several young Nepalese supporters. The prison police responded with knee-jerk alacrity but were distracted by the flames emanating from a torched hut. They lost their wits completely when two of their constables were shot in the crossfire. Risking their lives, the guerrilla warriors managed to cut the electric wires, enabling Jayaprakash and his team to escape. They managed to reach Bihar and then travelled to Calcutta and from thereon to Delhi. Jayaprakash disguised himself in European clothes and assumed a false identity.

Jayaprakash's freedom was short-lived. Caught off guard during a journey on the Frontier Mail from Delhi to Rawalpindi to meet Afghan insurgents, he was arrested near the Amritsar railway station by the Lahore police chief, William Robinson, on the morning of 19 September 1943, exactly ten months and ten days after his escape from Hazaribagh jail. He was taken to the Lahore Fort. It was a brutal, high-security jail with appalling living conditions. The government did its best to suppress the news of Jayaprakash's arrest, but with little success. His followers were gripped with paranoia even while he remained calm, ready to face long periods of sustained interrogation and torture with equanimity. It was not long, thereafter, before the guerrilla movement inspired by Jayaprakash petered out.

A few months later, in February 1944, Jayaprakash sent a written complaint to the home secretary, Government of Punjab, on his interrogation travails. 'I was arrested on the 18th September last year at Amritsar and brought the same day to this Fort. After about a month of my detention here, I was taken to the office where officers of the Punjab, Bihar and Bengal C.I.D.s were present. I was informed that I would have to answer certain questions that would be put to me and make a statement regarding my recent activities. I made it clear to the officers present that I was prepared to answer any question that did not relate to my recent "underground" activities, and as for the statement, I had no more to say than that I was an enemy of the British Empire of India (not of Britain or the British Commonwealth), that I was working for my country's independence and that I would continue to do so till either the object was achieved or death intervened.'[34]

Jayaprakash was taken for questioning several times during the day and night. He was not allowed any sleep. The interrogation went on relentlessly from 20 October to 10 December 1943. In a raw, blistering account of the lengths to which the interrogation team went, he wrote, 'From morning till 12 pm, I would be continuously kept in the office, then be taken to the cell for an hour, brought to the office again for an hour or two, taken back for an hour again and so on till morning. The interrupted portions of hours that I got in my cell could hardly bring me sleep, for, just as I would be dozing off, the time would be up and I would be brought out again. On paper the process perhaps does not appear to be so torture-some [sic], but I can assure you in all honesty that when [it] continues for days it is a most oppressive and nerve-racking experience.'[35] His only contact with the outside world were two British-owned newspapers, which were also heavily censored.

His spirit unbroken, Jayaprakash continued to speak the language of militant protest. The interrogation team eventually gave up trying to tease information out of him. He was given access to newspapers, books and journals and was allowed to write three letters a week. He spent more than fifteen months in solitary confinement, being allowed to move out of his claustrophobic cell, in handcuffs, for an hour each in the morning and evening to exercise. His cell was a 15-by-12-foot space with stark grey walls. The guards, under strict orders not to engage with him, pushed food in through the thick iron bars. He tried to keep his spirits up by watching the banal antics of 'Churchill', the local tomcat, named for his appearance that 'only lacked a cigar to equate it with that other famous face that is the hope of Europe—of that Europe, that is utterly dead but is frantically trying to live'.[36] His situation often drove him to extremes of despair and rancour.

'Yes, nothing happens in my cosmos that meets the eye,' Jayaprakash was to write in a brooding, meditative tone. 'Yet there are things that do happen here—things that neither I nor the sun's eye can see. But while walls can shut off sight, ears can see through them. So, sometimes as the sun goes down and darkness falls over men's deeds, I hear both the howls of the captive and the thudding of the ogre's blows, the ogre who rules over this cosmos. No, the ogre is not an individual. He is like Brahman—all-pervasive. He is a spirit, the spirit of a system, a system that makes brutes of men. When I hear those howls, a great many things happen to me. I find myself turning into a brute—a raging tearing, brutal vengeance wells up within my being. I fight hard to keep my humanity. It is difficult, very difficult, very difficult, and I am not sure I quite succeed.'[37] Despite the severe odds, he was far from dreaming about walking to freedom. In a letter to Gandhi he asserted, 'Although prison is not a place for human beings to live, still I assure you that I am neither counting the days of my release, nor thinking that I am engaged in any penance. In revolutions, it is inevitable that some die, some are ruined and some languish in jails. Where is the question of any kind of deliberation on this? Thousands are still languishing in jails—in future also thousands will continue to languish.'[38]

Jayaprakash's 'cosmos' changed for the better when Lohia was unexpectedly brought to his cell on 25 October 1944. 'It was a great moment for me—greater than the liberation of Paris or Europe. The walls of my cosmos were shattered for the moment, and I was no longer a captive in the grip of the ogre, but a human being, transported to the human world.'[39] Lohia had been brought to the Lahore Fort in May or June 1944. He, too, had been put through an unspeakable ordeal. After their brief reunion, the friends were allowed hour-long conversations every day.

Jayaprakash utilized his time in captivity by reading and writing. Two small rows of books by the side of his spartan bed on the floor were his lifeline. His books were rationed to about ten a month. His demand for books from close friends like Minoo Masani, Yusuf Meherally, Kamalashanker Pandya and Sri Prakasa, often outstripped the supply. His delight in receiving his book consignments was all too apparent in letters such as this one addressed to Minoo Masani. 'So your books were a feast to me and I fell to them with a shameless voracity. It was very kind of Yusuf (Meherally) to send me all those lovely books— nine of them (including these for the doc) Prabhavati told me that he has sent books worth nearly Rs. 10,000 to friends in prison. That is a service unique in its thoughtfulness and resource.'

His reading was eclectic. There were books by Bernard Shaw, Bertrand Russell, Douglas Reed, Romain Rolland, André Maurois,

Marcus Aurelius, books on Indian economy and polity like Baden-Powell's *Land Revenue Systems in India* and Agatha Christie's thrillers. Then there were books that provoked him into writing elaborate comments, running into several pages like Oscar Paul's *Underground Europe Calling*, René Guénon's *The Crisis of the Modern World*, Jim Phelan's *Jail Journey* and Louis Fischer's *A Week with Gandhi*; books that kept him entranced, like Hemingway's *For Whom the Bell Tolls* and Erich Fromm's *The Fear of Freedom*; also books by George Eliot that seemed to bore him to death.

Jayaprakash wrote with relentless momentum, getting under the skin of issues like Hindu–Muslim unity with piercing acuity and prescient intimation of what was to happen in the coming months and years. He maintained a cracking pace, writing longhand, with brilliant and disturbing flashes of insight, as he put together random jottings, letters and notes between September 1943 and January 1945, the period of his incarceration.[40] A long note titled 'A Revolution Is Disowned Because It Failed', written on 5 August 1944, was an assessment of the collateral damage of Gandhian politics in the context of Gandhi's open dissociation from the 1942 movement on account of violence. 'For many weeks now, since Gandhiji made his comments on the August movement, a great bitterness has been gnawing at my heart. I know it is fruitless to be embittered and, perhaps, I take things too seriously. Perhaps my fundamentally Socialist way of looking at things leads to my being completely possessed with political issues of the moment.'[41]

'All that happened was not violence,' wrote Jayaprakash, questioning Gandhi's reluctance to own a movement 'tainted' by violence. 'By far the greater part of those moving events was a non-violent mass demonstration—swift, elemental, cyclonic. Nothing like it had happened in 1921, 1930 or 1932. Great deeds of heroism, of non-violent heroism, were performed. They deserve to be made immortal in song and national history. But, I fear, they will rather be treated as ugly spots disfiguring the purity of the Congress name and flag. Already, those who performed deeds of sabotage have been condemned as enemies of their country's freedom. Those thousands of unknown soldiers of independence who participated in the stirring events of

1942 did not stop to consider whether the upheaval that caught them in its surge and flung them onward was technically, in accordance with the niceties of political formulae, a Congress movement or not.'[42]

Over the course of his writings, Jayaprakash also unravelled the contradictions at play in theories of Partition. Venting about an underlying feeling of disquiet, he said, 'We are unaware that the Muslim League's claim for partition is based on the theory that the Muslims in India constitute a separate nation, and, as such, should have their own independent state. We do not think this claim would bear any scientific scrutiny. If we take race, language, history, culture, geography, religion, tradition all together, then India forms one single nation much more truly and really than do the separate communities living in this country.'[43]

In a sharp riposte to the two-nation theory, Jayaprakash said, 'Let us concede for the sake of argument that the Muslims of India do constitute a separate nation. Does it follow necessarily that they should therefore separate from the rest of the country and constitute an independent state? Is it not possible for two nations to live together within a common state? Does not history afford examples of such common statehood? Do not the Scot, the Welsh and the English live together under one government, do not the German, the French and the Italian Swiss form one nation state, do not the British and French Canadians live together, is not the great American nation the result of the mingling of all the nationalities of Europe, are not practically all the South American nations multi-national in composition? It seems highly illogical to demand a partition of the country merely because the Indian Muslims consider themselves to be a separate nation.'[44]

Jayaprakash sent three petitions to the Lahore High Court to draw its attention to the brutalities to which prisoners were subjected in the Lahore Fort. 'I am conscious of the argument that those who believe in violence as a political method as I do must be prepared to be forcibly suppressed,' he wrote. 'I grant that, but there are lawful means even for such suppression. A political revolutionary may be executed for his offences when found guilty by the established law, but he may not be put to any torture for the extortion of information. War is the deadliest, most brutal and violent form of political conflict. Yet a prisoner of war has certain rights and immunities which civilized society scrupulously respects. The same person who would be most mercilessly bayoneted to death in the field of battle would be immune from ill-treatment in the war prisoners' camp and would receive such amenities as the standards of the countries concerned and his own status would warrant.'[45] Soon after the third petition was sent to Arthur Trevor Harries, the Chief Justice of the Lahore High Court, Jayaprakash was transferred to the Agra Central Prison in February 1945.

The Second World War ended in September 1945. Nearly all the members of the Congress Working Committee were released by June 1945 to enable them to deliberate on the Wavell Plan at a conference convened in Shimla. Gandhi, released earlier on 8 May 1944 on account of ill health, was not part of the deliberations. The viceroy's parleys with leaders of political parties for the complete Indianization of the Executive Council broke down when Muhammad Ali Jinnah insisted on retaining the exclusive right to nominate Muslim members. The exceptional tumult in the country added to the instability of the political environment. Numerous agitations and strikes flared up. These in conjunction with the peasant movements of Telangana and Tebhaga and the Indian National Army (INA) trials electrified the entire country.

An event that has been practically effaced from public memory was the mutiny of the Royal Indian Navy that broke out on 18 February 1946. By 19 February, sixty ships harboured at Bombay and eleven shore establishments, including the large Castle Barracks, pulled down the Union Jack and hoisted flags of the Congress, the Muslim League and Communist Party of India. By the dawn of 20 February, the strike had spread to Calcutta, Karachi, Madras, Jamnagar, Visakhapatnam, Cochin and other naval stations. The public support for the mutineers was reminiscent of scenes from Eisenstein's *Battleship Potemkin*. The Labour Party that was in power in England was completely rattled. It sent a three-member Cabinet Mission to India in March 1946 to work on a negotiated settlement of the political question. The mission comprised Sir Stafford Cripps, who in the past (March 1942) had led an unsuccessful delegation to negotiate with the Congress, Lord Pethick-Lawrence and A.V. Alexander (members of the British cabinet).

Gandhi remained tone deaf to the meaning of the mutiny, as did Patel who dismissively referred to the mutineers as a bunch of young hotheads messing with things they had no business being involved in.[46] Jayaprakash and his CSP comrades, on the other hand, saw the naval mutiny as a landmark event that openly challenged the might of the cruelly repressive government.

5

Parting of Ways

Jayaprakash continued to languish in the prison in Agra. His survival kit included precious parcels of books sent by Minoo Masani and thousands of pages of jottings. There were frequent attempts to secure his release as well as Lohia's, but Wavell, the viceroy, dithered. His reticence was prompted by an apprehension about the discord their release would foment. In particular, he was concerned about the effect it would have on compromise settlements, a startlingly prescient worry in hindsight. As a result, it was only around April 1946 when Wavell took a call.

Jayaprakash was opposed to the path of negotiations being pursued by Congress leaders and was clear that the country would have to be prepared to wage another struggle if negotiations failed. Soon after his release, he had a brief meeting with members of the Cabinet Mission at Delhi's Imperial Hotel on 13 April. Answering questions of the Associated Press two days later he said, 'The talks with Cabinet Mission are not the result of goodwill on the part of British Labour Government. It is the result of the greatest national upheavals since 1857 and also of outside pressure and world situation.'[1] Asked for his views about the Communist Party of India, he replied, 'I consider the Communists to be Russia's fifth columnist and as such a perpetual danger to the country, irrespective of what policy they may be following at a particular moment.'[2]

Jayaprakash's release made front-page news. Wherever he went, there were huge crowds waiting for him. The atmosphere was electric, and the adulation reached hysterical proportions when he reached Gandhi Maidan in Patna to address his first public meeting on 21 April 1946. An iconic image of that moment was of Jayaprakash, dressed in a white khadi dhoti-kurta, facing an unprecedented number of star-struck men and women, many with raised fists, the mood of elation washing over them. Senior Congress leader Sri Krishna Sinha presided over the meeting and national poet Ramdhari Singh Dinkar read a poem composed specially for the occasion.[3]

> *The future history is yours*
> *The entire sky is yours*
> *He who is Jayaprakash*
> *Is not afraid of death*
> *Seeing the flame dying out*
> *Plunges into the pyre himself . . .*

Jayaprakash's speech fired everyone's imagination: 'Although we adopted the "Quit India" resolution in August 1942, the British have not yet left the country. Our leaders say that Swaraj is coming and coming within a short time. I wonder what that Swaraj would be like. You know that independence of a country is not gained by negotiations. But what is today going on in Delhi is not just another round table conference. The cabinet ministers of Britain have come over here to negotiate with Indian leaders. This is a direct consequence of our fight for freedom inside the country and the brave efforts of the Azad Hind Fauj under the leadership of Subhas Chandra Bose. The question today is how to channelize this force and organize the people—the students, the kisans, the workers and others—for the coming fight for freedom.'[4]

The Patna meeting was followed by several others in different parts of the country. Wherever Jayaprakash went, he was given a rousing welcome. He kept appealing to people to prepare for the last struggle; to combat the smugness and false hope surrounding the quest for independence through protracted negotiations. For nearly six months, he observed the virulent sparring between the Congress and the Muslim League over the legal minutiae of the Cabinet Mission Plan. It was apparent that Gandhi had allowed the leadership of the Congress to pass into the hands of Nehru and Patel. Finally, Nehru announced that the Congress would enter the Constituent Assembly unfettered by agreements. When the plan was placed before the AICC in Bombay on 6 July 1946, Jayaprakash was all set to oppose it. Adding a touch of drama and poignancy, a visibly frail and tired Yusuf Meherally was pulled in on a stretcher to support his friend. 'The question before the country,' Jayaprakash thundered, 'is not whether to accept the so-called Constituent Assembly scheme sponsored by British imperialism but how to utilize the new forces released by the Quit India movement to drive the British out of India.'[5] This was followed by a long statement issued on 28 July, titled 'To all Fighters for Freedom—III', written on the pattern of two similar letters penned after his escape from Hazaribagh jail.

Jayaprakash stressed the need to prepare for the last offensive: 'The struggle for freedom does not cease with the acceptance of the British constitutional proposals. That struggle will continue. In fact, the character and scope of that struggle will become deeper and wider. To the struggle for liberty will be added the struggle for national unity and bread.'[6] He spoke of strengthening peasant and labour unions, volunteer corps, student and youth organizations, village republics, weavers' cooperatives and myriad other organizations that would help to develop the collective strength and consciousness of the people. He also stressed the need to revitalize the Congress, warning that, '. . . if the present Congress leadership persists in its attempt to transform the Congress into a mere parliamentary body with no constructive programme, relying entirely on governmental machinery to serve or to rule over the people, turning more and more bureaucratic, keeping its hold over the Congress organization by the distribution of patronage and largesse, we shall no doubt be unavoidably drawn into conflict with it. But, at the same time if we carry on our work amongst the people with energy and devotion, we shall undoubtedly be in a position to rally the Congress masses around us and resurrect the Congress from its parliamentary debris.'[7]

Jayaprakash's decision to not allow members of the CSP to join the Constituent Assembly was not endorsed by the majority.

They felt that the CSP could have secured a substantial representation in the Constituent Assembly, enabling it to push its socio-economic agenda in the constitution drafted by it. In retrospect, it does appear that Jayaprakash made an error of judgement and this became a subject of controversy in the higher echelons of his party. Once the interim government was formed on 2 September 1946, Nehru was keen to involve Jayaprakash in the Congress Working Committee. After declining the offer once, Jayaprakash was persuaded to accept the membership. Speaking to the press on 13 September 1946, he said, 'My joining the Congress Working Committee is a token of Congress solidarity. Furthermore, with all the prominent members of the working committee having joined the interim government, I felt there was need in some manner to emphasize the popular non-governmental, revolutionary character of the Congress. I need hardly add that if I ever find that my being on the Working Committee comes in the way of my present work of preparing for a revolutionary struggle, I shall not hesitate to leave the Committee, as I had left it for different reasons before.'[8]

Asked about the attitude his party would adopt towards the interim government, Jayaprakash replied, 'We were opposed to the whole constitutional scheme but when a decision has finally been taken and an Interim Government has been formed with Congress cooperation, we, as Congressmen, cannot oppose or obstruct it. Rather it becomes our duty to strengthen our organization in accordance with and in furtherance of the basic Congress policy of independence.'[9] He continued his uncompromising opposition to colonial policies, positioning himself against the Congress stand on several issues and crossing swords with Patel, now member, home, in the interim government.

Through all these events that were criss-crossing and feeding off each other, Jayaprakash's relationship with Prabhavati remained on an even keel. She continued to spend major chunks of her time with Gandhi and Kasturba. When Kasturba lay dying, after eighteen months of imprisonment at the Aga Khan Palace in February 1944, she asked for Prabhavati. At that time, Prabhavati was in jail in Bhagalpur but was permitted to join Kasturba and Gandhi. She looked after Kasturba and remained at the palace for nearly two months after the latter's death, happy that she was close to Gandhi. She wept copiously when she had to leave but survived her long period of imprisonment with tenacity and resilience. Asked by the jail warden about her commitment to the Congress, she replied that she had imbibed it from her father in her cradle and would never abandon it.[10]

Released from Bhagalpur jail in June 1945, Prabhavati returned to Gandhi, travelling with him to Poona, Uruli Kanchan and Delhi. She also visited Jayaprakash at the Central Jail, Agra, as often as she could. When Jayaprakash was released, Prabhavati was present at the Delhi Junction railway station to receive him. The same night, overcome by emotions that she could not deconstruct, she wrote to Gandhi: 'A few days earlier you told me that I should live with Jayaprakash and try to understand him and his ideas . . . He has come out of jail with I can't say what ideas. If I live with him, I would be able to understand him better . . . I would also be able to explain your ideas to him . . . I have always wanted Jayaprakash to be close to you . . . I dream of him being one of your foremost five followers . . .'[11] Gandhi replied that it was her dharma to live with Jayaprakash and look after him. He added a terse postscript, 'You should also think for yourself. What will you do after I die?'[12]

Meanwhile, the Muslim League, having failed to secure an assurance of its dominance over the interim government, withdrew its acceptance of the Cabinet Mission Plan and resorted to a programme of Direct Action, launched on 16 August 1946. This led to the outbreak of communal riots on a large scale. The riots started in Calcutta and then spread to Noakhali in East Bengal, resulting in the death of a large number of Hindus. The ferocity and suddenness of the violence was shocking. As immediate reaction, riots against Muslims broke out in Bihar between October and December. The area affected most was the Magadh region.

The interim government headed by Nehru recommended strong action against the rioters. Communal tensions kept rising, so much so that when Nehru toured through the affected areas between 4 and 9 November 1946, he was greeted with hate slogans and black-flag demonstrations. In a meeting at the Wheeler Senate House of the

Patna University (where my father was also present), when Nehru rose to address students, he was not allowed to speak. Jayaprakash, also on the podium with Nehru, rebuked them for their unruly behaviour. Arguing that those who indulged in rioting were enemies of freedom, he said, 'By creating such disturbance, these elements had proved to be "traitors" to their country . . . Why should anyone feel mercy for them?'[13] He was appalled when pro-Congress newspapers like *Searchlight* and *Indian Nation* also began to play the communal card.

Jayaprakash was convinced that the unfolding communal barbarity was the result of a conspiracy between the Muslim League and the British government. He felt that the Congress had fallen into a diabolical trap by settling for negotiations rather than mass agitation. He articulated to the students what he believed was at the root of the trouble. 'The mischief being done by the British rulers who were using the Muslim League as a pawn in their nefarious game of holding India in bondage. Communalism will take India fifty years back from where it stands today. Noakhali can be avenged only by driving the British out and making the country free. It is, therefore the duty of every patriotic Indian to foil that game by refusing to be led away by communal passions which are being stirred up deliberately.'[14] A day later, in an interview given to the Associated Press of America, he emphatically said that the only radical remedy for stopping communal violence was the uprooting of British rule.[15]

Jayaprakash toured the riot-affected areas in Bihar with groups of students in a desperate attempt to heal festering wounds, drawing Patel's ire when he helped stop police raids and searches of Muslim homes. He challenged Patel's line that there was no trouble in Bihar. The ferocity of violence in Punjab too saddened him no end. 'The present disturbances in the Punjab are carefully planned and are part of a conspiracy to install the Muslim League in office as a step towards the creation of Pakistan. It cannot be an accident that the districts where serious rioting broke out are precisely those districts which are ruled by British officers.'[16] As expected, his tirade against the role of British officers did not go down well with them. They alleged that Jayaprakash was using the deteriorating communal environment to foster rebellion even in organizations such as the police. In a note addressed to Wavell, the Bihar governor Sir Hugh Dow wrote, 'JP Narayan has again been stumping the country trying to suborn the police from their allegiance, stating that while all the constables were fine stout fellows whom the country could rely on in the coming struggle, all officers from the IG down to the assistant sub-inspector were dishonest and unreliable. Ramanand Tiwary[17] continues openly to urge the police constables to go on strike and to refuse to obey their officers.'[18]

In February 1947, Mountbatten was appointed the last viceroy with the specific task of transferring power as quickly as possible. Mountbatten's DICKIE Bird Plan, whereby each of the eleven provinces of British India and each of the 559 princely states would be given the option to join India or Pakistan or remain independent, was opposed by Nehru who felt that it would balkanize India. Mountbatten then whipped up a plan drawn up by Indian civil servant V.P. Menon, which proposed partition into two dominions, India and Pakistan, under the British crown. A Boundary Commission created East and West Pakistan on the basis of hastily devised plans and borders sketched by a British judge, Cyril Radcliffe, with the help of old maps and census figures.

The socialists kept themselves away from voting on the partition resolution in the AICC meeting. They hoped against hope that the Congress would reject the partition formula, resign from the interim government and face the British government on the question of the country's independence. The Mountbatten Plan unfolded on 15 August, with India and Pakistan as self-governing dominions within the British Commonwealth. Purna Swaraj was destined to remain a pipe dream till 1950.

The birth of India and Pakistan, an inevitable outcome of the imperial policy of divide and rule, was one of the darkest moments in Indian history with a resonance similar to the holocaust in terms of brutality. As writer Saadat Hasan Manto noted, 'normal mores of civilization were suspended',[19] and a million people were killed in the genocide that followed. Partition resulted in the migration of more than 13 million people, with countless deaths from disease in 600 makeshift refugee camps. More than 70,000 women faced sexual violence—many of them, savage death. India, hence, did not just wake up to life and freedom but a raging inferno of communal violence not only in Punjab, but also in Bengal, Bihar, Uttar Pradesh, Kashmir, Sind and beyond. Gandhi's desperate effort to douse the fire by fasting and praying in riot-hit areas did not help and eventually claimed his life. He was shot and killed by a Hindu fanatic at the time of his evening prayers at the Birla House on 30 January 1948.

By this time, Jayaprakash was once again challenging some of his own fundamental political assumptions by giving a quick spin to ideas based on lessons drawn from Marx, Gandhi and Western democratic values. In an article titled 'My Picture of Socialism', written for CSP's party journal *Janata* in 1946, he put forth the necessity of building the socialist movement within the contextual framework of Marxist thought, of world history since Marx's death, and India's own political history. 'Marxism is a science of society and a scientific method of social change that includes social revolution. As such, there can be no room for dogmatism or fundamentalism in Marxist thought.'[20]

Marx and his materialist view of history remained pivotal to Jayaprakash's thought even as his focus on democracy was unremitting. There could be no socialism without democracy, he wrote. 'It is a common mistake to think that there must be dictatorship of the proletariat in a Socialist state. This is against the teaching of Marx . . . Dictatorship of the proletariat has been considered in Marxism thought as essential for the transitional period . . . Once the transition is over, the state must become a fully democratic institution . . . Thus, my picture of a Socialist India is the picture of an economic and political democracy. In this democracy man will neither be slave to capitalism nor to a party or the state. Man will be free.'[21] He wrote with strident conviction about the need to disperse the ownership and management of industry and the necessity of developing villages into democratic republics to attenuate the looming danger of totalitarianism.

Jayaprakash continued to see in the CSP the inherent potential for becoming the chief instrument to develop socialism in India. 'The CSP is the party of Socialism in this country: the party of the future. Like the country itself, CSP too is passing through transition and must soon acquire forms that would represent and express the political, economic and social urges of the oppressed masses.'[22] He followed up his polemical writing on socialism with an article, 'The Transition to Socialism', written in January 1947.[23] Drawing on Marx's stand at the Hague Convention of the First International in 1872, he countered Marxists who maintained that violent revolutions were imperative. The article focused on two extremely divergent paths to socialism, one peaceful, where democratic conditions prevailed, and the other violent, where they did not. Which of the two paths should be followed depended upon the ground realities of a country at a given point of time. While Lenin took the path of violent revolution in Russia, the Labour Party in Britain, which had come to power in 1945, was putting socialist schemes into practice in a democratic way.

Jayaprakash viewed the transition to socialism as not a straight road, but a tangle of conflicting paths. Therefore, it was not possible to be doctrinaire about the policies of a transitional period such as this. 'I have reaffirmed my faith in democratic Socialism, which is the only true Socialism . . . But faced as we are with undemocratic forces which have to be defeated and destroyed before Socialism can be ushered in, I conceive a period of trouble and turmoil, a revolutionary phase of the transition, a phase in which not only the democratic revolution should be completed but also considerable progress made towards Socialism. A state and society emerging from such a revolution should then be able to pass in a democratic manner into full Socialism.'[24] This was a bold stand, an attribute for which Jayaprakash was well known. Replying to a related query about the role of Muslims in the revolutionary struggle for freedom, Jayaprakash asserted that their role was as significant as that of other Indians. The need of the hour was to take up and tackle the problems of the masses, not as members of this or that community but in their capacity as peasants and workers. He cited the case of Darbhanga, where 2000 Muslims had joined the Kisan Sabha.[25]

While the CSP was preparing to emerge as a full-blown political party, its differences with the Congress increased. The two were soon on a collision course. Reports of harassment and the arrest of socialist workers active in labour and peasant movements in Congress-governed provinces poured in. This included Jayaprakash's close friend Suraj Narayan Singh and Gita Singh, a young socialist leader of Bihar. Many of Jayaprakash's associates in the Bihar Socialist Party were arrested because of their role in the Jharia coalfield agitations for better wages.

Jayaprakash's relationship with Patel worsened. Something as innocuous as his address at a public meeting in Patna Police Lines on 10 October 1946—where Jayaprakash acknowledged the role of police constables in the freedom struggle while demanding the removal of officers who had acted inhumanely during the August revolution—became contentious. Ramanand Tiwary, the leader of the police strike at Jamshedpur in 1942, in which 700 police constables had participated, was present at the venue. A garbled version of Jayaprakash's speech was sent to Patel. Greatly incensed, Patel warned Jayaprakash in a letter, marked secret and dated 17 October 1946: 'I do not know how far this version is true, but would it not be unwise to agitate about this matter in this manner publicly, instead of approaching your own Ministry in the Province in a proper constitutional manner? Surely, you, as a Member of the Working Committee, would be expected to bring the matter to the Working Committee or the Parliamentary Board, if you have any grievance against the Ministry; but your agitation and propaganda of this nature is sure to embarrass the Ministry and also to some extent us here who are working under a very difficult situation, particularly owing to communal tension.'[26]

Jayaprakash wrote back saying that the facts about the meeting and his speech reported to Patel were 'somewhat misleading'. He enclosed a correct version of his speech. He also added that contrary to Patel's impression, Jayaprakash had met Sri Krishna Sinha, the Bihar chief minister, twice to discuss this festering issue and had written to him as well. However, the matter had not received the attention it deserved.[27] Patel also expressed annoyance with Congress socialists on the Naval Mutiny issue. Socialists like Aruna Asaf Ali were charged by the provincial Criminal Investigation Department with aiding and abetting the mutineers in direct contravention of the Congress stand on the matter.

Given Jayaprakash's misgivings with the Congress on a gamut of issues, it seemed logical for the CSP to function as an independent political party. The party dropped the word Congress from its name and retained just its socialist identity at its conference in Cawnpore

towards the end of February 1947. This was followed by the adoption of
a policy statement designed to provide new and necessary momentum
for progressive change. Jayaprakash's essays on socialism became the
substructure of the document, its backbone. The socialists also decided
to go for mass membership, making it possible for persons who did not
wish to be members of the Congress to join the party. Writing to Louis
Fischer about a month later, Jayaprakash said, 'One of the important
decisions was that we changed our name from the Congress Socialist
Party to the Socialist Party. This indicates the shift of emphasis from
the national to the social struggle.' Echoing Gandhi's views, he added,
'I think the best thing to do would be for the Congress to dissolve itself
so that new parties based on socio-economic programmes might come
into being.'[28]

While Nehru tried to bridge the chasm between the Congress
and the socialists, Jayaprakash's relationship with Patel continued to
fray. Provocation came from both sides. On a few occasions, it was
Jayaprakash who seemed to take the lead. For instance, while addressing
the Coimbatore district textile workers in April 1947, he remarked,
'Sardar Patel appeals to us not to leave the Congress. It was Sardar and
his friends who tried for five years to send us out of the Congress. But
we remained in spite of these efforts. We have now reached a new stage.
We do not want to exploit the name of the Congress, but will proceed
with policies and programmes of our own. The Socialist Party of India
will approach the masses on its own behalf.'[29]

An anguished letter from Patel to Jayaprakash, dated 26 April
1947, mentions his failed efforts to bring about a truce between
the socialists and the Congress. 'Since my release I have tried my
best to bring about a fusion between your party and the Congress.
Unfortunately I have failed to convert you, although I have succeeded
in convincing many important individual members of the correctness
of my views. I have done nothing either in thought or in action to
injure the cause of your party or to do any harm to any individual.
I can only say that I am sorry that I have not been able to convince
you of my bona fides. It is regrettable that at a time when we need to
stand together you are consciously or unconsciously trying to divide
our forces.'[30]

Jayaprakash's reply to Patel's letter was not without sting. Addressing him as he always did, as 'Sardar Saheb', he wrote, 'It is true that I had said that you were among those of our leaders who did not look with favour on the Socialists and even tried to destroy their influence in the Congress. I may be mistaken, but this is the impression that I have gathered during my many years of experience of inner Congress politics. Your sharp attacks on us within and outside the AICC, the activities of some of your trusted lieutenants like S.K. Patil and Shankerrao Deo and the attitude towards us of the entire Congress machine in every province which is under the control of the so-called right-wing—all these have conspired to create this impression in my mind.' He did, however, agree that differences needed to be resolved. 'I and my colleagues are prepared to sit down with you and some of our other leaders to thrash out this question of cooperation between the two wings of the Congress. We are as keenly conscious of the critical times ahead as any of you and should like to put our shoulders to the wheel and take full responsibility in guiding the country towards a safe destiny. When we were in Delhi last, both Bapuji and Jawaharlalji had called us and impressed upon us the necessity of working together and strengthening the Congress. We agreed whole-heartedly with the suggestion in principle but were doubtful of its being worked out in action.'[31]

Written from Mussoorie, Patel's response, dated 23 May 1947, to Jayaprakash was terse, bordering on the accusatory. 'On several occasions, I have made earnest endeavours to make reconciliation and to secure cooperation from you and your [sic] party, but every time we have met with a rebuff. It is my sad experience that although often you have agreed with our decisions or our policy when you were with us, you disagreed afterwards on grounds of party discipline or party interest. There are many in the Congress who feel that much of the indiscipline in the Congress is due to the existence of your party in the Congress and also of the party members working solely in its interest or for strengthening it. This naturally brings conflict and distrust, but so far as I am concerned, I have, since my release, said nothing or done nothing to come in the way of your working or your party's working in the manner you think fit, however much I may have disagreed with it.'[32]

The exchanges continued, laconic, polite, fractious, incendiary, revealing a bitter polarization. On 29 May, a strong rebuttal of all the issues raised followed. This included an elliptical reference to Patel's patronizing platitude about getting old. 'I thank you for your letter of May 23,' Jayaprakash wrote. 'In spite of its underlying bitterness, I am rather glad that you have enabled me to understand you better. You write that on several occasions you made earnest endeavours towards reconciliation and securing our cooperation but every time you met with a rebuff. This is a rather astounding statement. As far as I am concerned, I know only of vague talks in which remarks such as getting old and our taking your place were made, but I never knew of any serious attempt made to secure our cooperation. On the other hand, my personal experience has been that my cooperation has not been accepted even when offered at a critical time . . . The instances that I gave in my previous letter were to show that whenever I attempted to have cooperation translated into practice, I faced a blank wall.'[33]

Patel's next move was to 'ask' the socialists to take over the responsibility of administration of a single province and solve its issues instead of restricting themselves to agitational activities. This gauntlet was thrown at the socialists on 10 August 1947 in a meeting in New Delhi. Jayaprakash's press statement issued the very next day was part defensive and part churlish. 'We are not in a hurry to leave the Congress. We have not in mind the next elections. We are free to express our views like everybody else and carry on propaganda so as to create an atmosphere for the Socialist programme to be carried out by the National Government.'[34] What transpired between Jayaprakash and Patel was not restricted to paper-solecisms and debates. They clashed openly in different forums. The AICC session called on 14–15 June 1947 to ratify the Congress's acceptance of the Mountbatten Plan saw one such clash, when Jayaprakash and Lohia debated the partition issue with Patel and Nehru. When it was time to vote, the socialists abstained.

Their relationship reached a nadir when Gandhi was assassinated and Jayaprakash pointed to the culpability of Patel as the home minister. In a statement jointly issued with Lohia and Kamaladevi Chattopadhyay on 3 February 1948, Jayaprakash stated that the assassin was not one person, but a big and wide conspiracy of organizations like the Hindu Mahasabha, Rashtriya Swayamsevak Sangh (RSS) and the Muslim League. He insisted on the resignation of the government 'in symbolic atonement of the evil deed', and entrustment of the home portfolio to a minister who would have no other portfolios to administer and would be willing to curb and crush organizations fomenting communal hatred.[35] Clarifying their stand, Jayaprakash said that what they were demanding was not removal of Patel from the cabinet. Instead, they were questioning the wisdom of entrusting important portfolios of home, states and information to one person. 'Are there not sufficient person in India that one man should handle the three portfolios?' he asked. 'That clearly indicates that Sardar Patel seeks power which is likely to lead to dictatorship.'[36] In speech after speech he lashed out at the government: 'Why was it that the government realized the danger of Communalism only after Mahatma Gandhi's assassination? Where was the secret police? If the secret police did inform the government in advance about the real position, why was no action taken to meet the danger?'[37]

The acrimony with Patel did not stand in the way of Jayaprakash's continuing support of the Congress-led government at the Centre, thanks primarily to Gandhi's insistence on unity at a time when the scourge of communal politics was burgeoning. Jayaprakash addressed several meetings on the issue of communalism. He warned people that encouraging the idea of Hindu Raj would result in balkanization of the country. 'If you want to establish People's Raj, if you want to remove poverty, hunger, disease and illiteracy, if you want to build up a state where all may have equal rights and opportunities, then get rid of the canker of communalism. This canker has gone deep down and has poisoned the whole body-politic. It has not only divided the Hindus from the Muslim; it has divided the Hindus from Hindu. If allowed to go unchecked, it will spell disaster for the whole country.'[38] He urged the immediate banning of 'communal organizations' like the Hindu Mahasabha and the RSS.[39]

The socialists continued to resist the Congress's effort to enforce conformity. In what was perceived as a serious breach of political etiquette, they set up their own candidates for the Bombay Municipal Corporation elections, defeating many of those nominated by the

Congress. This was a landmark event in the history of the party that had, by March 1948, grown exponentially. According to the general secretary's annual report (March 1948), the total membership of the party stood at 5139 confirmed members and 3671 probationers with the highest numbers from Bihar—1150 confirmed and 1923 probationers. The number of trade unions under the influence of the party was 797 with more than 5 lakh members. Two national federations in the mining and sugar industries had been formed and two more in the textile and water transport industries were in the offing. The spectacular success of a general strike organized by the Bombay chapter of the party on 29 December 1947, involving about a million workers, was indicative of the strength of the socialist movement.

The strength of peasant movements was also growing. In Bihar, the Bakasht struggle over land appropriated by zamindars in lieu of failure to pay rents assumed the form of a mass movement with districts like Gaya, Darbhanga, Muzaffarpur, Bhagalpur and Monghyr acting as the epicentre. The provincial Kisan Sabha of Bihar, which was under the influence of the Socialist Party, had sixteen district branches, twenty subdivisional branches and 128 branches at the thana level with a membership of over 1,10,000. They were organized around issues like commutation of rent and opposition to conversion of peasants' lands into big farms by landlords. In Uttar Pradesh, Kisan Sanghs in forty-six districts were under the influence of the party. In Maharashtra, this number was nine. The party also had a considerable presence in a number of other states like Assam, Kerala, Bengal, Gujarat, Punjab and Rajputana.

It was a no-brainer that the training of workers was important. Schools for training trade union workers were established in several provinces with separate schools for women workers. A labour college was set up in Bombay. The Bihar branch of the party organized the autumn and winter school of politics. In Uttar Pradesh, several study circles and miniature think tanks were started. Indian participation was ensured in international socialist conferences at Milan and Antwerp. The radical literature published in the journals *Janavani, Sangharsh, Janamat, Janata, Socialist, Jagrati, Mazdoor, Krishak, Kranti* was at the forefront of global socialist writing.

Through all this, the party got next to no support from the Congress government. Quite the contrary. In a letter sent to Nehru on 11 January 1948, Jayaprakash wrote, 'The distance between us and the Congress is becoming wider every day . . . In Bihar, for instance, nearly 500 of our workers are either under arrest or wanted by the police.' Jayaprakash rued the fact that all those who wanted the Congress to be a body of voluntary servants of the people had lost the battle with calamitous results. 'Of course, there will be many to whom this issue will appear academic or dogmatic. They would say the main issue today is of national survival and building up a powerful state and a prosperous country. Only the other day Sardar Patel disparaged "isms" and denounced the parrot-cries of socialism. We do not think there is any contradiction between the issue of "isms" and the issue of national survival and national construction. Rather, not only is there no contradiction, but we believe that in building up the national state and new India, a consideration of isms is essential. We believe that on the basis of Socialism alone is it possible to build up a strong and prosperous India. Congress has become a source of power and personal advancement. Congress elections beginning with enrolment of members have become a racket and self-seeking and power politics have become rampant. This rising tide of selfish politics is the greatest barrier today in the path of the Congress advancing towards socialism.'[40]

The Socialist Party prepared its own draft of the constitution by December 1947, driven by the conviction that the Constituent Assembly was pro-capitalist in orientation. The draft was as much about freedom as equality. In a scathing attack on the assembly in his introduction to the draft, Jayaprakash wrote, 'Its deliberations have been dominated by cool and sedate lawyers who give no evidence that they comprehend the significance of the turmoiled birth of a nation. There have been no passionate controversies raised in the Assembly, nor have we witnessed the din and dust of a stubborn fight of interests and ideologies.'[41] The outcome, he observed, was a constitution that fell considerably short of the democratic principles enunciated in its preamble. It was highly centralized and was adversely impacted by the ordinance-making powers of the executive. Extraordinary powers were vested in the president and the governors under the emergency provisions. He pointed at several other fault lines that could, if left unaddressed, result in dangerous omissions and anomalies.

Nehru's decision to move from 7 York Place to the huge, palatial Flagstaff House on Delhi's Teen Murti Marg, built as the official residence of the British commander-in-chief, was also critiqued by Jayaprakash. 'In a meeting with him in December 1947 I asked Nehru if it behoved the Prime Minister of a poor country to live in a fabulous palace. I reminded him that on his return from a visit to the USSR, he had written in his book with obvious admiration that the great leader Lenin lived in a two-room small flat in the Kremlin. Nehru replied that the Russian Ambassador who had come to see him a few days ago had come in a magnificent limousine flanked by two equally grand cars. I protested that Russia was now a developed country and a big power but India was still in as early a stage of development as Lenin's Russia . . . The consequences of that initial mistake can be seen in the ostentatious pomp and grandeur of our rulers which mock at the millions of wretched dwellings in the name of the "dignity of state".'[42]

Their mutual distaste for power politics and genuine concern for the poor and dispossessed brought Jayaprakash and Gandhi closer ideologically. In fact, when Kripalani resigned as Congress president, Gandhi wanted Jayaprakash to take his place, but Nehru initially chose Patel and eventually offered the position to Rajendra Prasad. With Gandhi's death, the connection between the socialists and the Congress snapped completely, widening the cracks.

In February 1948, the Constitution Committee of the Congress decided to outlaw organized groups and parties with independent constitutions from Congress membership. Within a few weeks of this decision, at the annual convention of the party held in Nasik between 19 and 21 March 1948, the socialists finally separated from the Congress. One of the first events Jayaprakash organized was a hugely successful All India Labour Convention, in Bombay, in November 1948. From then, there was no looking back. Bringing in a new constitution, the party upheld Jayaprakash's belief in democratic socialism, non-violence, decentralization and constructive methods. Resolutions on national reconstruction, revival and regeneration strengthened the political foundations of the party, and Jayaprakash was confident that his new party would emerge as a credible parliamentary alternative to the Congress.[43]

The annual report Jayaprakash delivered as general secretary succinctly analysed where the party was headed. He began by assuring valued friends in the Congress that their bonds of personal and ideological attachment would never snap. 'There is much in common between Congress and the Socialist Party: their faith in secular democracy brings them nearer together than any other two parties in the country. This naturally means that the Socialist Party shall ever be ready to fight for the defence of the state and of democracy and against the forces of communalism and reaction; and in this fight it would be happy always to join hands with the Congress.'[44]

Following these comments with a no holds barred critique of Congress compromises and miscalculations, Jayaprakash reminded those who had not come to terms with the decision to leave the Congress that the CSP had been formed as a reaction to the growth of 'Parliamentary mentality' in the former. Commenting that accepting partition was political adventurism of the worst kind, he said, 'If partition had not been accepted, the Congress would have had to resign from the Interim government and face the British once again on the issue of full independence and an undivided India.'[45]

The most passionate and visceral portion of the report dealt with the role of ethics in politics and the close relationship between ends and means, reflecting how far Jayaprakash had moved from orthodox Marxism and how close to Gandhi. He repudiated the view that all politics was power politics as also the assumption that the state was the only instrument for social good. This marked the beginning of a new phase in his political thought, which was to culminate later in his abdicating power politics altogether. Looking back at the factors that propelled this momentous decision, Jayaprakash said, 'At that point it was apparent that try as we may, we would not have been able to change the essentially conservative character of the Congress. At the very best it would have become a bourgeois-liberal party.' He added wistfully, 'It was only Jawaharlal who could have done something with our help.' He also recalled that when he met Gandhi a day before his death, Gandhi had warned him about the difficult times ahead.

6

Emergence of New Fault Lines

The rift with the socialists left the Congress with wounds that took years to heal. They continued to be bitterly polarized on most issues, the tone and texture of their debates going beyond acceptable political differences. In all fairness, Nehru tried to glue some of the broken pieces together, but was caught in the overwhelmingly conformist culture of the older party. Thus, he was compelled to sidestep most of the important points of difference.

Writing to Jayaprakash on the eve of the Nasik session on 15 March 1948, a visibly emotional Nehru spoke of the need to stay together. 'You are meeting soon and are likely to take vital decisions. What you decide will naturally have an important effect on the country. You have sometimes discussed these matters with me in the past and I told you how I feel about them. I think the time has come when you must decide for yourself and no one else should seek to interfere with your decision. So I do not propose to say anything about it. But I should like, if I may, to express the hope that whatever the decision may be, it will be taken in a friendly spirit to others and with a desire to cooperate to the fullest extent possible. The internal situation is difficult enough, the external one is full of peril . . . so we must try our utmost to pull together and face these two dangers together.'[1]

Jayaprakash echoed Nehru's sentiments by speaking of ties that were deep and resonant. Reminiscing about their long association, he said, 'I should like to point out here that while we often played the role of a left minority within the Congress, there were many occasions on which we were completely at one with the majority. Particularly, during periods of national struggle, members of the Party acted as zealous soldiers of the Congress and worked as one team with other Congressmen. This positive aspect of our work is often overlooked by critics. Summing up the total result of our work within the Congress, one might say that we acted as a check on the politics of compromise; we strengthened the organisation as an instrument of struggle, and we were able to produce a climate of Socialism within the Congress. The fact that every Congressman today is anxious to describe himself as a Socialist, whether or not he is actually one, is a tribute to the work of our Party. I am conscious that when we leave the Congress, we shall leave behind many friends and valued comrades with whom our bonds of personal and ideological attachment shall never snap.'[2]

This was on 19 March 1948. In a letter sent to Nehru a little over a week later, he again said, 'I need hardly say what a personal wrench it has been to most of us to separate from old friends. What it means personally for me I can hardly express. But I have no doubt that politically, there was no alternative and I hope that in the act of separation, we have done nothing that would embitter our relations. I, together with many other senior members of the Socialist Party, do fervently hope that we will continue to receive inspiration and guidance from you and that the personal bonds and loyalties will continue.'[3]

The idea that the bond would not snap was somewhat delusional. The country was in economic stasis. While addressing the many failings of the government, Jayaprakash was convinced that socialism would bring about a decisive rupture with past practices and provide a radical alternative to capitalism and the Congress. Nehru on his part advised his colleagues to not say or do anything that might result in a widening of the breach. He wrote another emotionally charged letter in August 1948 offering to consider how the gulf between the two parties could be bridged. 'I am greatly distressed at many things in India. But perhaps what distresses me most is the wide gap which is ever growing between many of us and the Socialist Party.'[4]

Nehru was convinced that the political path Jayaprakash was following demonstrated a serious error of judgement. He was 'apt to go astray very often and act in an irresponsible manner. But he is one of the straightest and finest men I have known, and if character counts, as it does, he counts for a great deal. It seems to me a tragedy that a man like him should be thrust, by circumstances, into the wilderness.'[5] Untainted by prejudice, Nehru recognized the strength of Jayaprakash and saw in him a future prime minister.[6] He continued to work on Jayaprakash by saying that his premature leftism could lead to reaction and disruption. His letters took on an achingly poignant tone as he wrote, 'I cannot, by sheer force of circumstance, do everything that I would like to do. We are all of us in some measure prisoners of fate and circumstance. But I am as keen as ever to go in a particular direction and carry the country with me and I do hope that in doing so I would have some help from you.'[7]

By-elections held in the constituencies where the socialists had resigned, most of which were in Uttar Pradesh, shattered illusions of a rapprochement. The levels to which Congress leaders like Govind Ballabh Pant stooped astonished Jayaprakash. Carrying out a virulent smear campaign, Pant, a right-wing polemicist, alleged that the socialists were self-seekers who left the Congress for personal advancement and that to vote for them was like voting for the Razakars and the frontier tribesmen raiding Kashmir. Using an extremely divisive tone, he further alleged that if voted to power, the socialists would replace Hindi with Hindustani and would ensure that temples would cease to exist.[8] What irked Jayaprakash, in particular, was Pant's repeated assertion that 'opposition' was a Western political concept, completely unsuited to India.

The socialists lost in most constituencies not because they were not an electoral force. Rather, their losses were attributable to a deliberate attempt to create an atmosphere of fear in which people were afraid to exercise their franchise freely. Even a leader of the reputation and calibre of Narendra Deva was defeated. Jayaprakash poured out his anguish in an article titled 'Towards Fascism' written for *Janata* on 4 July 1948. 'I had thought that there were certain things that were common ground between us and the Congress, such as, defence of freedom and democracy, a clean and decent public life, opposition to communalism and racialism. In a democracy, unless opposition parties have some common basis of this sort, democracy cannot function.

If the Congress begins to pander to communalism just to catch votes, what will happen to India?'[9]

In another article on the election, published in *Janata*, he underscored the importance of 'harder work and better and better organisation'.[10] Jayaprakash's core group included leaders like Narendra Deva, Yusuf Meherally, Achyut Patwardhan, Ram Manohar Lohia, Asoka Mehta and Madhu Limaye. They agreed that the organizational structure of the party needed to be revamped to make it truly mass based. Contesting the argument of a faction in the party that was against the unchecked influx of members, Jayaprakash argued that nothing in Marxist theory ordained that a socialist party must restrict its membership to a chosen few.

Jayaprakash contrasted the Indian situation with the state of affairs in Russia, arguing that in the absence of democracy in czarist Russia there was plausible reason for the Bolshevik Party to organize itself on the basis of restricted membership. The Indian context, with a democratic constitution on the anvil, did not justify this. The party needed to be modelled on the British Labour Party, as a bastion for working-class organizations of peasants and workers. Resolving their inner differences and contrarian views through fiery discussions and debates, the socialists endorsed a new constitution on 8 March 1949, amplifying many of Jayaprakash's core ideas. Membership was thrown open to individuals interested in the objectives of the party, but Jayaprakash's proposed affiliation with organizations of peasants and workers did not materialize.

Jayaprakash continued to work to build a grassroots movement. His political report, presented to the Madras conference of the Socialist Party in July 1950, was critical in shaping positive outcomes.[11] Placing the core values of socialism at the heart of this report, he said that in a clash between the core values and theories of socialism, the former must prevail. Socialism could not be reduced to a quest for nationalization of industry and collectivization of agriculture alone, but had to bring into its ambit the end of exploitation, injustice, oppression and insecurity, leading to equality of opportunity for everyone. Before the session ended, it adopted a programme for national revival presented by Madhu Limaye, which included known socialist and Gandhian objectives, like reducing the gap between rich and poor, village reconstruction and social integration.[12]

The debate that followed reflected the differences simmering within the party. Voicing serious discontent, B.P. Sinha, a member from Bihar, said, 'I am not satisfied with the definition of democratic methods given by the General Secretary. I want to ask him if by democratic methods, he means peaceful methods only. I believe that democratic methods include armed insurrection also.'[13] Kulomani Mohapatra from Orissa alleged that Jayaprakash had looked at every problem in a 'pedantic Gandhian' way. 'Our ideal cannot be achieved merely by reforming Gandhian ideas and dressing them up with Marxism.'[14]

Calling Jayaprakash's report 'singularly remarkable for its vagueness', Gobind Das (also from Orissa) queried, 'The report is an ethico-politico utopia . . . was it not on account of these utopian conceptions that social democracy failed in Europe?'[15] Raising the issue of affiliated membership, D.S. Mahajani from Bombay remarked, 'It is not possible to persuade unions to affiliate because we cannot explain to the workers what democratic socialism means. This is again due to the fact that we ourselves are not clear about it.'[16] Amolesh Mazumdar, a delegate from Bengal, argued that insurrectionary methods were perfectly democratic if they had the backing of the demos, the people. Standing on most issues with Jayaprakash, Bihar's Karpoori Thakur called all those who were opposed to democratic socialism 'pseudo-revolutionaries', and said they were bookworms, not fieldworkers.[17]

The year 1950 was a disquieting one in Jayaprakash's life. In March, Achyut Patwardhan, one of his closest comrades, decided to leave active politics to focus on educational work. On 2 July, another comrade and close friend, Yusuf Meherally, died after a long illness at the age of forty-seven. Inconsolable, Jayaprakash wrote, 'After Mahatma Gandhi's death, Yusuf Meherally's death has given me the greatest shock. The country would not see another Meherally, a pillar to the Socialist Party, friend of all, lovable and faithful to his ideals.'[18] Jayaprakash's relationship with Lohia was on the ropes because of his continuing proximity to Nehru. Lohia believed that Nehru was using Jayaprakash to keep the conservative groups in the Congress (headed by Patel) at bay.[19] Jayaprakash's differences with Aruna Asaf Ali were also escalating. It was no secret that she disagreed with his rendition of the objectives of democratic socialism. It was not long before she sent in her resignation and joined the CPI.

Jayaprakash's personal life was calmer. No longer pulled by contrarian impulses, by 1948, Prabhavati and he managed to settle down to some level of domesticity. She agonized over his schedules and was awake to his needs. She nursed him when he fractured his right arm in a road accident near Daltonganj on 1 April 1949. She was with him during his long fast in Pune in 1952, a time that stirred up memories of her ashram life. She accompanied him on most of his travels: at mass rallies of railway workers, through the famine- and flood-affected areas of north Bihar, at sit-ins and marches and hundreds of public meetings. In her white khadi sari, relatable and accessible, she quietly defined her boundaries as political discussions and debates on socialism reverberated around her. Her small rented home was always ready to welcome their associates and party workers. She would take care of their needs, proffer advice when it was sought and listen to their stories.

This is how Jayaprakash's close associate Kamaladevi Chattopadhyay described Prabhavati's role in Jayaprakash's life. 'She was deeply attached to him and intensely proud of him. I had often watched her looking at him when her eyes held almost an adoration. Nevertheless she was conscious of his weaknesses and foibles, when her reaction was one of amused, restrained indulgence. There was the eternal clamour over his contrary demands. He would sternly ask to travel light, which she had learnt after some bitter experience to ignore. "You see all what he calls the extras that I am asked not to carry are the essentials he cannot dispense with. So I have to carry the unwanted even at the cost of his irritation. He becomes like a child on such occasions."'[20]

Prabhavati had the ability to lighten up a heavy moment and leave everyone convulsed with laughter. One of her favourite anecdotes was about her first train journey to Sitabdiara with her father-in-law soon after her marriage. When she entered her first-class coupe, she found the windows shut, to keep her away from public gaze. Feeling claustrophobic, she opened the windows only to find her father-in-law shutting them again. This went on till Harsu Dayal realized that he was dealing with a strong and independent young girl.

Her relationship with the spinning wheel was almost as old as her relationship with Gandhi, and equally intimate. During meetings, conclaves and sit-ins, she could be seen sitting in a quiet corner, working on her spinning wheel. When she moved to Patna, she started 'charkha' classes in tiny shacks near the Socialist Party office in Kadamkuan and near Patna College in Patna City, encouraging women and young girls to spin for their independence as well as the country's. Once these classes moved to the building that currently houses the Mahila Charkha Samiti, the women were in a space they could call their own. In 1957–58, she also started a Montessori school named after Kamala Nehru with seed money collected as donations from friends.

Jayaprakash travelled from one end of the country to another to strengthen the party and extend its influence in the trade union movement. The constant travel also played a vital role in fund collection for the party and its network of allied organizations. As president of three major national unions—railway personnel (the All-India Railwaymen's Federation), telegraph workers and civilian employees of the defence ministry—he had to lock horns with the government on several labour issues. He ended up facing the ire of the CPI, which accused him of soft-pedalling issues and working in league with the government to stave off strikes.

The communists were not completely wrong. Even though Jayaprakash strongly critiqued government policies, if the national interest was involved as in Kashmir and Hyderabad, he was not averse to working with the Congress. He was behind the Socialist Party's unstinted support to the armed resistance movement in Hyderabad and supported the state's merger with India. Even his supporters were surprised by his pro-government stand in advising the All-India Railwaymen's Federation to desist from going on strike. His naive belief in the commitment given by senior Congress leader Rafi Ahmed Kidwai, minister of communications in 1950–51, on a matter related to the salary of post and telegraph workers when they were on strike, also led to a lot of criticism.

Jayaprakash's focus was party work. Joining hands with colleagues, he coordinated several peasant marches and rallies and took the lead in organizing the kisan and mazdoor panchayats, both of which were

affiliated with the Socialist Party. The extent of his involvement with
peasant and workers' movement was evident from his management
of struggles like the one in the Dalmianagar sugar factory in Bihar.
The workers' union at the factory was headed by Basawan Singh,
Jayaprakash's long-cherished socialist associate. A seemingly
unresolvable issue related to the reinstatement of approximately 2500
workers, who had been dismissed during a long strike, was settled
through arbitration by Rajendra Prasad, but not before Jayaprakash
went down on his knees before Nehru.

What rankled Jayaprakash most was the attitude of the
government. Not only was it impervious to the demands of workers,
but it was openly conspiring to weaken the socialists by promoting
the Indian National Trade Union Congress as a rival. 'The chief role
of the Congress Unions today is that of strike-breaking. They talk of
Gandhian methods, but they are no better than the Communists in the
matter of bogus membership, and they do not stop at hooliganism,'
complained Jayaprakash.[21] He cited the example of the dock workers
in Bombay who demonstrated peacefully before the Port Trust on an
issue related to recruitment. Their leaders were hauled up and thrown
into prison under the Public Security Act on the 'fictitious plea' that
a breach of peace was anticipated. He was also upset by legislation
outlawing strikes and essential services, describing it, in a telegram sent
to Nehru on 2 March 1949, as a blot on Nehru's administration and
an ugly example of growing Indian fascism.[22]

In dealing with issues related to widening social and economic
inequalities, Jayaprakash realized that he needed to go beyond available
political literature and emotive texts. This led to the foundation of the
Khoj Parishad in Calcutta in April 1948. One of the earliest ventures
of the foundation was organizing a conference of leading economists
in Calcutta in August 1948. Just a few days before the conference,
Jayaprakash spoke of how independence had turned into dust in the
mouth of the people. 'The miseries and the muddles, the ascendant
corruption and self-seeking, the runaway profits and the profiteering,
the killings and the war, and, above all, the supreme blunder which
cost us the life of the Nation's father have made of that independence
festival a historic mockery.'[23]

Addressing a public meeting in Calcutta, Jayaprakash continued to express his concern at the deteriorating economic condition of the country. Not enamoured by the mixed economic growth model or the Industrial Policy Resolution of 1948, he focused his lens on falling industrial production, scarcity of goods, exploding unemployment rates, rising costs, chronic poverty and growing corruption. Jayaprakash blamed the administration for this appalling situation. He wrote to Nehru with anguish, 'You are a believer in first things first, and I thought the very first thing you would do was to reform the system of administration and the services. You cannot make the present system yield results which it never was intended to do. There was corruption under British rule against which all of us spoke strongly. There is more corruption under Congress rule and I see no instance of any serious attempt being made to root it out or even to check it. Nepotism and favouritism are prevalent in the highest quarters, and it is often the corrupt civil servant, who being conversant with the art of pleasing his masters whoever they may be, that prospers.'[24]

Making an inventory of government failures on the economic front, which if not corrected would lead to a 'mess similar to that of Kuomintang China' or even to fascism, Jayaprakash was severely critical of Nehru's leadership. His letters to Nehru took on a bitter tone: 'There is no doubt that you will hold fast to the faith that you are leading the country to Socialism, but let me say without malice or rancour that in spite of your best intention, the country is drifting in the opposite direction. You are trying to ride two horses which may be possible in circuses but not in a historical evolution. History can move only in one direction and not two at the same time. You want to go towards Socialism, but you want the Capitalists to help in that. You are bound to fail in that. If you want Capitalism to play its role in industrializing the country, it will demand its price and if you pay the price you will give a go by to Socialism. This is exactly what is happening today.'[25]

Another issue that worried Jayaprakash was the worsening state of civil liberties in the country. In the same letter dated 10 December 1948, Jayaprakash spoke of his experience during a visit to Nagpur in connection with a meeting of the railwaymen's federation. As Section

144 was in force, the local branch of the Socialist Party applied to the magistrate for permission to hold a meeting but was refused. The socialists then approached the home minister of the state. He also said 'no' on grounds that communists had been denied permission. Giving expression to his anguish, Jayaprakash said, 'There is nothing that I ask for apart from freedom—no dividends of any kind; but at least I expect to enjoy the ordinary freedom of a citizen in a free society. If there is danger of the peace being disturbed as a result of my speech, then all I can say is that in that case, the peace deserves to be disturbed.'[26]

Jayaprakash also expressed anguish and outrage at the arrest of Achyut Patwardhan, when the latter was about to address a rally which was disrupted by a group of Congress goons. Horrifyingly, the local administration arrested Achyut instead of the rogues and took him in an open truck to the police station and later to the Nasik prison where he was kept with undertrials.

The arrest of Achyut Patwardhan was followed by the arrest of Lohia and fifty other socialists on 25 May 1949, for demonstrating in front of the Nepal embassy, demanding the release of Nepalese leader, B.P. Koirala. Jayaprakash issued a strongly worded press statement against the arrest the next day. 'Free India is being slowly converted into a vast prison . . . Citizens in a free country possess the fundamental right to assemble peacefully and the right cannot be taken by the simple device of declaring such assemblies as unlawful. There are more restrictions on the liberties of citizens in Free India today under Congress rule then under the worst of British despots. This must cause deep anxiety to all freedom lovers in this country and perhaps the day is not distant when they all must join together irrespective of party creeds to save this country from fascism.'[27]

Two of Jayaprakash's close associates, Ganga Sharan Sinha and S.M. Joshi, were arrested in Gwalior during a local disturbance even though they had no role in it. In an angry letter addressed to Patel, he called this an act of madness.[28] Another case that anguished Jayaprakash was the arrest of Baleshwar Dayal whose grassroots work for the Bhil tribe of central India had been of outstanding merit. He was arrested at the height of an agitation against newly imposed tax on grass, firewood and timber that was wreaking havoc on the Bhil economy. Jayaprakash wrote to Nehru with a degree of sarcasm, 'All I can do is to wonder how far apart we have travelled in looking at things.'[29]

Harangued by increasing personal attacks, Nehru justified what was happening by saying that if a choice had to be made between the security of the state and the liberty of its citizens, the former would take precedence. Sounding like Patel, he alleged that the socialists were acting irresponsibly. 'They seem to be all frustrated and going mentally to pieces.'[30] The irony of his words was not lost on Jayaprakash. 'That is exactly how dictators endeavour to justify suppression of liberties and their own dictatorship,' he said in a letter addressed to Aruna Asaf Ali.[31]

Jayaprakash commented freely on events taking place on the world stage. He condemned American intervention in the Chinese civil war and questioned the North Korean invasion of South Korea. He supported Tunisia's struggle for freedom. He questioned India's decision to stay in the Commonwealth. 'The decision to stay in the Commonwealth would mean tying India's foreign policy to the apron strings of the British Foreign Office and joining a fraternity of nations like South Africa and Australia which practise racial discrimination against Indians. Over and above this, India would become a perpetual enemy of the Soviet Union since she would be joining the American Bloc.'[32] Replying to Jayaprakash's contention, Nehru spoke of the practical support that an association with the Commonwealth would secure for at least two or three years. That more or less sealed the debate.

The rapid exodus of Hindus from East Pakistan also plagued Jayaprakash. He issued a strong press statement saying that if India's attempt to stop this exodus failed, it would need to resort to military intervention. He was attacked by a section of the press for warmongering, but became something of a hero in West Bengal. His stand changed when he found that the RSS and the Hindu Mahasabha were trying to communalize the issue. In a complete turnaround on 29 March 1950, he said what his supporters expected from him. 'We do not want that India should wage war against Pakistan. We must create confidence among the Muslims in India that their lives and properties are safe and secure and that they have equal rights and opportunities for self-expression and self-development along with Hindus. We hate communalism. We reject all notions of Hindu Raj. We reject the theory of a theocratic state in India.'[33] He visited the riot-affected areas and set up a cadre of peace workers. Meanwhile, Nehru responded to the mounting war fever between India and Pakistan by entering into a pact with Pakistan's prime minister, Liaquat Ali Khan. Jayaprakash welcomed the Delhi Pact, signed on 8 April 1950, the outcome of six days of talks to create an atmosphere of peace and safeguard the rights of minorities.

The struggle for democracy in Nepal under the leadership of B.P. Koirala, former president of the Nepal National Congress, became the subject of several letters exchanged between Nehru and Jayaprakash. Koirala was a close friend of both Jayaprakash and Lohia from his student days in India in the early 1930s. When Koirala came to Delhi to seek military support, Jayaprakash tried to secure arms aid for the Nepal Congress by writing to socialist leaders in Burma. His closeness to B.P. Koirala and his wife Sushila, however, did not stop him from chastising the former for not supporting his elder brother Matrika Koirala, the prime minister of the interim government formed by King Tribhuvan.

The Socialist Party suffered a big setback during the first general elections held in the winter of 1951–52. Despite the cult of personality around Jayaprakash and other leaders, the socialists did not mount a serious challenge to Nehru, whose popularity soared. It seemed that voters across the political spectrum could not get enough of him. The Congress was an unstoppable force. It perfected its demographic and geographic strategy and won 364 of the 489 seats in the Lok Sabha. The party's victory was perceived as a personal referendum in Nehru's favour.[34] A.K. Gopalan of the Communist Party of India led the opposition bloc by winning sixteen seats while the Socialist Party won twelve.

The odds were stacked against the socialists from the word go. Jayaprakash tried to draw Nehru's attention to the possibilities of intimidation and the tampering of ballot boxes. He campaigned around the country, foregrounding social and economic issues that the Congress had ignored. He critiqued not only the Congress but also the Jana Sangh, condemning the latter strongly for raising irrelevant slogans about Indian culture being under threat: 'The Jana Sangh is raising a slogan that culture is in danger. If communal parties continue to have sway in the political field, real issues like poverty, starvation and economic emancipation will be thrown into the background.'[35]

Allegations and counter allegations flowed. What outraged Jayaprakash most was the attempt by some Congress leaders to malign the socialists by calling them American agents, a mischievous slogan that was in vogue in certain constituencies in Bihar: 'America *ke teen dalal,* Mehta, Lohia, Jayaprakash.' He was also outraged by the rumour that Lohia had brought back thousands of dollars from America to fund the election campaign. But what possibly hurt him most was the contents of a speech delivered by Nehru in Patna, in which the latter insinuated that the socialists had entered into a pact with the Jana Sangh. This influenced Jayaprakash's decision to support the opposition candidate in the first presidential election and put aside his long association with Rajendra Prasad.

The election verdict cast a dark shadow on Jayaprakash's leadership. The mood within the party was one of anxiety, defensiveness and reproach. Party hardliners tried to vilify him. The first salvo surprisingly came from Ramanand Misra, an old associate with whom he had escaped from Hazaribagh jail. Misra circulated a note at the party conference in Bihar holding the top brass of the party squarely responsible for the defeat. Everyone present understood whom he was pointing to. Several other delegates made the same point. Jayaprakash was devastated. As he walked out, my father, present at the meeting as a young socialist, saw him struggling to hold back his tears, looking woebegone. It was clear that he had lost his hold over the party.

A stronger attack awaited Jayaprakash at the Pachmarhi convention of the party held between 23 and 27 May 1952. Jayaprakash accepted the blame for the electoral defeat, but was extremely defensive about the party's policies and programmes. 'I have been, for good or ill, mainly responsible for the development of party policy and programme. It is for me, therefore, to take full responsibility for what happened at the elections. And it is to me more than anyone else that your criticism and censure should be directed. It is not so much the defeat, but the reaction to it, in the ranks of the Party, that is worrying me. I was pained at this reaction and I tried to explore and re-examine and locate the errors in policy. But I did not find any such error. There was nothing wrong with the policy or programme of the Party.'[36] If Jayaprakash was defensive, Lohia emerged as a powerful theoretician, capable of challenging the former's hegemony as the party's chief ideologue.

The political differences between Jayaprakash and Lohia remained relatively muted at this convention. Lohia did not blame Jayaprakash directly but spoke about the need to build a firm doctrinal foundation for the party. 'It should never be an auxiliary team of the Congress Party nor should it ever act as the sappers and miners of the Communist Party.'[37] Bringing the complexities of the defeat to life with unmatched intellectual rigour, he pointed out that of all the candidates, the socialists were the youngest; the party had every now and then adopted a facing-both-ways policy; its record of constructive work and struggles had not been too impressive; and it had spent barely any money on the elections. Barring money, all other reasons for the defeat could be worked upon. It was a temporary reverse. He closed his speech with the following words, 'Those who set out to build a new civilisation must be ready for defeat, ready to struggle and be defeated and yet to struggle again.'[38]

Defending the doctrinal foundation of the party at the convention, Jayaprakash said that while it was not possible to carry on with canned ideas and ready-made doctrines, Marxism was not a dogma. It was a scientific method of studying changes in society and bringing about social change. For the Indian context, Jayaprakash sought to meld Gandhian praxis with Marxian thought to create an ideology that was wholly the country's own.[39]

Jayaprakash tried to talk himself into believing that the electoral debacle was not the result of a calamitous midlife crisis. The party was after all only four years old. It needed to reinvigorate itself, and it could do this by blending Marx and Gandhi in a seamless and organic way. But the relentless personal attacks, with disparaging references to the socialists' 'soft corner for Nehru', continued to devastate him. Inflicting a heavy emotional blow on the socialists, a section of the press and Congressmen even tagged them as 'Nehru's B Team' and 'Nehru's Second Eleven'.

A deep sense of hurt and underlying despair was reflected in the tone of Jayaprakash's letters to Nehru during this time. He accused Nehru of weakening the party. 'What pained me is what you did to Socialism. I wonder whether you have paused to consider the harm you have done to the cause in which you profess such faith. It is remarkable that on the one side you went on declaring yourself a Socialist and, on the other, opposing and ridiculing Socialism. You have on occasions criticised all extant forms of Socialist thought and practice, but I have searched in vain in your recent writings and speeches for your own picture of Socialism.'[40]

Nehru's reply was terse. 'You say that I have done harm to Socialism. I am no judge of that. But I think I have never said a word against Socialism. Rarely in the course of the election addresses I referred to the Socialist Party. This too was chiefly in connection with their foreign policy and their alliances in India. I do not pretend to be a Socialist in any formal sense of the word but surely Socialism is not the monopoly of any particular group.'[41]

Jayaprakash stunned everyone by announcing that he would fast for self-correction in Pune for three weeks, beginning 23 June 1952.[42] It was a quintessential Gandhian moment, but with no indication of what would follow. Under the care of Dr Dinshaw Mehta[43] and his clinical team, he handled the fast well, but the inordinately long period caused anxiety and heartache to innumerable friends and followers. Nehru too seemed deeply anxious. His letters to Jayaprakash were warm and exculpatory in tone. In the first one, dated 8 July, he wrote, 'I have hesitated to write to you during the ordeal which you have imposed upon yourself. You have made us very anxious and my thoughts have been with you. I earnestly hope that you will pass through this ordeal successfully and that your health will not suffer because of it in future. It is some comfort that you have the best advice and the conditions are as favourable as they can be for such a supreme test. Your life is too precious for all of us and for India.'[44]

Jayaprakash's joy, on receiving Nehru's letter, was boundless. He wrote back with a deep sense of love and gratitude, 'Dear Bhai, I was very happy to receive your letter. All these days I have been missing this word of love and cheer from you. You write of embarrassment.

You need have felt no embarrassment at all because I am not fasting against you, your government or any of your colleagues.'[45] Nehru replied two days later, inviting him over not for a brief and hurried talk, but for 'something more'.[46] A few days later, he wrote again, inviting Jayaprakash for a retreat at Mashobra or to Kashmir for a period of quiet rest.[47] His birthday wishes were also full of pep: 'I am writing to you rather early to send you all my love and good wishes on the occasion of your coming birthday, when you will complete half a century. I used to think [of] that age [as] quite respectful. But now that I am 62, it appears to me very youthful.'[48] Jayaprakash also received letters from Sushila and B.P. Koirala that went beyond ritual exchanges and helped forge a lasting bond between him and the couple.

Jayaprakash lost seventeen pounds, but the process of introspection and soul-searching, prompted by the fasting, strengthened his conviction about the importance of ethics in shaping human society. In a note titled 'Aphrodisiacs vs. Real Vitality', he urged his socialist comrades to use the slogan 'Back to the Village' for village-based constructive work. 'Let us give up this quest for the new and striking, let us become pedestrian and plodding for a while. "Back to the village" may be an old slogan, yet, I am confident that if we seriously set out to put it into practice, such a flood of strength and vitality would surge into the party that Socialism would soon become irresistible.'[49] He emphasized the importance and need for constructive work, not only for the village but also for urban areas. He appealed to party leaders to convert it from the tail end to the vanguard of the party's agenda.

More importantly, he felt the stirring of an impulse to distance himself from orthodox Marxism. The reasons were not hard to find. The news of Stalinist repression, his purges and massacres had already reached Jayaprakash's ears from reliable communist sources. His belief in the Gandhian idea that the means always equate the ends had implications that were absolutely revolutionary. He began to feel that materialist philosophy was not capable of accommodating the non-material urge to acquire and practise goodness, which was at the heart of human progress. 'For many years, I have worshipped at the shrine of the goddess—dialectical materialism—which seemed to me intellectually more satisfying than any other philosophy. But while the main quest of philosophy remained unsatisfied, it has become apparent to me that materialism of any sort robs man of the means to become truly human. In a material civilisation, man has no rational incentive to be good. It may be that in the kingdom of dialectical materialism, fear makes man conform, and the party takes the place of God. But the God himself turns vicious; to be vicious becomes a universal code.'[50]

Jayaprakash's disillusionment with dialectical materialism may have baffled many of his socialist followers, but it strengthened the synthesis of socialism and Gandhism in his mind. This is best illustrated in his address titled 'The Ideological Problems of Socialism', at the First Asian Socialist Conference in Rangoon on 7 January 1953, where he spoke about the importance of human values and strongly endorsed the thesis of Lohia to apply the test of immediacy in the socialist movement.[51] He picked up several issues that indicated the distorted development of Marx's ideas. First, he noted a singular failure to deal with value systems and their implications for political and revolutionary actions. Second, he cited Yugoslavia's attempts to deinstitutionalize the rule of the communist party by converting it into the League of Communists without considering the benefits of a multiparty system for democracy. Third, he emphasized the dangers of exploitation of the working class through collectivization and bureaucratization in the Soviet Union. Fourth, he highlighted Marxism's reluctance to open up to alternative historical possibilities, such as democratic new social movements. For this, he used the example of India's localized land reform movements (Bhoodan, Gramdan) to show that social revolutions can take place peacefully and voluntarily and the road to socialism via capitalism was not prescriptive.[52] This was something deeper than a critique of the Stalinist obduracy that reduced socialist philosophy to a crass Machiavellian code of conduct, bereft of any sense of right or wrong, good or evil. It was, rather, a leap of faith, conditioned by contingent events and Jayaprakash's commitment to reorient socialism in a way that would be congruent with Gandhism.

The change in Jayaprakash's outlook facilitated the merger of the Socialist Party with the Krishak Majdoor Praja Party (KMPP) led by J.B. Kripalani who was considered closer in political outlook to the Congress than to the socialists. Ever since the electoral debacle,

Jayaprakash, Lohia and Asoka Mehta had been thinking of a larger political consolidation in order to create a better political balance in the country. It was anything but an ideological coming together. Their strategic merger in the form of Praja Socialist Party (PSP), in September 1952, evoked some amount of wariness in socialist hardliners like Narendra Deva even as Jayaprakash assured party workers that the PSP was committed to the creation of a democratic socialist society, free from social, political and economic exploitation. Kripalani was appointed chairperson of the party, and Asoka Mehta, the general secretary. Later, a section of the Forward Bloc merged with the newly formed party. The party began addressing issues related to economic precarity and the oppression of marginalized groups. It also acted as a political conduit for peasant movements and for a while the merger seemed to work well.

Jayaprakash's only regret was that the decision was taken without consulting senior leader Narendra Deva, who was at that time touring China as a member of the first Indian goodwill mission to that country. Since Deva had been privy to earlier discussions, it was assumed that he would support the merger. The fact that he did not, upset Jayaprakash. There were other issues too that re-emerged to create strong divisions in the old socialist group, leading to attacks on Jayaprakash. Shortly after the formation of the PSP, a series of meetings took place between Nehru and Jayaprakash, Kripalani and Narendra Deva to explore the chances of working together. Speaking on their behalf, Jayaprakash assured Nehru that their approach to socialism was not doctrinaire, hidebound or conservative. Speculating about the reasons behind Nehru's move to ask for their cooperation, he said, 'If it means only this that a few of us are to be added to your cabinet and some state cabinets to strengthen the government and your hands in carrying out your present policies, the attempt would not be worth making. But if it means launching upon a bold joint venture of national reconstruction, it might well have been a historic move.'[53] Lohia, a bitter critic of Nehru, was not a part of these deliberations.

Nehru's dream of a radical reconfiguration of the planning process resulted in the launching, on 2 October 1952, of community development projects and, in 1953, the national extension service.

In speech after speech he was heard saying, 'I will not rest content unless every man, women and child in this country has a fair deal and attains a minimum standard of living . . . Five or six years is too short a time for judging a nation. Wait for another ten years and you will see that our plans will change the picture of the country so completely that the world will be amazed.'[54] Driven by the quest for an equitable order, he promised that steps would be initiated to reduce disparities in income and wealth, weaken private monopolies and disperse the concentration of economic power in the hands of a few individuals. To Jayaprakash, this seemed like the perfect socialist manifesto and so when Nehru invited him, seeking his cooperation in the national reconstruction process, he was delighted.

Nehru and Jayaprakash met in the first week of February 1953 to discuss the objectives and principles of national reconstruction. They seemed to agree on most issues but Jayaprakash felt that an explicit, written agreement in terms of a common programme was essential for effective cooperation. He took some time in deciding areas of cooperation. Finally, a densely typed fourteen-point draft policy was prepared and sent to Nehru on 4 March 1953. In an accompanying letter, Jayaprakash acknowledged that Nehru's proposal for cooperation was a bold and unusual one because the Congress, '. . . stood in no need of a coalition either at the Centre or in most of the States. But you rose above partisan considerations and took a statesmanlike step. What you proposed was, to my mind, not a parliamentary coalition in the accepted sense of the term, but a joint effort to build a new India. Therefore a great deal would depend on how you conceived your own move in asking for our cooperation.'[55] Placing what he termed an 'ideological consideration' before Nehru, he said, 'China and India are the two countries in Asia to which all of Asia and Africa are looking. If India fails to present anything but a pale picture of a welfare state, I am afraid the appeal of China would become irresistible, and that would affect the lives of millions and change the course of history disastrously.'[56]

The draft policy proposed constitutional reforms followed by administrative reforms that would facilitate devolution of power and decentralization of authority, effective mechanisms against corruption, reforms in the legal system, redistribution of land, transformation of the rural economy into a cooperative economy, nationalization of banks and insurance companies, progressive development of state trading, promotion of small-scale industry, nationalization of coal and other mines, association of workers in the management of state enterprises, unified trade union movement organized on the basis of the union shop, scaling down salaries in government services and promotion of the spirit of swadeshi.

Nehru replied to Jayaprakash's letter on 17 March 1953, 'Reading your letter, I realized not only how much we had in common in regard to our basic outlooks, but also the differences in our approach.'[57] It was evident from the text of the letter that Nehru was not thinking of anything revolutionary at this stage. He certainly did not wish to be tied down to specific commitments. 'I feel, after reading your letter and after my talk with you, that perhaps, any kind of a formal step at the present moment would not be helpful. We have to grow into things, not to bring them about artificially. You have sent me a draft programme which includes, among other things, basic constitutional changes. Now, obviously, it is not possible for me to bring about these changes even though I may not be opposed to them. But surely, it is beyond me both as Prime Minister and as the President of the Congress to deal with such vital matters and give assurances with regard to them. Many of these may be logically justifiable and yet there may be other reasons which come in the way. Again, one can hardly take all these things in a bunch.'[58]

When they met, Nehru tried to initiate a dialogue on cooperation once again. What was he thinking? Following the death of Sardar Patel in 1950, was he seeking a closer relationship with Jayaprakash, or was the dialogue a brief dalliance with the socialists to counterbalance the remaining conservatives in his party? Whatever his reasons, Nehru's attitude provoked righteous indignation in socialist leaders who refused to settle for incremental changes. Jayaprakash's own response was measured. He continued to meet Nehru, dispassionately agreeing to cooperate on common objectives. The meetings, bristling with ideas, far from being clandestine, resulted in a political storm. Clarifying his stand to the press, Jayaprakash said: 'Today no single party can build up this country. There must be close cooperation between all democratic and progressive forces in the country.'[59]

During the PSP convention at Betul on 14–18 June, Jayaprakash's associates bitterly criticized what they felt was an acquiescence to Nehruvian ideas. Jayaprakash was defiant in his reply: 'If someone seeks my cooperation I will never deny it, provided there is agreement on the purpose of the cooperation. Some have spoken as if the Congress was dying for our cooperation. Make no mistake about it. The Congress is as much afraid of blurring its features as some of you are.'[60]

Lohia, the most trenchant of Jayaprakash's critics, was busy setting the news agenda with a series of incendiary stories. His doctrinaire belief in equidistance from the Congress and the communists became a rallying point for many young socialists. Backchannel negotiations for a settlement between Lohia and Jayaprakash entered a turbulent new phase. In the ferocity of attacks, what possibly rankled Jayaprakash most was a whispering campaign that he was trying to acquire a position in the cabinet to emerge as Nehru's successor.

The recriminatory atmosphere in party meetings singed Jayaprakash. Feeling betrayed, he sent his resignation from the national executive of the PSP on 15 June, proposing that those opposed to cooperation with the government could come forward and take up organizational responsibilities. Asoka Mehta and three joint secretaries of the party joined him. The onus of preventing a bitter break-up was now on Lohia. He rose to the occasion by asking them to continue, annotating his brief appeal with these words, 'Jayaprakash and I, what else can I say about our relationship except in the past we have both faced bullets together. Beyond saying that I have no brother of my own it is unnecessary to say anything more.'[61] However, the Lohia faction of the PSP unequivocally declared its opposition to the Congress in December 1953. Even though Jayaprakash was persuaded to withdraw his resignation, his sense of alienation was apparent.

This was a turning point in Jayaprakash's life. His deepening disdain for power politics was evident from the first all-India conference of the PSP convened in Allahabad in January 1954 where he uncharacteristically chose not to speak at all. The PSP too was never the same again. Differences between pro and anti-Congress members kept surfacing. Swords were crossed over minor issues. They stumbled from one nadir to the next, using socialism as a rhetorical weapon.

The Travancore–Cochin story was a case in point. When elections were announced there, the PSP, putting aside ethics, struck an electoral alliance with the communists, professedly to prevent a Congress majority. The Congress played its cards well and offered to support the PSP to keep the communists out. The PSP accepted the offer. Even though the PSP's share of seats was only nineteen in a house of 117, the local PSP chief Pattam Pillai formed the first socialist ministry of the country in April 1954.

The matter did not rest with the formation of the ministry. In a political environment bedevilled by factionalism, the mishandling of an agitation for the merger of Tamil-speaking areas of Travancore-Cochin with Madras, that led to the death of protesters, drew fire from Lohia. He sent a telegram asking Pillai to resign, thus widening the gulf between the pro and anti-Lohia factions.

The incident snowballed into a big crisis when Pillai refused to resign. The national executive of the PSP, which had been kept out of the picture, felt that Lohia should not have precipitated the crisis. Even as behind-the-scenes deliberations for a settlement were on, a new crisis began brewing when Asoka Mehta openly welcomed the 1955 Avadi Congress resolution for establishing a socialist pattern of society. Lohia and his group called the declaration a colossal fraud. In a situation rapidly spiralling out of control, Madhu Limaye launched a vicious personal attack on Asoka Mehta, leading to Limaye's suspension. The Uttar Pradesh PSP executive, however, backed Limaye and invited him to address their conference at Ghazipur. In response to this act of extreme indiscipline, the entire state executive was suspended.

Lohia and Madhu Limaye formed a new Socialist Party in December 1955. Jayaprakash's sustained efforts to reunite the party failed. Finally, in 1957, he gave up his membership, ending his tryst with party politics. Hopelessly divided, mired in vicious infighting and several political missteps, the PSP faced an ignominious rout in the fiercely contested third general election in 1962. By 1965, prominent members like Sucheta Kriplani, D.P. Misra and Chandra

Shekhar left the party to join the Congress. Asoka Mehta too left to join as deputy chairman of the Planning Commission. The socialist movement was on life support and it would be a while before it got back on its feet.

7

From Socialism to Sarvodaya

Socialist ideas were in historic disarray. Tired of the struggle for political power, Jayaprakash was once again drawn to Gandhian praxis. The non-statist movement of social reconstruction led by a Gandhian, Vinoba Bhave, that had the potential to radicalize agrarian politics and energize grassroots dialogues and movements for change, gripped his consciousness. What he was seeing was nothing less than revolution by non-violent mass action. He wrote paeans to Vinoba's quiet genius and found in the latter's Sarvodaya-Bhoodan movement the kernels of a partyless form of democracy in which consensual decision in conjunction with 'lokniti' (politics of the people) was possible.

The story of how the movement began in Pochampalli village in Telangana on 18 April 1951—with the voluntary donation of 100 acres of land to the landless by an elderly village patriarch, Ram Chandra Reddy—moved Jayaprakash. This was at a time when communist guerrillas were trying to break the land monopoly of rich landlords by violent means. In speech after speech, he spoke of Bhoodan—or the movement for land redistribution to the landless through persuasion—with deep and inspiring conviction. 'What do we see in Bhoodan to be so moved? To superficial observers Bhoodan is just an agrarian reform movement, which at best is preparing the ground for legislation. To those who have looked deep, it is a far more significant movement. It is the beginning of an all-round social and human revolution—human because it aims at changing man along with society.'[1]

Bhoodan proved the validity of non-state forms of socialism based on the idea of people's sovereignty, empowerment, autonomy and agency. Jayaprakash felt it was a great experiment in democracy, perhaps the greatest in history. It was the first step towards a total revolution— social, political, economic, moral and intellectual. Bhoodan echoed the Marxian ideal—from each according to his capacity, to each according to his need.

More land was distributed to the landless by August 1953 than through all the land reform laws passed by the legislature. Jayaprakash was confident that a new consciousness was dawning upon the landless and the dispossessed. They were realizing that they had as much right to land as the landlords, that land belonged to the community, and everyone who worked upon it had a right to share. Jayaprakash saw the kernels of an economic revolution in their refusal to till land. He even found resonance with Gandhi's salt-satyagraha in their moral fight for the triumph of right over wrong.[2] The movement led to the formation of a cadre of non-violent revolutionaries known as the Sarva Seva Sangh.

Bhoodan gave shape to a new idea when a district in Orissa donated nearly all its villages. Thus was born the 'Gramdan' movement for voluntary communization of land. Landowners were persuaded to give up their rights of ownership, and to donate a portion of their land to the landless and a part of their produce to the village treasury. Wage earners were asked to contribute a day's salary to the village treasury and a day's free labour to a village project. Another interesting offshoot of Bhoodan was 'Sampattidan' or the signing away of a portion of personal wealth (a minimum of one-sixth of their income), an application of Gandhi's idea of trusteeship.

Jayaprakash spent a good deal of time meeting the industrialists of Bombay in a serious effort to convince them of the idea of redirecting a fraction of their wealth, as what they considered to be their wealth was the product of social cooperation. This was the genesis of philanthrocapitalism, eliciting a positive response from people like J.R.D. Tata who sent him a cheque of Rs 25,000 from the Dorabji Tata Trust and another cheque of Rs 12,500 from Tata Industries. Even the labour unions of TISCO agreed to contribute one day's wage. Bihar's

sugar mill owners volunteered to pay Rs 5000 per mill. This money
was used to rehabilitate landless families on Bhoodan lands. One of
the earliest contributions came from the colliery owners of Bihar who
donated 15,000 tons of coal.

When Jayaprakash renounced party politics and embraced Jeevandan,
the absolute commitment of one's life to a cause, at a Sarvodaya conference
in Bodh Gaya on 19 April 1954, his supporters were stunned. Present at
the occasion, Prabhavati found it difficult to remain composed. She had
spent almost her entire lifetime waiting for this day. Wiping away her
tears, she whispered, 'If Bapu (Gandhi) had been alive, he would have
been so happy.'[3] Jayaprakash's socialite associates distanced themselves
from what they saw as inchoate Sarvodaya ideas, incapable of solving
developmental challenges. A section of the press reported that his
decision to withdraw from politics was the result of Lohia's opposition to
his approach. Calling out the press coverage as baseless, Jayaprakash said,
'It is true that there are certain differences between me and some others,
including Dr. Lohia. But to say that my Gaya decision to withdraw
from what is ordinarily known as politics was the result of Dr. Lohia's
opposition to my approach is being unfair to Lohia and to me and to
the party.'[4] When asked if he had given up politics forever, he said, 'I
am neither engaged in politics at present nor would involve myself in
any party politics in future. I may occasionally attend party meetings
and give my advice, if it is asked for.'[5] Jayaprakash also spoke about the
need to create conditions for the withering away of parties but added
that till such time this actually happened, he would continue with his
membership of the PSP.

Jeevandan took the shape of a small movement. Within days, a small
community of volunteers who pledged their lives to Bhoodan added
to the strength of the Sarvodaya volunteers of the Sarva Seva Sangh.
Jayaprakash appealed to students to donate a paisa out of every rupee
spent and commit to spending at least a month every year to Bhoodan-
related work. He implored them to wear only khadi and promote it as a
symbol of simplicity, self-reliance, non-violence and self-restraint.[6]

Jayaprakash's effort to widen the base of the movement propelled
him in an ambitious direction. He wrote to President Rajendra Prasad
to give up his office, 'for the sake of the country, especially for the

creed of non-violence and social reconstruction'.[7] He told him that it was imperative for him to repay his debt to Gandhi. However, the unseemly controversy that erupted around Sampattidan took away some of its sheen. It began when Jayaprakash was addressing the press in Bombay. He announced that top industrialists including J.R.D. Tata, Dharamsey Khatau, Madan Mohan Ruia and K.S. Cambata had joined the Bhoodan movement and were ready to participate in Sampattidan, an important step towards a Sarvodaya economy. J.R.D., however, issued a quick rebuttal to make his stand clear, 'While it is not an uncommon thing in the western countries for industrial leaders to make large grants for charitable purposes, it must undoubtedly seem strange that one in my position should publicly commit himself to ending the capitalist system which he represents.'[8] Clearly when he had signed up for Sampattidan, it was for the limited purpose of philanthropy.

Jayaprakash's reply was polite but preachy: 'I never thought that you were so keen to preserve that system. The capitalist system, no doubt, has many virtues and has performed certain historic functions. But no sensitive person can be blind to its injustices, its blighting faults. No one should be proud of being its representative in this age.'[9] Tata was not the only one to take this stand. Dharamsey Khatau too reacted in a similar way.[10] But both of them continued to make generous contributions to sustain the movement, as did other Sarvodaya supporters like Sir Purushottamdas Thakurdas.

In May 1954, Jayaprakash formed an organization called the 'Gram Nirman Mandal' to establish an ashram where Sarvodaya workers could live and carry on village reconstruction. The ashram was built near Sukhodewara, a village in Gaya. Over a hundred families had gifted approximately 300 acres of land as part of Bhoodan, following a process known as 'Sarvaswadan'. Out of these 300 acres, a 60-acre site, that was uncultivated, was earmarked for the project, and the remainder was distributed to the landless of the village.

There were several daunting odds. The area was rocky and the nearest railway station was 30 miles away with a dusty, muddy, bullock track as the approach. But Jayaprakash, Prabhavati and their team led by Brahmanand, M.P. Kurian and Gita Singh, set about organizing work at a fevered pace. Huts made of palm fronds, shaded by gulmohar and mahua trees, were erected in no time. A fruit orchard was planted and a *goshala* with more than a hundred cows was built. Over a period of time, model centres for weaving, carpentry, manufacture of charkhas and other village industries such as oil pressing, pottery and soap making were created. The ashram also ran an agriculture project that encouraged innovations, and a programme for the development of village cooperatives. A centre for treatment of leprosy (endemic in the area), an ayurvedic dispensary and a small maternity clinic were set up. The Kawakol area near the ashram with a large proportion of tribals and backward communities was selected for development of agro-industries.

Jayaprakash and Prabhavati's own house was fenced with bamboo, with a beautiful frangipani tree with clusters of fragrant yellow flowers leaning against the fence. There were two rooms: one with wooden cots with white, hand-spun, khadi covers, and the other with a low writing desk, a four-spindled ambar charkha, reed floor mats and several books on a simple shelf.

The idyllic haven attracted social scientists, student volunteers and activists from several countries. Of them, a couple from Australia, Wendy and Allan Scarfe, both in their mid-twenties, visited the ashram in 1957. Encouraged by Jayaprakash, they stayed back for six months to introduce ways of teaching beyond learning by rote. They sailed back to India again, two years later, for a two-and-a-half-year stint as teachers in the ashram's experimental rural school. Their book, *A Mouthful of Petals: The Story of an Indian Village*, part memoir, is a delightful description of the time spent in Sukhodewara. Of the community library with Upendra Maharathi-inspired Buddhist murals on the ochre walls, of enchanting birds on arches of fresh leaves, of lantern lights streaming through big, barred windows, stories of wasps, scorpions and snakes crawling into the classrooms during monsoons and the cry of jackals at night, and dark tales of extreme rural poverty and misery.[11]

In addition to the regular school, they set up night classes for students and landless labourers from nearby villages in an improvised classroom with walls whitewashed with limestone brought from the surrounding forests. In a sense, this was where Jayaprakash's vision of continuous revolution, which begins in the heart of man, was taking shape. It was an austere utopia with no luxuries, not even electricity, and where everyone was expected to log specific hours of manual labour. There were no freeloaders. However, the time spent in the ashram was energizing and astoundingly peaceful. It was an ideal getaway for rest and recuperation, reading and writing. The ubiquity of Jayaprakash's daily routine is reflected in this somewhat quirky entry in Prabhavati's diary: 'JP loves trees. In the afternoon when trees were being planted, he left his writing work to see what was happening. He said—"I love watching this. I was probably a tree in my last birth."'

The Bhoodan–Gramdan movement drew incredible international attention and acclaim. Its ambitious milestone of 25 lakh acres of voluntary donation of land by April 1954 had been reached. Louis Fischer said that it was the most creative thought coming from the East. Writing for the *Observer* in 1959, Arthur Koestler observed that the movement presented an Indian alternative to the broken Nehruvian model of development. By 1969, the Gandhi Centenary Year, a large number of villages in Bihar took the Gramdan pledge, laying the foundation of Gramswaraj, a non-pyramidical structure of village self-government, approximating to Gandhi's oceanic circle. But Jayaprakash's emotional hunger for transformative change remained, even as the movement started losing momentum. Much of the donated land was of poor quality, barren, rocky and completely unfit for cultivation. In a vast majority of cases, there were insurmountable legal hurdles in transferring property, and, predictably, a number of donors had second thoughts.

The deadline for distribution of 50 million acres by 1957 came and went. Vinoba, who had begun by asking landowners to donate one-sixth of their land, progressively reduced the amount to one-twentieth. He rejected Jayaprakash's suggestion of using non-cooperation as a strategy to put pressure on landowners. Vinoba wanted Bhoodan to be a social revolution by consent—no matter how long the process took. He had walked for several years asking for land for the landless; he could walk for several more. Bhoodan, however, would soon cease to be the force that it once was. His appeal to students and teachers to join the movement for one year was mostly ignored. In 1970, when

Jayaprakash went to Musahari, in Bihar, to study issues related to the Naxalite movement, he found that a majority of the villages had been donated in 'bogus gramdan'.

Even though Jayaprakash had taken what seemed like a sabbatical from active politics, he continued to agonize over issues that were at the forefront of the country. He was in a gladiatorial space with Nehru over a brutal incident of police firing in Patna University campus on 12 and 13 August 1955, that followed a student agitation against a rise in bus fares. BN College was riddled with bullets. When the vice chancellor tried to address the students, tear-gas shells were fired. Jayaprakash stood with students and tried to get his voice heard over the clamour of propaganda against them. Nehru supported police action. As usual, several points and counterpoints were made. The attacks became personal, prompting an emotional response from Nehru, 'You have made a number of statements which have amazed me beyond measure and which I consider wholly incorrect as well as most unfortunate. I can only express my deep sorrow that you should have this opinion of me.'[12]

A major issue that engaged Jayaprakash was the matter of states reorganization, more specifically the Samyukta Maharashtra Movement(SMM). The SMM cut across ideologies. It was championed by socialist leaders like S.M. Joshi and supported by veteran Congress leaders like C.D. Deshmukh, trade union comrades like Shripad Dange, social reformer Prabodhankar Thackeray and members of the Republican Party. The SMM was also a cause that Narendra Deva was passionate about. Unfortunately, he died on 19 February 1956, creating a huge void in Jayaprakash's life. A day later, Jayaprakash sent an anguished letter to Nehru highlighting the unjust treatment of Maharashtrians: 'I feel that you have been ill served by your advisors on the Bombay question. Morarji bhai and other Gujarat leaders should have shown greater generosity and high-mindedness.'[13] He also shot off a letter to Morarji Desai protesting his handling of the situation.[14] His unsolicited advice remained unacknowledged.

Jayaprakash continued to offer his contrarian views to Nehru, on the Bengal–Bihar merger issue, and the festering Kashmir issue, bordering very often on the incendiary. '95% of Kashmir Muslims do not wish to be or remain Indian citizens. I doubt, therefore, the wisdom of trying to keep people by force where they do not wish to stay. This cannot but have serious long-term political consequences though immediately, it may suit policy and suit public opinion. From the point of view of the desirability of establishing a peaceful social order, it cannot but prove disastrous. I do earnestly wish that this question be considered more from a human, rather than a nationalist point of view.'[15]

Deeply unsettled by Jayaprakash's strong words, Nehru responded immediately. 'I am absolutely convinced that your information about 95% Kashmir Muslims is completely wrong. If one takes the population of the whole of the state, apart from the part occupied by Pakistan, I think it is rather doubtful which way a majority would lie. I think there is a fair possibility of a majority being in favour of India . . . I am sure any change in the present position of Kashmir would lead to dangerous consequences, large migrations, great bitterness between India and Pakistan and probably war.'[16] He shut Jayaprakash up by saying, 'I have written to you briefly about this matter. The story is a long one and a very complicated one. But it seems to me clear that your sources of information are not good.'[17]

As always, Jayaprakash remained invested in global issues. In February 1956, Nikita Khrushchev's secret speech, exposing Stalin's crimes to the twentieth Soviet Communist Party Congress, opened a can of worms. Party ideologues like Rajani Palme Dutt dismissed Stalin's 'errors' as 'spots on the sun' and rebuffed critics with formidable statistics of Soviet pig iron production. Convinced that Stalin's horrible excesses were possible because of the socio-economic and political systems created in the name of Marxism, Jayaprakash addressed a letter to his 'Communist friends' dated 5 November 1956. 'The first question that the Communists must answer for themselves is how it could be possible that they were kept in the dark so long about the facts that Khrushchev has recalled. Was not the whole non-Communist world talking about these facts for nearly three decades? The revelations of Khrushchev were indeed no revelations at all. It is impossible that the Communists—at least their leadership—did not know the facts. Why did they remain silent so long?'[18]

Whatever little attraction Jayaprakash had for Russia dissipated during the October 1956 Hungarian counter-revolution that began with a massive student protest on the streets of Budapest. Within days, Soviet armed forces moved into the city using their formidable T-54 tanks to destroy rebel strongholds. What left Jayaprakash aghast was Nehru's silence and his chief adviser on foreign policy Mr Krishna Menon's statement that the Hungarian question was the domestic affair of the Hungarian people.[19] When Nehru continued to remain silent, Jayaprakash tried to draw his attention by saying, 'If you do not speak out you will be held guilty of abetting enslavement of a brave people by a new imperialism more dangerous than the old because it masquerades as revolutionary.'[20] Nehru broke his silence on the same day (5 November), at a UNESCO conference in Delhi by condemning the Soviet conduct.

However, Krishna Menon, acting ostensibly on his own, abstained from voting at a UN resolution condemning the Soviet Union for the use of force. But soon after, Nehru's speech in the Lok Sabha on 19 November, delivered without text or notes, once again condemned Russia. In the words of a BBC correspondent, 'Never before has Mr. Nehru spoken out so positively against Russian imperialism and the oppressed peoples behind the iron curtain.'[21] Nehru's fundamental ambivalence on this issue remained, in no small measure due to the veiled threat in Khrushchev's remark that Hungary was as close to Soviet Union as Kashmir was to India. Untouched by compromises propelled by realpolitik, Jayaprakash continued to critique India's stand on Hungary.

In a different context, the Soviet government's refusal to allow Boris Pasternak to receive the Nobel Prize for Literature in 1958 outraged Jayaprakash. He supported Nehru's protest as chairperson of the Indian Academy of Letters, the Sahitya Akademi. The news of the arrest of Olga Ivinskaya (immortalized as Lara of *Dr Zhivago*) and her daughter Irina on absolutely flimsy charges also spiked Jayaprakash's disillusionment with Russia. One of Boris Pasternak's closest companions and lovers, her arrest came soon after the author's death and was extremely discomfiting. Jayaprakash issued a statement to the press condemning the arrest.[22]

An issue where Jayaprakash felt that Nehru was on the wrong side of history was the Chinese occupation of Tibet. Jayaprakash felt the occupation violated the right to self-determination of the people of Tibet, their need for democracy and unfettered freedom of speech. Addressing the Bihar State Tibet Convention on 9 March 1959, soon after the crushing of the Tibetan uprising, he said: 'Tibet stands as an outstanding case of ruthless suppression of the freedom of weak and defenseless nations by strong and aggressive powers. Tibet is, and has been throughout history, a separate country and not the "Tibet region of China" as the imperialist formula goes, and the Tibetans are, and have always been, a distinct and separate nation. As such, they are entitled, as any country and nation, to freedom and full sovereign rights. No moth-eaten page of imperialist history can controvert that truth or undermine that sovereign principle.'[23]

An Afro-Asian convention on Tibet, organized by him on 9 April 1960 at Vigyan Bhawan in Delhi, was a resounding success. Attended by around seventy foreign and twenty-five Indian delegates, the convention managed to arrive at a consensus to fight for the rights of not only Tibetans, but of all people living under colonial regimes. Jayaprakash went on a month-long tour of East Africa, spending a major portion of his time in Nairobi, joining hands with the Kenyans in their struggle for freedom.

It was the eve of the second general elections. Jayaprakash had more or less renounced party politics. However, he continued to speak against Nehru's government. In his speech on the need for an effective opposition, delivered in Begusarai on 27 January 1957, he blamed Nehru for failing to lay the foundation for a strong opposition as Kemal Ataturk had managed to do in Turkey. In a press statement issued soon after the Begusarai speech, he said, 'The position today is that for the last ten years the Congress party has enjoyed complete monopoly of power and huge majorities in the legislatures. I regard the continuation of this position—quite apart from the merits or demerits of the Congress—to be fraught with serious danger to India's democracy and wellbeing. I regard the altering of this position as the main task in the coming election.'[24] His letters to Nehru were visceral and accusatory.

Nehru mockingly chastised him for playing hide-and-seek between the pillars of politics and Bhoodan. He complained that Jayaprakash's letters were so long and dense that sometimes even contemplating a cohesive reply was difficult. 'If I attempted to deal adequately with the various points you have raised that would mean discussing a multitude of internal and external problems. Indeed, that would mean writing something in the nature of a little book.'[25] Nehru was clearly not amused by JP's sustained attacks. While addressing a public meeting in Madras on 31 July 1957, he said that it was strange that he was being expected to help in the foundation of a strong and responsible opposition. He mocked Jayaprakash's analogy of Turkey. 'With all respect to Jayaprakashji, the example is not a good one. There is no democracy in Turkey, real or even unreal . . . does he want that kind of thing to happen to India . . . our friends like Jayaprakashji have gotten so entangled in their dislike for the Congress that they have forgotten the good of India . . .'[26]

Jayaprakash continued to speak about the absoluteness of Congress power that made even constitutional checks and balances something of a mirage. He refrained from actively campaigning for the 1957 general elections, but continued to appeal to the electorate to vote with the idea of building a strong opposition. Nehru was hurt by what he felt was an unjust denigration of his policies. He hit back at Jayaprakash: 'I have had a feeling for many months, if not more, that there was a widening gap between our views about various matters. Almost everything that I thought important and emphasized was criticized by you in strong language. I do not object, of course, to that criticism. But I am merely pointing out that this difference in our viewpoints had grown so much that there were not many points of contact left. I was left in some state of amazement whenever I read your reported speeches or statements. I thought that you had completely lost grip of the situation in India as well as in the world, and what you said had no reality at all . . . We spoke different languages . . . your language seemed to be a special one which I could not make much of. It seemed to me to be the result of being cut off from reality and a result of woolly thinking.'[27]

Nehru's words, especially his comment on 'woolly thinking', cut Jayaprakash to the bone. Deeply wounded, he retreated into himself but eventually sent a cryptic reply. Addressing Nehru as 'Dear Sir' instead of the familiar 'Dear Bhai', he wrote: 'I was prepared for all manner of outbursts from you, but not for outright abuse. At Madras you found me to be lacking in good sense and said so publicly. Now you call me woolly minded.'[28] Keen to paper over their differences, Nehru wrote, 'I do not remember, though I perhaps may have a short memory, of ever having allowed my personal relations with anyone to be affected because of differences of opinion, however strong these latter might be. I feel no reason I should do so in your case, even though you may feel otherwise. And so, I shall continue to address you as before and have affection for you . . . it is true that I expressed my views strongly and criticized what I considered your views equally strongly . . . I ventured to call you "woolly minded". I would not personally call that a term of abuse. All of us are supposed to suffer from this from time to time, certainly I do.'[29]

Nehru's letter had a placatory tone that worked its magic on Jayaprakash. When he met Nehru at the Gramdan Conference at Mysore, Jayaprakash was overcome with emotion. He wrote: 'It was after a long time that I saw you at the Gramdan Conference. As I sat looking at you there, many old feelings welled up within me and I felt overwhelmed. I wanted to say something to you there, but you were naturally cold and I did not feel up to it. Even now, it is not possible for me to put down on paper what I feel. But I do wish to say this much that it was very wrong of me to have written to you in the manner I had done in one of my letters and I do beg you to forgive me for it. I have no doubt that you will not want me to change my views because you do not like them, but I have no doubt I should not have used the tone and language that I had done to express them.'[30]

Nehru's reply was the last word in charm. 'There is no question of your apologizing to me for anything. All I want is your affection and you can hold any views you like. I am sorry that I appeared cold to you at the Gramdan Conference. We really had no occasion of meeting by ourselves. Sometimes, at public functions, one develops a certain exterior aspect which is perhaps a manner of self-protection lest one's feelings get the better of one. You know that you will always be welcome, however our views may differ about anything.'[31] This, in essence, was the story of the relationship between these two exceptionally bright individuals, a story of rebuffs, rapprochements and deep, layered emotions.

Jayaprakash also made an effort to reconcile with Lohia. Addressing the press after a meeting with Lohia in Lucknow on 15 July 1957, he commented, 'We met as old friends and had a very cordial talk with each other. We talked about many things, including the possibility of a single party of Socialism in India. This should not be taken to mean the usual things like merger.'[32] Optimistic about the outcome of his effort at forging socialist unity, Jayaprakash also dashed off a letter to Ganga Sharan Sinha (at this point the chairperson of PSP).[33] Lohia and he met again in Calcutta and exchanged several letters. The unity remained chimeric, but their meetings cleared the air. 'My work is over,' reported Jayaprakash to Achyut Patwardhan. 'One good result of my fruitless endeavour has been that the bitterness for me that I developed in Lohia's heart has been reduced to a great extent. It is a big gain for me.'[34]

Jayaprakash managed to stay away from the blinkered preoccupations of the PSP for nearly three years. On 25 October 1957, he decided to reset his political compass by resigning from his sleeping membership. His parting letter to members of the PSP ran into fifty-four closely typed pages and was captioned, 'From Socialism to Sarvodaya'. It traced the linear trajectory of his journey from non-cooperation to Marxism, from Marxism to democratic socialism, finding a final niche in Sarvodaya. Considered seminal, the text of his letter was serialized and carried in leading newspapers.

The tone of the letter was emotional. 'After long deliberation, I have decided to write this letter. It has not been easy for me to do it because it is never easy to cut oneself away from an association of a lifetime. We have worked together, and together we have suffered imprisonment, lived through the adventures of the underground, and tasted the ashes of independence. We have all far to travel yet. But I, on my part at least, find myself at a point of the journey where I must decide to part company and walk it alone. It would have gladdened my heart beyond measure had I been able to persuade you to come along with me but I realize that is not possible—at least for the present. I hope, however, that our paths will often meet and that at the journey's end, they will merge together. We may not live to see that consummation ourselves but I feel confident if the world were ever to reach the port of peace and freedom and brotherhood, Socialism must eventually merge into *Sarvodaya*.'[35] Jayaprakash admitted that, in a sense, Sarvodaya was also political. But it was the politics of the people as distinct from 'rajniti'—not embedded in power and leading eventually to the withering of the state.

Jayaprakash went on to say that the past course of his life might well appear to the outsider as a zigzagged and tortuous saga of unsteadiness. But as he looked back, he discerned in it a uniform line of development. The groping undoubtedly was there, but it was far from being blind; there were clear beacons of light that remained undimmed and unaltered from the beginning. He was not apologetic about the unconventional journey, constantly questioning himself and his beliefs. His big regret was the same as Prabhavati's—that his voyage should have reached the definitive point of Sarvodaya after Gandhi's death.

By the end of September 1959, Jayaprakash was ready with the draft manifesto on the 'reconstruction of Indian polity'[36] which read like a theses on partyless democracy. It carried echoes of 'Swaraj'— Gandhi's dream of village self-government based on grassroots democracy, mutual cooperation and voluntary efforts—and ideas inspired by the writings of Walter Lippmann, considered the dean of American political journalism; Maurice Duverger, French political scientist; Salvador de Madariaga, Spanish diplomat, historian and social philosopher; and Erich Fromm. Initially only meant for private circulation, Jayaprakash sent a copy to Nehru, with the wry hope that his critique of parliamentary democracy might appeal to him. Copies were also sent to Indira Gandhi, Rajendra Prasad, Dr Radhakrishnan, Morarji Desai, Lal Bahadur Shastri and other leaders including those who belonged to the Jana Sangh and the CPI.

At the outset, Jayaprakash rejected the Western model of parliamentary democracy on the grounds that it functioned as democratic oligarchy. He felt that the time for a communitarian, partyless, grassroots democracy to re-enter political conversation had come. A theoretical abstraction, partyless democracy worked as the antithesis of parliamentary democracy. It negated all that was wrong with party politics. 'Party rivalries give birth to demagoguery, depress political ethics, put a premium on unscrupulousness and manipulation and intrigue. Parties create dissensions where unity is called for, exaggerate differences where they should be minimized. Parties often put party interests over the national interests. Because centralization of power prevents the citizen from participating in government, the parties, that is to say, small caucuses of politicians, rule in the name of the people and create the illusion of democracy and self-government.'[37]

How then could people be empowered? How were they expected to achieve equality, freedom and peace? Jayaprakash found his answers in the Gandhian village economy model that he had earlier questioned and derided. At the base of the new social organization would be self-governing, self-sufficient, agro-industrial communities. They would come together to tackle common issues and build regional communities. The regional communities would join to form district communities which would federate into provincial communities—that in turn would form the national community. A radically transformed social and political order such as this would not happen overnight. There would have to be a period of transition, during which elections would be conducted in a manner so as to ensure that political parties would not play any role up to the district level. Even at the state and national levels, the candidates would be selected by the people themselves and not by parties. The latter would be allowed to support candidates only after their election by the people. This would gradually reduce the role of parties in political processes and increase that of the people, eventually leading to partyless democracy.

Jayaprakash had already flagged many of these ideas on different platforms. Addressing members of Parliament, he had spoken about the need to let people select their own candidates for elections, somewhat like in the American primaries. He deplored the fact that even though non-availability of food, hunger and malnutrition remained major unfinished tasks, there was unnecessary dissipation of energy in fighting about 'unreal things and letting real things slip away'. He asked the MPs, 'Which of you really functions as selfless servants of the people which is today the greatest need of the hour, above parties and above elections?'[38] The real guarantee of democracy, he was convinced, lay in the strength of the people. The more people engaged, the greater the possibility of developing an informed, nuanced democracy.

The years 1958–60 were, in a sense, epochal for the state-led process of democratic decentralization. Following the Balwantrai Mehta study team report recommending decentralization, all the states passed panchayat acts, facilitating the creation of more than 2,17,300 village panchayats. Jayaprakash continued to focus on the problematique of what he perceived as the unmixable elements of parliamentary democracy and panchayati raj, fearing that one would dominate the other. Wryly agreeing with Nehru that panchayati raj was no less than a political revolution, he added that its potential to usher in a true revolution depended on its role in making the people self-governing by creating democratic, decentralized communities. He feared that the movement would get bureaucratized and succumb to party politics. His wish list for participatory democracy included social education, devolution of power, people's control over revenue administration, at least partial control over financial resources and exercise of authority over civil servants.[39] As president of the All India Panchayat Parishad, he appealed to Sarvodaya workers to take interest in grassroots institutions.

Jayaprakash's utopia was not predicated on the idea of partyless democracy alone, but on a new kind of economic structure based on voluntary limitations of wants. For communitarian democracy to function as something more than a shell, there had to be a real devolution of economic power. This was the genesis of 'Swaraj for the People',[40] a document published in 1961. There was a measure of synergy in what he proposed: a decentralized, labour-intensive economy that would depend on a comprehensive programme of rural industrialization. Villages would be developed as agro-industrial communities based on the organic blending of agriculture and industry. For production of different commodities, area-specific choices based on aggregates and averages would drive the setting up of village, block, district, state and union-level industries. The state and union industries would be large-scale. Ruling out any Sisyphean tension in this model of decentralized growth, he advocated a mass-based skill development and entrepreneurship development programme with a special thrust on training in modern agricultural techniques.

Jayaprakash travelled to Europe and West Asia for four and a half months between the middle of May and September 1958. He was accompanied by Prabhavati. They spent more than a month in England on the invitation of the British Labour Party and several independent socialist groups. They visited every country in Western Europe except Spain and Portugal. Of the communist nations, they travelled to Poland and Yugoslavia, and in West Asia, Egypt, Lebanon, Syria, Iraq and Israel, meeting a large number of political leaders, leaders of trade unions and cooperatives, writers, thinkers, peace workers and others engaged with radical experiments in ways of living and thinking.

At most places they received a rapturous reception. A meeting that Jayaprakash never really stopped reminiscing about was with Sicilian social activist Danilo Dolci, a darling of the European left who stirred up the local government in Palermo and the national government in Rome with Gandhi-style hunger strikes and non-violent demonstrations. Jayaprakash addressed a group of Hungarian students in Vienna on the relevance of Satyagraha and discussed the dynamics of the Bhoodan movement in an address delivered at FAO (Food and Agriculture Organization) in Rome. His visit to the community of ragpickers in Paris moved him, as did his meeting with nuclear physicist Niels Bohr. He spent a memorable evening with Albert Camus, discussing a gamut of issues, including Nehru's ambivalent stand on Hungary. Camus's disappointment with Nehru's approach was reflected in what he said to Jayaprakash: 'We all felt terribly let down by Mr. Nehru who had been our hero.'[41]

One of the highlights of Jayaprakash's European tour was an interview given to the London correspondent of *Manchester Guardian* on 7 June 1958. The correspondent asked whether he would agree to take office if, after Nehru, India was faced with choosing between extremism of the left and right. Jayaprakash answered that he had no desire to go back to party politics. No office, however exalted, had any attraction for him. 'But if there was an emergency, yes, he would be ready to answer the call—not as the leader of a party but as a man whom the Indian people had asked for counsel and guidance.'[42] What was he thinking? Was he seeing himself in the role of a seer, not unlike Gandhi, who would change the political narrative by bringing in a radical agenda? He gave unsolicited advice to Nehru to step down to re-establish direct personal contact with people. A couple of years later, he made another startling statement at a meeting in Patna, saying that Nehru should give up prime ministership so that the question of who would be his successor could be settled in his lifetime.[43]

Addressing a meeting of members of Parliament upon his return from Europe, Jayaprakash said, 'I went to Europe seeking certain things, certain ideas, certain solutions of problems with which we are faced. I carried with me certain ideas with which all of you are familiar—and I am sure many of you believe in those ideas as much as I do myself— ideas which Mahatma Gandhi, during his life and work, placed before us and the world . . . They do not know how to put those ideas into practice in their own complex, highly industrialized, technologically developed societies; yet they evinced a great deal of interest, and I am sure out of this interest, something of great value is going to emerge.'[44]

Communal discord continued to rip through the country. Instances of rioting that had somewhat decreased in the 1950s began to rise in the 1960s, with 1964 being a specially bad year. With the outbreak of violence in East Pakistan, the influx of refugees on Indian soil saw a dramatic increase, leading to riots in Calcutta, Rourkela, Jamshedpur and other areas in eastern India. Calling such incidents bestial, shameful and unthinkable, Jayaprakash said, 'If Indian Hindus kill Indian Muslims for no reason than that Pakistani Muslims have killed Pakistani Hindus, it is (among other things) a complete vindication of the two-nation theory. It simply means that we affirm in action what we loudly repudiate in words. As a Hindu, who is proud of his religion, I cannot think of a greater blasphemy than to clothe these crimes that degrade man with the sanction of dharma. Whatever of dharma is left in the present atmosphere of creeping materialism, benumbed ethical sensibility, pseudo-science and undigested vulgar modernism would surely bleed to death if brother continues to knife brother only because he worships God differently.'[45]

Addressing the selective reporting by parliamentarians of atrocities perpetrated upon Hindu minorities in East Pakistan, he wrote to both houses of Parliament asking them to depute a study team to assess the story on the Indian side. His study of the riot-affected areas in Jamshedpur convinced him that Hindus had no reason to feel smug.

They needed to face the truth about their own premeditated mass cruelty. 'I visited all the affected areas in the city but did not have the stomach to visit more than 2 of the 17 Muslim refugee camps. A member of the Lok Sabha is reported to have broken down while speaking about the atrocities committed in East Pakistan but I doubt if any sensitive person could have stood the sights and stories of atrocities in Muslim refugee camps in Jamshedpur . . . the same may also be said of Rourkela. One of the major diseases from which we suffer as a nation is the weakness, which after all deceives no one, of appearing holier than we actually are.'[46]

Jayaprakash continued to speak about the dangers of communalism in different forums. When asked, during a press interview, whether he would like to propose a ban on communal parties, he said that the real remedy lay in political education. 'I think this is something on which all nationalist, secular, democratic parties should get together, forgetting their ideologies and personal differences, struggles and so on. They should join hands on at least this one programme and meet the challenge of Hindu, Muslim or any other communalism, because communalism of any kind is anti-national and a danger to the country.'[47]

Jayaprakash's interest in Kashmir deepened at this point. He had, in the past, lent his support to the 'Quit Kashmir' movement steered by the National Conference led by Sheikh Abdullah. Ferociously attacked on several occasions for his unwavering support of the idea of Kashmiri self-determination, Jayaprakash attributed the historical genesis of Sheikh Abdullah's demand for plebiscite to the promise made by Nehru in a broadcast on 2 November 1947. Nehru reportedly said, 'Let me make it clear that it has been our policy all along that where there is a dispute about the accession of a state to either Dominion, the decision must be made by the people of that State. It was in accordance with this policy that we added a *proviso* to the Instrument of Accession of Kashmir.'[48] Later, in the same broadcast, Nehru had announced, 'We have declared that the fate of Kashmir is ultimately to be decided by the people. That pledge was given, and the Maharaja has supported it, not only to the people in Kashmir but to the world. We will not and cannot back out of it. We are prepared when peace and law and order have been established to have a referendum held under international auspices like the United Nations. We want it to be a fair and just reference to the people and we shall accept their verdict; I can imagine no fairer and more just offer.'[49]

Firm in his belief that there was no credible proof that the people of Kashmir had accepted the legal fact of accession, Jayaprakash said that constitutional accession had little meaning in the absence of emotional integration. He felt that emotional integration was on shaky ground after Sheikh Abdullah was cast out of power in 1953 and put behind bars for no apparent reason. It took nearly five years for charges to be framed against him, and another four before they were brought to a court. Jayaprakash began a nationwide campaign against his detention and demanded his immediate release.

This surprised people who were aware of Jayaprakash's stand on the arrest and subsequent death of Jana Sangh leader Dr Syama Prasad Mukherjee in a Kashmir jail, in which he had held the state government responsible for criminal negligence.[50] Sheikh Abdullah responded angrily to Jayaprakash's statement, stating that a Hindu leader like him had no right to interfere in the affairs of Kashmir. Later, realizing that he had made a big mistake by alienating a well-wisher, the Sheikh made an emotional appeal for rapprochement, saying that Jayaprakash was the conscience keeper of India to whom people of Kashmir looked to for support after Gandhi.

Jayaprakash continued agitating against Sheikh Abdullah's imprisonment. He flagged the unpopularity of Bakshi Ghulam Mohammad's regime, juxtaposing it against 'the great and widespread popularity of Sheikh Abdullah'.[51] Eventually when Sheikh Abdullah was released on 8 April 1964, Nehru's statement that, 'If a damned thing can't be proved in four years, in six years, there is obviously nothing to be proved,'[52] was a vindication of Jayaprakash's stand.

During the 1964 parliamentary debates on Kashmir, Jayaprakash defended the Sheikh's proposal to reunite Jammu and Kashmir and ascertain the will of the people, if not through plebiscite then through free and fair elections. His comments unleashed an avalanche of protest from both Jana Sangh and Congress members of Parliament. A prominent Congress MP even asked for his arrest.[53] But he continued to speak his mind and issue press statements that generated unprecedented heat.

Jayaprakash's strong opposition to Partition did not come in the way of his quest for harmony with Pakistan. In September 1962, he founded and chaired a body named India–Pakistan Conciliation Group with his friend J.J. Singh, former chairman of the India League of America, as secretary. One of its first major initiatives was leading a goodwill delegation to Pakistan in September 1964 headed by Jayaprakash with J.J. Singh, B. Shiva Rao, member, University Grants Commission, and S. Mulgaonkar, editor of *Hindustan Times*. The delegation met President Ayub Khan and representatives of the opposition. Though Jayaprakash declined to be drawn into any discussion on Kashmir that involved Pakistan, he came back carrying the impression that the attitude of the Pakistani government was not as rigid as it appeared, leaving ample scope for meaningful negotiations.

Jayaprakash felt that both countries needed to work together on areas of common interest. Once that happened, even an issue like Kashmir would not appear forbidding and insurmountable.[54] He also felt that the Indian press needed to be objective and careful while reporting misbehaviour with minorities in Pakistan. He reminded the press that communal disturbances were also taking place in India and the suffering of minorities was no less real or intense in human terms. Unsparingly precise and with piercing acuity, he said, 'It is time we shed our conceit and pretence and face the truth squarely: that we are no better or worse as human beings than our brothers across the border. This facing up to the truth is an indispensable step for strengthening the moral fibre of our nation and cleansing it of the canker of communalism.'[55]

Jayaprakash's optimism received a jolt when the Pakistan army started Operation Desert Hawk in the Rann of Kutch. As disappointed as he was, when he heard that Prime Minister Lal Bahadur Shastri was going to attend the Commonwealth Prime Ministers conference where Ayub Khan was sure to be present, he addressed an urgent letter to him, enclosing in a separate envelope a note on the Kutch dispute prepared by my father. Urging Shastri to take the initiative of inviting Ayub Khan to a quiet luncheon or dinner to pick up the threads of 'personal exploration and understanding', he wrote, 'Another matter. By separate "urgent" cover I am sending you a note on the Kutch dispute that has been prepared at my request by a friend and relative of mine, Dr. Bimal Prasad, Reader, Indian School of International Studies. I hope you will have time to glance through this revealing document. Many things contained in it you are no doubt acquainted with, but I am sure it also brings out facts that might have not come to your notice—at least no awareness to these facts could be discovered in the Parliament debates on the subject.'[56]

The Rann of Kutch was, however, just the beginning. Pakistan began infiltrating Kashmir on 5 August 1965. About 30,000 infiltrators crossed the line of control, sparking off the Indo-Pak war. It was only on 22 September that a UN-mandated ceasefire put an end to the war. Pakistan's attack on Kashmir in August 1965 radically altered Jayaprakash's views. He admitted that Pakistan's 'feigned' concern for the people of Kashmir was only a smokescreen behind which it made plans to annex the state. He, however, continued to have faith in conciliation efforts.[57]

Jayaprakash's effort for meaningful dialogue on Kashmir came to a standstill when Sheikh Abdullah showed appalling political incorrectness in meeting Chinese Prime Minister Zhou Enlai at Algiers. The Sheikh's passport was impounded and he was asked to return immediately. Anticipating his arrest, Jayaprakash wrote a letter to Prime Minister Lal Bahadur Shastri: 'Sheikh Abdullah's re-arrest at this juncture will be yet another mistake for which the country will have to suffer for many years to come.'[58]

On Sheikh Abdullah's rearrest in May 1965, Jayaprakash raised his voice again against the arbitrariness of the move, saying that the Sheikh had not been given a chance to clear himself of the charges made against him. In June 1966, he sent a long, emotional letter to the new prime minister, Indira Gandhi, urging her to consider his unconditional release. 'We profess secularism, but let Hindu nationalism stampede us in trying to establish it by repression. Why do I plead for Sheikh Saheb's release?' Jayaprakash asked. 'Because that may give us the only chance we might have of solving the Kashmir problem.'[59]

Jayaprakash came around to the view that the Kashmir issue could only be resolved by the people of Kashmir and the Government of India. He told Sheikh Abdullah that what was possible before 5 August 1965 was now not tenable. Speaking at a convention organized by the Sheikh to discuss the state's future in Srinagar on 10 October 1968, he was absolutely candid. 'This convention must understand clearly that after the 1965 conflict no Government of India can accept a solution that places Kashmir outside the Union of India. These are unpleasant but inescapable realities and as your friend and well wisher I am bound to speak the truth as I see it.'[60] But he also continued to warn the Government of India that repressive policies would fail to succeed in Kashmir.

Jayaprakash made a significant contribution to the peace process in Nagaland in his capacity as member of the Nagaland Peace Mission in 1964–65. The peace mission, set up with the support of the Naga Baptist Church Council, with B.P. Chaliha and Michael Scott as its other members, held several rounds of talks with underground leaders at Chedema and Shillong. Working for peace in an area that remained turbulent for nearly seventeen years, ten of which were marked by severe repression, was not easy. The mission managed to secure acceptance of ceasefire terms, bringing about a transient truce. Jayaprakash resigned from the peace mission in February 1966, when he felt that he had forfeited the confidence of leaders of the Naga Federal Commission by advocating the need for a negotiated settlement. He was invited to Kohima by the Nagaland Baptist Church Council and the Peace Centre a few months later, and was overwhelmed by the warm welcome accorded to him. Speaking at a public reception, he justified the Government of India's stand and said that a sovereign state of Nagaland outside the Indian union was untenable.[61] The Naga issue kept him engaged till it was resolved as did the anti-colonial movement in Goa, though the latter was resolved much sooner through Indian military action in 1961. He saw the military action in Goa as a severe compromise on India's declared policy of peaceful resolution of international issues.[62]

Jayaprakash's largely elusive search for peaceful ways to settle disputes was admired by many young dreamers. Gopal Gandhi, who at this point was a student of English literature at St Stephen's

College, wrote a charming letter to Jayaprakash. 'My admiration for your courage and statesmanship—always high—has arisen enormously ever since you have taken this noble and gracious stand on the India–Pakistan question. This is to tell you that you are not alone in your mission and that there are several people who would be only too glad to help you further the noble cause of Indo-Pak amity. I am young and inexperienced and [a] mere student. But if there is anything I can do for this work, you have to only let me know.'[63] Sending a reply about a month later, Jayaprakash wrote, 'You ask what you can do to help. Try to make as many young men as possible to look at things with your eyes of sanity. Even if you succeed in one case it would have been a good job done.'[64]

An incurable romantic, Jayaprakash felt that India's border issues with China could be settled through mediation. 'I suggest that India's border dispute with China should be referred to an impartial arbitrator with both sides committed to accept the award. It would not be difficult to name three or four such independent persons even in the present divided world.'[65] Jayaprakash also proposed the leasing of the disputed Aksai Chin area to China as a possible settlement. When queried on Jayaprakash's statement, Nehru's reply was ambivalent. 'These questions are seldom arbitrable. But I would not rule it out if circumstances are proper and both parties are agreed and a suitable arbitrator is appointed.'[66]

By the closing years of the 1950s, the India–China border issue had turned into a live bomb waiting to detonate. Chinese maps brazenly showed large slices of Indian territory in eastern and western sectors as part of China. The Chinese were no longer saying that the maps were merely reprinted versions of the old Kuomintang maps. In Lok Sabha debates, Nehru emphatically said that in the north-east, the McMahon Line was the frontier by treaty, by usage and by geography. In the western sector, the disputed area of Aksai Chin, where the boundary was not clearly demarcated in some stretches, was on a different footing and could be perhaps settled by negotiation. Neither Nehru nor the defence minister, Krishna Menon, thought there was need for alarm or panic. In Parliament he was extremely vague, saying that there could be no greater folly than two great countries getting into a major conflict for the possession of a few mountain peaks. It would take another three years for his illusions to be dispelled.

When the Chinese finally advanced into Indian territory in October 1962, an aggression that Nehru had clearly not seen coming, Jayaprakash issued a provocative, recriminatory statement saying that it was India's policy of appeasement that resulted in Chinese aggression and the ignominious defeat of Indian troops. 'The first mistake was committed when India accepted Chinese sovereignty over Tibet. It was even a mistake from the moral point of view. When the question of "cultural genocide" committed by China in Tibet was raised by some nations in the UN, India preferred to remain neutral on the issue. I was perhaps the first man in this country who raised my voice against the Government of India's policy towards Tibet.'[67] He continued to blame Nehru for basic errors of judgement in failing to see the necessity of containing Chinese expansionism in 1947 and 1948.[68]

By May 1963, Jayaprakash was planning a friendship march from Delhi to Peking, confident that it would help overcome the hostility and hate. People from the USA, England, Austria, Japan, East Africa and a few other countries who were part of the World Peace Brigade (of which he was the co-chairperson) were to participate in the march. Comparing his pacifist move to Gandhi's Dandi March, he remarked wistfully, 'Whoever dared imagine in March 1930 that from the womb of the Dandi March would emerge the great Salt Satyagrah that shook the very foundation of the British empire?'[69] In the end, the march did not take off because of Pakistan's refusal to allow passage through East Pakistan and Britain's through Hong Kong.

Pakistan's rebuff in the form of a letter from Zulfiqar Ali Bhutto came dripping with derision. 'The problems in East Pakistan created by Government of India's unrelenting and inhuman policy of evicting thousands of helpless Indian Muslims from their homes in Assam and Tripura and forcibly throwing them across the border into East Pakistan have brought about an atmosphere of disquiet and uncertainty with the result that the feelings of the people have become highly exacerbated and the general situation in this area has, during the last few months, tended to become more and more sensitive.'[70] Jayaprakash was not prepared for this. He nonetheless focused on forming an India–Pakistan

Conciliation Group similar to the one formed in India in September 1962. Crusading for peace, he said, 'To work for peace is not cowardice. Quite to the contrary, it requires the highest type of moral and physical courage.'[71] Calling Kashmir the chief irritant in Indo-Pak relations, he felt that a positive approach would help transcend the deep-seated distrust between the two countries. This could only happen through a dialogue on areas of common interest in which the two countries would commit to work together for their mutual benefit.

The news from Nepal was not good. King Mahendra dissolved the democratically elected government in December 1960 and put B.P. Koirala in prison, giving Jayaprakash sleepless nights. 'I think history will show and perhaps sooner than it is expected that King Mahendra, by his action, has injured not so much democracy as monarchy itself and particularly his own throne and dynasty. King Mahendra has made himself ridiculous by claiming to have taken this action in the defence of democracy. This is unsurpassable double talk. The faults of parliamentary democracy are well known but no democrat will doubt that this kind of democracy is far better than the personal rule of a King or dictator.'[72] He met Mahendra in Kathmandu and pleaded for the restoration of democracy. Garlanded with shoes by the king's supporters and with absolutely no support, he kept issuing statement after statement hoping that Mahendra would respond.

Nehru's death on 27 May 1964 devastated Jayaprakash. He was in Calcutta when the news reached him. Prabhavati scribbled the following words in her diary on 28 May: 'Jayaprakash took a flight to Delhi yesterday night and went straight to Panditji's house. It was overflowing with mourners. He went today morning also and sat quietly for two hours. Later he went to Shanti Ghat where he looked extremely disturbed.'[73] She was privy to Jayaprakash's suffering the next day when she reached Delhi. 'I went to Shanti Ghat and later to Indira. In the evening a huge condolence meeting was organized at Ramlila grounds. Jayaprakash was requested repeatedly to speak. But he could not speak. He was extremely sad.'[74] And then her description of the final farewell at Allahabad on 8 June: 'We went on a special boat to watch the ashes being immersed in the Sangam . . . in the evening went to meet Indira at Anand Bhavan. Reminiscing about the old days, we grieved for a lost part of our lives.'[75]

Nehru's death was a solitary experience for Jayaprakash. Nehru had been his beau ideal over two very significant decades of his early life. He struggled for days to regain his equilibrium, confessing to my father and friends like J.J. Singh that something had died within him. His official tribute to his 'bhai' may have been clichéd—'The captain of the ship is no more. The leader has left the people desolate and forlorn. The tragedy, the nation had feared these past months has at last overtaken it'[76]—but he managed to reclaim the appropriate words to write a moving letter to Nehru's daughter Indira. Indira lost no time in reverting. 'I have received so many letters of warm sympathy all over the world from people who know and loved him,' she wrote. 'Yours brings me special comfort for I know you share our sorrow in a deeply personal way.'[77]

The abyss that opened up after Nehru's death was difficult to bridge. Sixty-year-old Lal Bahadur Shastri, Nehru's trusted cabinet colleague, was sworn in as the next prime minister on 9 June 1964. He inherited a rapidly deteriorating economy, a restive polity and equally restive neighbours. He was dead within nineteen months, on 11 January 1966, under suspicious circumstances, a day after signing a peace treaty with Pakistan at Tashkent soon after a full-scale military attack on Pakistan in response to its audaciousness in infiltrating Jammu and Kashmir. In accordance with the treaty, both countries agreed to withdraw their armies to their pre-1965 position and to restore normality in their mutual relations. Jayaprakash's warm obituary summed up the sense of deep loss that once again gripped the nation.

Replacing the interim prime minister Gulzarilal Nanda, Indira Gandhi was elected leader of the Congress Parliamentary Party on 19 January, in a compromise between the party's right and left wings. She was barely forty-nine. 'You have taken on a tremendous burden, and my heart goes out to you in this hour of trial and anxiety,' wrote Jayaprakash, offering her his full support, looking forward to a new dawn.[78]

Another close comrade, Lohia, passed away in October 1967. Pushing aside their differences, Jayaprakash focused his tribute on Lohia's unique place in the history of modern India. 'Death has cut short an extraordinary political career—a career that was yet to reach its summit. But even in the comparatively short span of 57 years he had made for himself a unique place in the history of modern India. He was one of the fathers of Indian Socialism, both as the theoretician and organiser. He more than anyone else gave to democratic Socialism, the weapon of militancy.'[79]

Through the rumble of history and politics, Jayaprakash's life oscillated constantly between the quotidian and the monumental—and that's what makes it so special. He campaigned for a building grant from the education ministry for the Nritya Kala Mandir in Patna, wrote to the chief engineer, Public Works Department, to complete work on a bridge before the monsoon, and appealed for the proper care of B.P. Koirala, ailing in a prison in Nepal, all with equivalent intensity. A routine letter of thanks to the Dalai Lama for sending him a copy of his book *My Land and My People* went hand in hand with a fervent request to people to donate money for flood-affected areas of Bihar. A deeply felt petition was sent to the central and state governments to review the use of the draconian Defence of India rules to put down civil disturbances[80] on the one hand. On the other, he sent a letter to his close friend J.J. Singh about a small accident near the Ganga embankment in Patna which led to some torn ligaments.[81]

In August 1965, Jayaprakash was awarded the Ramon Magsaysay Award for his constructive articulation of a public conscience for modern India. The citation mentioned his personal modesty wedded to clarity of thought and force of personality. More compellingly, it also mentioned his contribution towards dispelling myths of formulas that offer trite solutions. There was a clamour for his name as the consensus candidate during the 1967 presidential elections. Far from being pleased, Jayaprakash was discomfited to the point of being appalled. He was immensely relieved when the Congress nominated Dr Zakir Husain as its candidate. Jayaprakash offered his unqualified support to Dr Zakir Husain by mounting a vigorous campaign in his favour.

Throughout the 1950s, especially the latter half of the decade, Jayaprakash was dogged by the perception that he would be the next prime minister. On the eve of his overseas departure when he was asked by journalists to respond to Nehru's wish to unburden himself of public responsibilities and take a vacation from office, his wry and rather angsty response that Nehru should place someone of his own choice in the hot seat resulted in wild speculations that he was the chosen one. And even though he was often called 'Nehru's foremost critic', in private conversations Nehru was quoted as saying that Jayaprakash was indeed the chosen one.

An early portrait of
Jayaprakash Narayan

JP's wife,
Prabhavati

Another portrait of
Prabhavati

At the launch meeting
of the Congress Socialist
Party in Bombay,
21 October 1934

JP during his
fast in 1942

JP spinning in solitude at
his home in Sukhodewara
Ashram, Gaya

Prabhavati with
Mahatma Gandhi

Prabhavati and JP with
Vinoba Bhave at the Paunar
Ashram in Wardha

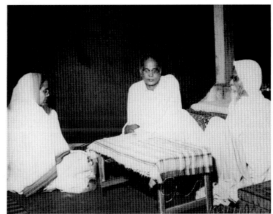

The torched Searchlight building, 18 March 1974

Women's silent protest, April 1974

On the roads of Patna in an open jeep

In a bus with detainees, 4 November 1974

Attacked by the police, 4 November 1974

Credit: Raghu Rai

People aboard a train to Patna, travelling to join the movement

Addressing a mammoth rally in Gandhi Maidan: 'The struggle must continue'

Credit: Raghu Rai

Credit: Raghu Rai

People's Lok Nayak

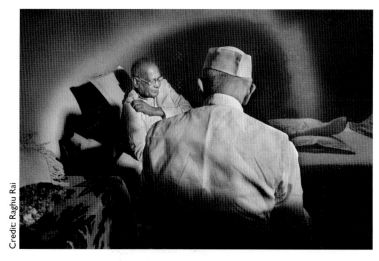

Morarji Desai
with JP

The Rajghat
Pledge, with JP
and J.B. Kripalani
in the foreground,
24 March 1977

JP with
Jawaharlal Nehru

Indira Gandhi's meeting with JP at his residence at the Mahila Charkha
Samiti in Patna, 14 August 1977

Bimal Prasad with the ailing leader in 1979

8

The Sting in the Tail

The months leading up to, and after, the elections of 1967 were enveloped in a fog of chaos, intrigue, and violence. Addressing a turbulent election meeting in Bhubaneswar in early February, Indira Gandhi was struck in the face by stones, hurled by young men who were shouting and jeering at her. Growing up in a small sub-Himalayan town, Ramachandra Guha recalls a slogan that was very popular at the time: 'Jana Sangh ko vote do bidi peena chhorh do, bidi mein tambaku hai, kangresswala daku hai.'[1] My own memory, charged with emotion, is of prancing around two very elegant men in starched white khadi kurtas discussing the run of watershed events, convinced that the turbulent economic and political headwinds that were sweeping through the country would blow Nehru's petite daughter away: my father and Jayaprakash at our tiny home at the rear end of Sapru House, Delhi.

The Congress, clinging to its worn-out shibboleths, was battered by the rise of non-Congress populist coalitions which, far from being stable, faced internal dissension and floor-crossing by legislators in search of power and money. Indira contested from Raebareli, Feroze Gandhi's constituency, reaching out to people as a traditional 'bahu'. The strategy worked and she won with a huge margin. The party's seat tally, however, went down to 283. The Congress was also voted out in several state elections, collapsing in UP, Bihar, Kerala, Punjab, Orissa, West Bengal, Rajasthan and Tamil Nadu. The sceptics watched, as Indira was sworn in as prime minister on 13 March 1967.

As the country lurched from one economic crisis to another, Indira found herself in a thicket of thorny issues. The quiet crisis of the economy in the 1950s and early 1960s was assuming epic proportions. Agricultural production, more or less wholly flat since 1960, was affected by a succession of severe droughts in most parts of the country. The population was growing by 2.5 per cent at over 13 million a year. The per capita income was less than $80 a year. Unemployment had quadrupled. There was near stagnation in industrial production, which hovered around 3.3 per cent during 1965–70, and a massive trade deficit. There was an exponential increase in inflation—prices continued to rise, by as much as 22 per cent in 1972–73. There were food shortages, rice riots and masses of desperately poor Indians.[2]

Indira sized up the situation and immediately took control. By May 1967, she was ready with a radical, socialist, left-of-centre programme of reforms that included plans to discontinue princely privileges by abolishing privy purses; guarantee of minimal wages for rural and industrial labour; nationalization of the insurance sector; social control of banking institutions; state trading in foodgrains and removal of monopolies. These plans found ideological resonance with the socialist group within the party led by Young Turks like Mohan Dharia and Chandra Shekhar.

By 1969, Indira was ready to defy the 'Syndicate', a caucus of Congress bosses who had sidelined Morarji Desai in their move to install her as prime minister. Their decision was motivated by the rather misogynistic perception that she would be dumb and compliant. In a thinly veiled attempt at tearing her down, even Lohia used the sexist term 'goongi gudiya' (dumb doll) to describe her. She proved them all wrong. Ambitious, with a penetrating eye for the realpolitik of the day, her learning curve was exponential. Having proven her political acumen in 1959, when, as party president she plotted the overthrow of a democratically elected communist government in Kerala, she was ready to take off from the moment she assumed charge. Politics was part of her DNA. Even during her student days at Oxford's Somerville College, she was active in the student wing of the British Labour Party and was a Red Cross volunteer when World War II began, driving ambulances through heavy artillery firing. Closer to home, in the leadership contest with Morarji Desai by secret ballot on 19 January 1966, she won 355 votes to his 169.

There was palpable dissonance between the Syndicate and Indira as early as the summer of 1966. To counter the balance of payments crisis, she decided to devalue the Indian rupee by a sharp 57 per cent, acting independently of the party and risking being called an American and World Bank stooge. Condemned from all sides, Indira explained her position in a radio broadcast on 12 June 1966. 'The decision to devalue the rupee was not an easy one . . . there are times in the history of every nation when its will is tested and its future depends on its capacity for resolute action and bold decision.'[3] On 16 July 1969, in a lightning strike, she divested Morarji Desai of the finance portfolio. On 19 July, she nationalized fourteen large commercial banks by a presidential ordinance to accelerate bank loans in agriculture. It was clear that she alone was calling the shots as prime minister. She overrode the Syndicate in getting her nominee, Dr Zakir Husain, made President.

Indira was expelled from the Congress on 12 November 1969 for backing a requisition to oust S. Nijalingappa, who had replaced Kamaraj as Congress president in 1968. Another reason for her ouster was the equally grave sin of asking for 'a vote of conscience' for the election of labour leader V.V. Giri as President when the Syndicate was backing N. Sanjiva Reddy. Indira once again outmanoeuvred the Syndicate. In an epochal decision, she split the ageing party. Out of 429 Congress MPs in both houses of Parliament, 310 chose to stay with her in the new Congress Requisitionist (R). A no-confidence motion brought in by the Syndicate's Congress Organisation (O) was defeated with the support of the communists and regional parties. As Jayaprakash watched from the wings, the stage was set for her complete control over the working committee and the parliamentary board. She cemented her hold on power with a decisive victory in the midterm polls of 1971, winning 352 seats to the opposition's twenty-five. There was no more doubt about her political instincts as she was sworn in as prime minister for the third time. This was the Indira wave backed by the powerful slogan of 'garibi hatao', and she, the poster girl of a personality cult that would have few equals.

Having known Indira intimately since her childhood, it can easily be speculated that Jayaprakash was thinking of dipping his toes into mainstream politics as Indira's adviser or mentor. He may have imagined that she would establish with him the same sort of relationship that Nehru had with Gandhi. But Indira had her team of advisers or 'sutradhars', a term recently used by Jairam Ramesh,[4] already in place: diplomats T.N. Kaul and D.P. Dhar, economist P.N. Dhar, security adviser R.N. Kao and the chief sutradhar, fifty-four-year-old, London School of Economics-educated P.N. Haksar. They were mockingly called the Panch Pandavas behind their backs. She also depended on leftist friends like Romesh Thapar.

At this point, Jayaprakash's position vis-à-vis Indira was not of an adversary but also not of an ally; he was not someone she trusted entirely. And yet there was warmth and charm in their relationship, a certain effervescence in their regular exchanges. For instance, in a letter written on 6 July 1966, she thanked him for sharing his views on Kashmir and proposed a meeting. 'I wonder if you are likely to come to Delhi sometime next month so that we could discuss the matter. I should welcome such an opportunity.'[5] Jayaprakash's reply, coming after her trip to Cairo and Moscow, exuded reciprocal warmth: 'I should like to congratulate you on the success of your foreign trip . . . I hope you have returned in good health because immediately you will have to face heavy work in Parliament as well as in the Government.'[6]

There were sweet, informal letters with birthday wishes. 'Dear Indu, it was only last night when I heard on the radio about birthday felicitations offered to you that I realised that yesterday was your 50th birthday. At my age, 50 still seems to be young, and though I pray that you should live to ripe old age, I wish you will always remain young. Wishing you again long life, happiness, fame and success.'[7] Enveloped letters from Indira to thank him for his support in drought-relief operations in Bihar: 'The purpose of this letter is to thank you for the wonderful work that you have done in organizing the drought relief operations in Bihar and in galvanising both official and non-official agencies into action. You have also not spared yourself in traveling around the country to raise funds. Your zeal and example were an inspiration to many others.'[8]

Nearly all the districts in Bihar suffered from a drought of apocalyptic proportions during the main kharif season between July and October 1966. It was unlike anything Jayaprakash had witnessed in his lifetime and was compounded by heavy floods in north Bihar during August–September. Altogether, 36 per cent of the area of the state was declared to be in the throes of famine and 30 per cent of the area where the yield had been less than 50 per cent of normal production 'scarcity affected'.[9] Approximately 34 million people were fighting for survival. To supplement government operations that included wheat imports from the United States and its distribution through 20,000 fair price shops, a relief committee was set up by Bihar chief minister Krishnaballabh Sahay. This committee, working under Jayaprakash's direction, started a network of free kitchens and food distribution centres by deploying relief workers at the district, block and panchayat levels and using home guards provided by the state government for relief distribution.

Jayaprakash lost no time in issuing urgent appeals to individuals, institutions and corporates to donate liberally, involving friends like David Astor, editor of the *London Observer*, for international publicity and support. The response from international agencies—Oxfam, Catholic Relief Services, CARE, American Peace Corps and several other smaller organizations—was stupendous. A large number of young university students from Britain, France, West Germany, the Scandinavian countries, Canada, the United States and Australia joined relief operations as volunteers. They distributed food packets and medicines; they blasted rocks and dug wells. Jayaprakash thwarted the Union government's attempts to downplay the crisis by issuing regular updates on the extremely grim situation. An irrigation programme was set up for two years, with plans to construct 5000 tube wells, 10,000 open borings in dug wells and 10,000 surface percolation wells.

Communal fault lines in Bihar and elsewhere were as fractious as ever, resulting in frequent orchestrated violence. Figures released by the National Integration Council showed an alarming escalation of incidents, with as many as 346 cases reported in 1968. Travelling to riot-hit areas, Jayaprakash did not even have time to mourn the death of his close friend and comrade Rambriksha Benipuri.

In a trenchant response to the Ranchi riots of August–September 1967, Jayaprakash said, 'There must be something terribly wrong with our upbringing, with the religious beliefs that have been inculcated in us, the education that is being imparted, the group attitudes that are being developed by assiduous propaganda to make it possible for normal human beings to change suddenly into bloodthirsty monsters.'[10] He expressed warm approval of those who had managed to keep away from religious extremism and who even at the height of rioting did not lose their humanity. He had special words of praise for minister, Ramanand Tiwari, 'whose amazing bravery, deep humanity and firm leadership saved hundreds of threatened lives'.[11] Turning the torch on Muslim separatism, he argued, 'Unfortunately there are still Muslim organisations, who under the guise of religious or cultural activity, emphasise the separateness of the Muslim community, ignore Hindu susceptibilities and keep aloof from the mainstream of national and social life . . . I fear that what I am saying may [sic] arouse bitter anger. I should be sorry, however, for those who would be angry, I am speaking as a friend, as one who is deeply concerned about the future of Indian Muslims and of the future of our country as a nation.'[12]

In his presidential address to the Eleventh National Convention against Communalism organized in New Delhi on 28–29 December 1968, Jayaprakash was extremely bitter about Hindu communalism. Talking about majoritarianism gone awry, he said, 'India being a country of many religions, almost every religious community has its own brand of communalism. They are pernicious, but Hindu communalism is more pernicious than the others. One reason is that because the Hindus constitute a great majority of the population of India, Hindu communalism can easily masquerade as Indian nationalism, and denounce all opposition to it as being anti-national.'[13] The speech created a furore. But before the furore could die down, a massive riot broke out in Ahmedabad between 18 and 24 September 1969. For an entire week, even as the country prepared for Mahatma Gandhi's centenary celebrations, arson attacks, vandalism and orchestrated killings left thousands homeless and hundreds dead. The majority of those killed were Muslims and nine out of ten homes and business enterprises destroyed belonged to them.[14] Anguished beyond measure, Jayaprakash wrote a deluge of op-eds about the juggernaut of the Hindu communal propaganda machine that was 'poisoning the Hindu mind by distorting history, by painting Muslims as aggressors and enemies of the country, by arguing that having asked for and obtained Pakistan, the Muslims have no right to live in India'.[15]

Writing to Frank Moraes, editor-in-chief of the *Indian Express*, Jayaprakash said, 'We Hindus have been prone to take shelter behind the loftiest structures of thought built by some of our distinguished forefathers, and behind that screen we continue to practice a form of religion and rituals that are millions of miles away from the spiritual insights of the Upanishadic rishis. It is this self-deception, this self patting of our backs that stands between the Hindu society of today and enlightenment and progress. Let us be frank with ourselves and confess that ours is a decadent society which perhaps needs a new Buddha to cleanse it and release it from the cobwebs in which it is caught.'[16] Jayaprakash renewed his commitment to initiate peace dialogues in areas that had experienced sectarian violence through Gandhian peace brigades—the Shanti Senas and their youth counterparts, the Tarun Shanti Senas. He made plans to commemorate the birthday of Khan Abdul Ghaffar Khan as Insani Biradari or Human Brotherhood Day. He also took urgent steps to set up a small organization known as Insani Biradari to work for social cohesion and peaceful resolution of conflicts in areas riven by communal volatility.

The year 1968 was one marked by revolution and social conflicts across the world. In the United States, students were besieging street after street in protest against the 10,000-day war in Vietnam. In March, 1227 girls of Smith College went on a three-day fast against the war. Students and professors opposed to the war fasted at Harvard, Princeton and other universities. In May 1968, 5,00,000 protesters marched through the streets of Paris shouting 'Adieu, de Gaulle'. In London, Vietnam-war protesters led by Tariq Ali and Vanessa Redgrave marched outside the US embassy at Grosvenor Square. There were spasms of protests in Germany, Italy, Spain, Poland and Northern Ireland. A mass movement in Mexico, resulting in the infamous massacre of Tlatelolco Square, and the rebellion at Prague, with students throwing burning torches on Soviet tanks brought in to quell the democratic uprising, became enduring images of the upsurge.

Accepting an impressive line-up of invitations to address conclaves and seminars, Jayaprakash spent seventy days travelling through Europe, the United States, the Soviet Union, Japan and Afghanistan with Prabhavati. In these revolutionary movements, he glimpsed the possibility of leading a non-violent social movement led by students in a not too distant future in India. For the moment he was happy introducing himself as a 'revolutionary', finding in it an 'assertion of the human spirit for freedom, for joy, for self-realisation'.[17]

Back home, following the death of President Zakir Husain on 4 May 1969, Jayaprakash was urged to accept a nomination for the presidency, but he laughed off the proposal saying that he had no desire to live like a bird in a golden cage.[18] Instead, he began working to usher in a politics of consensus, advancing the view that competitive politics needed to be substituted, or at least supplemented, by politics of consensus. He organized a national convention on unity and democracy between 21 and 23 February 1969 at the India International Centre in Delhi. A majority of the delegates were representatives of major political parties like the Congress, Jana Sangh, Praja Socialist Party, Communist Party of India, Samyukta Socialist Party (SSP), Communist Party of India (Marxist) and the Republican Party, along with leading academics and journalists. Two study groups were formed. One on national unity, with sociologist M.N. Srinivas as convener; the other on constitutional and administrative changes, with B. Shiva Rao and my father as conveners.

Setting the tone for deliberations, Jayaprakash said, 'The question now is, can the parties engrossed in the struggle for power be persuaded to agree even to the limited idea of supplementing their competitive politics with a measure of cooperative politics?'[19] Everyone present endorsed the need for consensus but nothing tangible was achieved for lack of agreement between parties, even on basic matters. A few noncontroversial proposals, like strengthening the Election Commission by appointing a few more election commissioners and constituting an interstate council for settlement of disputes, were accepted and implemented much later.

In 1969, the world celebrated the centenary of Gandhi's birth. To commemorate his life and work, Jayaprakash took Gandhian ideas to different forums. He spoke about the socio-political ideas of Gandhi at a seminar organized by the A.N. Sinha Institute of Social Studies in Patna and at the Gandhian Institute of Studies at Varanasi, an institution founded by him in 1960. He spoke about Gandhi's unfinished revolution at the Jadavpur University in Calcutta; on his politics of decentralization at the centenary celebrations in Canberra; on his global legacy at a seminar in Kabul. He was also invited to speak at Gandhian dialogues and conferences in the United States and Australia. In nearly all his lectures, Jayaprakash said that Gandhi's work, far from having ended with India's independence, was about to begin, when he was killed. 'It is clear that he was preparing to launch a second revolution— this time a non-violent economic, social and moral revolution. Alas, the assassin's bullets deprived India and the world of a unique experience.'[20] What remained unsaid was that Jayaprakash was preparing to step into his mentor's shoes to create such a movement and take it forward.

By this time, a new form of politics in the shape of radical dissent led by armed, largely clandestine guerrilla groups came alive in Naxalbari, Telangana and Srikakulam and, by 1970, in the Musahari block of Muzaffarpur district of Bihar. It had its roots in the raging agrarian crises. Ironically, Bihar was the first state to legislate on land reforms in 1950. Despite this, several landholders retained holdings in excess of the ceiling area. Skewed provisions in land reform measures allowed zamindars to hold on to astonishing amounts of homestead land and property for the purpose of trade, commerce, storage, etc. It was not surprising, then, that together with their rural counterparts, several young urban idealists fell under the spell of a movement that, despite its violent narrative, had the romantic resonance of Yoko Ono's lyrics in Lennon's song 'Imagine'.[21]

The movement seemed to stir in Jayaprakash, too, an awakening of hope. In an address to the National Conference of Voluntary Agencies on 8 June 1969, he spoke of the extreme inequity in society and the positive work being done by Naxalites to eradicate it. 'They are violent people. Alright. But I have sympathy because they are doing something for the poor. If the law is unable to give to the people a modicum of social and economic justice, what do you think will happen, if not nonviolence erupting all over?'[22] Speaking about the need for a non-violent social revolution to address rural poverty and related problems, he asked, 'With all the programmes and activities in this Gandhi Centenary Year, if the problems of the people are not solved democratically, what other recourse do the people have except violence?'[23] Jayaprakash's maverick line on violence and his support for a movement that was considered subversive came as a big surprise.

Jayaprakash was pulled into the vortex of the movement in June 1970, a few months before his seventieth year, when he received news that Naxalites in Musahari were about to annihilate two Sarvodaya workers. Jayaprakash confessed that he was both shocked and elated at the news. Shocked at the danger to their lives. Elated at the intoxicating possibility of a new level of engagement. He felt that the Sarvodaya movement was losing its fire 'and we, its workers, were becoming stale and flabby of spirit. Our work was so bland that it involved no personal danger to us.'[24] When the state government offered security, Jayaprakash was appalled. 'I feel greatly distressed at the security arrangements being made for me. I consider them entirely unnecessary and a waste of public money. Besides, they are most annoying and amateurish.'[25] The movement at Musahari led by leaders like Satnarain Singh, Ram Deo Paswan, Taslimuddin, Ashok Singh, Sripat Mahto and Raj Kishore Singh had earned substantial notoriety with the murder of half a dozen landlords in quick succession. The red flag emblazoned with a hammer and sickle, and slogans like 'fasal kabja karo aur zamin kabja karo'[26] (seize the crops and the land), mirrored the mood of the Maoist movement.

Accompanied by Prabhavati, Jayaprakash moved from hut to hut, hamlet to hamlet, village to village addressing small meetings along the way. It was difficult to mitigate the discontent arising out of destitution, but their presence, even if momentarily, lit up the lives of many. The meetings were crucial for Jayaprakash's own understanding of some of the basic issues that underlay social unrest. 'I had not buried myself in this manner before in a limited rural area. I must confess that socio-economic reality in the village, on close examination, is ugly and distressing to the extreme. My first reaction in coming face to face with the reality was to realise how remote and unreal were the brave pronouncements of Delhi or Patna from the actuality at the ground level. High sounding words, grandiose plans, reforms galore. But somehow, they all, or most of them, remain suspended somewhere in mid-air. They hardly touch the ground—at least not here. In the end what meets the eye is utter poverty, misery, inequality, exploitation, backwardness, stagnation, frustration, and loss of hope.'[27]

Surviving the challenges and privations of their daily life with infinite cheer, Jayaprakash, Prabhavati and the Sarvodaya followers did their best to implement Gramdan. In a few months, they covered seven village panchayats and forty-three revenue villages, farming out undistributed Bhoodan land, establishing gram sabhas, gram koshas (village fund) and shanti senas or peace brigades. For the time they were there, the block administrators did whatever they could to mitigate the social unrest arising out of rural destitution—mainly in terms of ensuring tenancy rights. What worked was not only his but also his wife's strong-willed presence and incredible personal charisma. Their jeep driver in Musahari, Jaleshwar, recalled that even in the bitter chill of winter nights, Prabhavati would drive to remote areas to visit the homes of jailed Naxalites like Raj Kishore Singh and Taslimuddin to see if their families needed anything, foregoing her needs to meet theirs.

Jayaprakash issued a press statement from Musahari on 23 December 1970 condemning the death sentence awarded to four Naxalite leaders of Andhra Pradesh and Orissa—Nagbhushan Patnaik, Narela Sekhar, G. Paidayya and L. Lachhanna. He said, 'I hold no brief for Naxalites or Naxalism, but I certainly would not lump them together with ordinary criminals . . . Gandhiji was not an admirer of violence, even when used for the most commendable purpose, but he spared no efforts to save Sardar Bhagat Singh and his two fellow-soldiers of freedom, Shri Rajguru and Shri Sukhdev.'[28] Musahari was, however, only the beginning of protracted agrarian tension in Bihar in areas like Darbhanga, Champaran, Sitamarhi, Purnea and Samastipur; with the presence of Naxalite guerrilla squads at its most intense in Bhojpur. Challenging the complacent government in an address given to the National Conference of Voluntary Agencies, Jayaprakash said,

'My Sarvodaya friends and my Gandhian friends will be surprised to read what I publicly say now. I say with a due sense of responsibility that if I myself am convinced that there is no deliverance for the people except through violence, then Jayaprakash Narayan will also take to violence. If the problems of the people cannot be solved democratically, I will also take to violence.'[29]

Stripping away the accretions of myth enveloping the Naxalite movement, Jayaprakash argued that the ground for violence was prepared by persistence of merciless exploitation, chronic poverty and accumulated injustices. He reserved the brunt of his fury for politicians, administrators, landowners and moneylenders. 'It is not the so-called Naxalites who have fathered this violence, but they who have persistently defied and defeated the laws for the past so many years—be they politicians, administrators, landowners, moneylenders. The big farmers who cheated the ceiling law through benami and fictitious settlements; the gentlemen who grabbed government lands and village commons; the landowners who persistently denied the legal rights of their share-croppers and evicted them from their holdings and who underpaid their labourers and threw them out from their homesteads; the men who by fraud or force took the lands away from the weaker sections; the so-called upper-caste men who looked down upon their Harijan brethren and ill-treated and socially discriminated against them; the moneylenders who charged usurious interests and seized the lands of the poor and the weak; the politicians, the administrators and all the others who aided and abetted these wrongs—it is they who are responsible for the accumulated sense of injustice, grievance and hurt among the poor and downtrodden that is now seeking its outlet in violence.'[30] He feared the counter-violence that the state would unleash was likely to lead to some form of despotism.

Jayaprakash extended his support to a parallel movement started by the CPI, PSP and SSP to seize 'gair majurwa'[31] and ceiling-surplus land in possession of village landlords to distribute it to the landless and poor peasants. The only worrying aspect of this movement, as he saw it, was the CPI's advice to the landless to come to meetings and processions with sticks, spears and swords. 'This kind of action is an open invitation to violence and cannot be described as a democratic people's movement.'[32] Taking on critics of the movement who raised questions of morality, Jayaprakash hit back: 'There were no such questions raised, no hue and cry about land grabbers, no "democracy in danger" slogans when the stronger elements in the villages illegally and stealthily stole hundreds of thousands of acres to which they had no right whatsoever.'[33]

Jayaprakash wrote an essay on Musahari and was momentarily pleased by the response from Indira. 'Your experiment is a golden attempt to explore the possibilities of non-violent change at ground level,' she wrote. Seeming to concur with Jayaprakash's main propositions, she said, 'I agree that Naxalism is primarily a challenge to find a non-violent way of eradicating poverty and exploitation and only secondarily, a law and order problem. I also have been emphasizing that Naxalism cannot be superseded by counter-violence, it can be tackled by a crusade against poverty and exploitation which provide a favourable ground for the growth of political extremism.'[34]

Till about 1970, the disagreements between Indira and Jayaprakash were without rancour. He thought it perfectly legitimate to expose her inconsistencies and inadequacies. Indira continued to humour him by discreetly sidestepping to avoid confrontation. But cracks of discord began to appear. In a congratulatory letter written after Indira's electoral successes, Jayaprakash was critical of her stand in the presidential elections. 'Although I knew it was a moment of political life and death for you, I did not like your political conduct at the time of the presidential election.'[35] Indira's reply showed the first simmering of differences that would accentuate in coming years. 'Thanks for letter of congratulations. You wrote that you did not like my conduct at the time of the presidential elections although you considered it necessary for my political life. I was pained reading this. I was pained especially at the thought that you know and understand me so little. I have never worried about my political or any other kind of existence. The question at that time was related not to my future, but to the future of the Congress and, therefore, of the country.'[36]

Kashmir continued to engage Jayaprakash. This is where his mind returned in between his other preoccupations. In 1966, he took Indira's permission to visit Sheikh Abdullah, who was detained at Kodaikanal, and stepped up his campaign for the latter's immediate release. In a statement to the press on 13 April 1967, he said, 'Detention without trial for indefinite periods for men with deep convictions not only defeats its avowed purpose but is utterly repugnant to all democratic principles and practices.'[37] When the Sheikh was released from detention on 4 January 1968, Jayaprakash congratulated the government for doing the right thing and began pressing for an early settlement on Kashmir; based on internal autonomy for the state within India, and autonomy of Jammu within the state. He remained convinced that Sheikh Abdullah had the capacity to influence public opinion in the Valley.

The Sheikh returned to the Valley to a tumultuous welcome and revived the activities of the Plebiscite Front, set up in 1964. He requested Jayaprakash to send a study team of scholars and leaders to Kashmir for ten days in June 1968 for a dispassionate assessment of all the fault lines. The team consisted of philosopher A.R. Wadia; sociologist S.C. Dubey; president, Sarva Seva Sangh, M.M. Choudhury; socialist leader and scholar Moinuddin Harris; economist P.N. Dhar and my father. They reached Srinagar on 23 June and met leading figures in the political life of Jammu and Kashmir, including Sheikh Abdullah and Mirza Afzal Beg, and interacted with a number of university teachers, students and bureaucrats not as interlocutors, but independent, nonpartisan observers. They also met and spent time with many of the locals in Srinagar and nearby towns and villages. The committee noted two particularly disturbing trends: escalation of communal tensions, and growing radicalization of students. 'Ideologically and organisationally, the students are potentially an uncertain factor in Kashmir politics. In anger and frustration, they may acquire hardened communal attitudes,' the team reported.[38] It was evident from the report that the underlying disillusionment with India's democratic facade was poised to instigate serious dissident responses in coming times.

When Jayaprakash visited the Valley on 10 October 1968, he received a 'hero's reception'.[39] But the public meeting that he and Sheikh Abdullah jointly addressed took an ugly turn. The Sheikh cited commitments made by Gandhi and Nehru to support his demand that the people of his state be allowed to shape their destiny in accordance with their wishes. Crossing swords with him on this issue, Jayaprakash reminded the audience that after the 1965 conflict, no government, even if it were headed by him, could accept a solution that placed Kashmir outside India. As a friend and well-wisher, he advised the people of Kashmir to seek a solution within the framework of the Union of India. Referring to the demand for self-determination, he said, 'It is extremely difficult to define and geographically demarcate "a people".' He then asked, 'Are the Kashmiris a people? Then what about the Dogras and the Ladakhis? Where will you draw a line?'[40] Jayaprakash's 'plain speaking' provoked an angry retort from Sheikh Abdullah. He said, 'Freedom is never given as a gift, it has to be snatched. The question is not what the government of India is willing to give us but what people of Kashmir want. They will get it with force. Hundreds of young men will be prepared to be hanged. If we have power, we will get it or we will destroy ourselves.'[41] When he arrived in Delhi, Jayaprakash told reporters that the Sheikh's speech was fundamentally meant to appease the restive radical elements in the Valley.

Notwithstanding the Sheikh's turnabout on the issue of a plebiscite, Jayaprakash's affection for him and faith in his leadership remained unwavering. The Sheikh gave him another major jolt in 1971 when he tried to draw a parallel between Kashmir and Bangladesh. Reiterating his stand on Kashmir, Jayaprakash said, 'I have to confess with a heavy heart that Sheikh sahib's attitude towards the freedom struggle of Bangladesh and his attempt to draw a parallel between the Kashmir and Bangladesh issues have sorely disappointed and disillusioned me. After all that has happened since 1947, it is futile for any Kashmiri leader to keep on harping on Jawaharlal Nehru's assurance to hold a plebiscite in the State when normalcy was restored there. The plebiscite issue is dead for ever. Even the Sheikh cannot put back the clock of history . . . The only question that may still be considered to be relevant is that of the quantum of autonomy that Jammu & Kashmir should enjoy within the Union of India, and Jammu and Ladakh regions, in their turn, should enjoy within the constitutional framework of the State.'[42] He was, however, crestfallen when Sheikh Abdullah and other leaders were externed from the state on the eve of parliamentary elections in 1971. In a letter to Indira on 26 March 1971, he said, 'It was a pity that Sheikh sahib and his friends were not allowed to participate in the parliamentary election. Had that been allowed, it would have contributed greatly to the easing of tensions in the valley and strengthen the hopes of its people that their democratic aspirations could find fulfilment within the present constitution.'[43]

In the increasingly fluid and unpredictable political environment, a revolutionary movement for political autonomy in East Pakistan led by Sheikh Mujibur Rahman emerged as a major area of concern. The suppression of the movement and trial of Mujibur Rahman on charges of treason generated stormy protests. Jayaprakash issued three press statements in support of the movement and appealed to friendly countries to act urgently and effectively to ensure that 'no country gives any armed assistance to the military dictatorship in Pakistan nor any facilities to her armed forces and for supplies being moved from the West to the East'.[44] He also met a group of leading journalists in New Delhi on 4 April 1971 to discuss the possibility of according immediate recognition to Bangladesh. The journalists present at the meeting were Frank Moraes, George Verghese, Girilal Jain, Kuldip Nayar and Dilip Mukherjee. The consensus that emerged was that the case for recognition was premature since there was no palpable political body or structure that could be called a government. Jayaprakash had to eventually concede that the question 'Whom to recognise, does seriously weaken, if not demolish, the recognition case'.[45]

A genocide of epic proportions in Bangladesh claimed millions of lives, displaced 30 million people, with an exodus of more than 9 million refugees to India. Jayaprakash appealed to Indira to take the lead in mobilizing world opinion against Pakistan. Indira dispatched senior cabinet ministers to several countries 'to waken the conscience of the world'. She also encouraged Jayaprakash to travel to cities like Cairo, Rome, Belgrade, Moscow, Helsinki, Stockholm, Bonn, Paris, London, Washington, New York, Ottawa, Vancouver, Tokyo, Jakarta, Singapore and Kuala Lumpur to draw attention to the holocaust. When Jayaprakash returned to India, his impatience with Indira's delay in 'taking action' was reflected in a press statement issued on 29 June. 'Everyone I met abroad was full of praise for the prime minister's restraint and statesmanship in dealing with a difficult crisis. I too admire her for that. But she must decide now if the time for action has not arrived.'[46]

Jayaprakash organized an international conference on Bangladesh at Sapru House in New Delhi on 18 September. A hundred and fifty foreign delegates from twenty-four countries took part in the deliberations. The conference was a huge success. It unequivocally recommended the recognition of Bangladesh by the governments of the world. Jayaprakash's impatience with Indira's inaction continued to grow. In an article written for the op-ed page in the *Indian Express*, he complained, 'It is difficult to imagine a greater and completer failure of our national leadership in the face of the gravest crisis this country has faced since independence.'[47] While Indira's delay was stoking resentment, Jayaprakash managed to annoy Indira as well, when he put together a joint front to agitate for the recognition of Bangladesh. The front eventually remained a pipe dream, with the Marxists pointedly refusing to align with parties like the Jana Sangh.

Indira, meanwhile, waited for the opportune moment with utmost circumspection. Aware that open support to the Mukti Bahini, a secessionist organization, would be condemned as interference in the internal affairs of another country, she supported them clandestinely. They were trained, organized and armed. Not giving a damn about the US and China's support of Pakistan, Indira checkmated Pakistan when she signed the Indo-Soviet treaty of Peace, Friendship and Cooperation on 9 August 1971, during the visit of Andrei Gromyko, the Soviet foreign minister, to India. She travelled to a number of countries to speak about the deepening crisis. Her meeting with President Nixon may have been nothing more than dialogue with the deaf, but she was a rage when she spoke at Columbia University's School of International Affairs on 7 November, warning that with more than 9 million refugees pouring across her borders, India had reached the limits of her endurance.[48]

Indira did not have to wait much longer. On 3 December, Pakistan launched Operation Chengiz Khan against India. The Pakistani air force struck airfields all along the western border in Amritsar, Pathankot, Srinagar, Avantipur, Jodhpur, Ambala and Agra. Seven regiments of artillery attacked positions in Kashmir. This was exactly what Indira was waiting for. Led by the Chief of Army Staff, General Sam Manekshaw, and commander-in-chief Eastern Command, Jagjit Singh Aurora, the Indian army invaded East Pakistan. Two weeks later, the Indian army marched into Dhaka triumphantly, culminating in the surrender of Pakistan's top military commander, Lieutenant General Amir 'Tiger' Niazi and over 93,000 officers and men.

This was a proud moment in Indian history, a moment that finally managed to obliterate the humiliation of the 1962 Sino–Indian war. Indira won begrudging appreciation from even her strongest detractors when she announced the recognition of the Republic of Bangladesh on 6 December 1971. Jayaprakash was exuberant. 'I find it difficult to hold back my tears of joy on hearing that the prime minister has announced in parliament today that the Government of India has formally recognised the Government of the Republic of Bangladesh. This is a truly historic event that will change the shape of things not only in the Indian subcontinent but in the whole of South Asia.'[49]

Caught in the happy tide of events, for a while Jayaprakash was able to push aside his worries about Prabhavati, who was battling a serious lung condition. She was screened for lung cancer at AIIMS Delhi and the Tata Memorial Hospital in Bombay. Although the test results were negative, she continued to be unwell. His own condition was far from satisfactory. He was suffering from agonizing sciatica. His borderline diabetic condition was also worsening. But he continued to work at a feverish pace. My mother, who was visiting a convalescing Prabhavati at the time, recalled the sound of his pounding typewriter in the mornings. A month later, on 16 November, he had a sudden heart attack while on a tour of rural Bihar. This led to prolonged bed rest. He sought existential solace in reading, promising Prabhavati that he would take a year-long exile from public activities. But before that could happen, Jayaprakash reappeared in the national news in the unlikeliest of contexts.

In April 1972, Jayaprakash was involved with the voluntary surrender of more than 400 dacoits of the Chambal valley—an area covering several thousand square miles bordering the states of Uttar Pradesh, Madhya Pradesh and Rajasthan—under a partial amnesty approved by the government. The desperadoes, in their combat fatigues and handlebar moustaches, had eluded armed police and paramilitary units for decades. The story of their surrender began in October 1971, when a burly and raffish man came to see Jayaprakash at his Patna residence and pleaded with him to take up the festering issue of their surrender. Jayaprakash tried to fob him off but the man would not take no for an answer. He turned out to be the much feared, hot-headed dacoit Madho Singh who carried a price of more than a lakh on his head.

Jayaprakash began this onerous mission by writing to the chief ministers of Madhya Pradesh, Uttar Pradesh and Rajasthan. Weakened by his heart condition, he was not in the best of health. His cardiologists were appalled when he announced his decision to spend several weeks in the ravines of Chambal to coax the rebels to surrender. Simultaneously, his team also began work in the Bundelkhand area. This was an unusual campaign that relied on the complicity of the administration. At the centre of the campaign was the Chambal Ghati Shanti Mission formed by Jayaprakash in October 1971 for establishing contact with rebel gangs and persuading them to surrender. By the middle of March 1972, the dreaded gangs of Kalyan Singh, Makhan Singh, Harvilas, Mohar Singh, Sarup Singh, Tilak Singh, Pancham Singh and Kali Charan were contacted and persuaded to surrender.

Speaking to Minoo Masani for the *Illustrated Weekly of India*, Jayaprakash said that even if their acts were reprehensible, '. . . 75 percent of those who are surrendering, are persons whose families were victims of some socio-economic injustice on the part of some petty revenue or police officials. Being hot tempered, the provocation led them to some violent action after which they took shelter in the ravines. This is not therefore a mere law and order problem but a socio-economic and psychological problem.'[50] The fact that the dacoits were also a potent weapon in the hands of the dominant classes for negotiating their individual position in the power hierarchy and that most of them were either Thakurs or Gujars tied up in sordid land disputes, was glossed over. Jayaprakash chose to see them as symbols of heroic resistance, as revolutionary challengers of the hegemony of upper castes. His work, hence, did not end with their surrender. He put together funds for their legal defence, the education of their children and other contingent expenses. His mission maintained contact with them in prison to work on their internal development, and his joy knew no bounds when, in November 1973, the dacoits were moved to an open jail.

Even though Indira was deeply appreciative of Jayaprakash's efforts, there was trouble brewing in their paradise. It began right after Indira's overwhelming victory in the 1971 parliamentary election, called fourteen months ahead of schedule. Coming after Indira's triumphant war with Pakistan and backed by the catchy and politically shrewd slogan of 'garibi hatao', the election was more of an emotive referendum. The opposition did not stand a chance. One can't but agree with Sudipta Kaviraj's view that 'promises of reform outflanked the left just as much as patriotism outflanked the right'.[51] However, even as celebrations were ongoing, there were murmurs and allegations of mass rigging, especially in states like Bengal, Bihar and Kashmir. The Jana Sangh noted with grave concern the 'ruling party's determined attempts to smother democracy, annihilate opposition parties by unscrupulous use of government machinery and money power'.[52] Joining the chorus, Madhu Dandavate, general secretary of the Socialist Party, said that Indira's style of functioning was utterly alien to parliamentary democracy.[53]

Commenting on the government's actions in Kashmir during the elections, which he saw as nothing less than tyranny of the state, Jayaprakash expressed outrage. 'To arrest and extern people on the very eve of a general election lays the ruling party open to the charge not only of negligence in dealing with anti-national elements, but also of using a convenient ruse to put its opponents out of the way so as to ensure its victory at the polls. A great deal of praise has been showered in recent months on the central leadership, particularly on the prime minister, for their political maturity and finesse. But I am constrained to say, with due respect, that the leadership has neither shown political maturity nor finesse in its present handling of the Kashmir situation.'[54] Jayaprakash spoke about other electoral malpractices like impersonation, booth capturing and the use of money power that had reduced elections throughout the country to a colossal farce.

Jayaprakash was also miffed at Indira's continuing electoral alliance with the CPI. Not having got over his near-pathological aversion to the

Soviet Union, he looked upon the CPI as a party that would supplant the country's democratic fabric by a totalitarian system. He was equally appalled at the increasing subversion of democratic norms. By now, Indira had centralized decision-making and, as historian Bipan Chandra noted, virtually destroyed the federal structure of the party developed during the freedom struggle and carefully nurtured after 1947 by Jawaharlal Nehru.[55]

Jayaprakash equated Indira's dominance with democratic centralism, a Russian euphemism for dictatorship of the leader, towards which she seemed to be headed. In a scathing attack on the Congress and on Indira's style of leadership, Jayaprakash said, 'Paradoxical though it might sound, the Congress, despite its massive electoral victories of 1971 and 1972, is today a little more than a hollow shell. It has no inner strength and substance, and is presently kept going on huge doses of funds and the charisma of its leader. There is little or no internal democracy left in it and its state leaders and chief ministers are mostly handpicked men . . . The present state of affairs might suit Indira Gandhi's style of leadership but spells ruin for the Congress as a democratic organization and ipso facto for Indian democracy itself.'[56]

The right to dissent, one of the most important rights guaranteed by the Constitution, was under threat. Jayaprakash wrestled tirelessly against the drowning of dissenting voices in universities, government funded research bodies and the press. He said, 'Dissent is not just an intellectual luxury but a necessary catalytic agent to which society owes its progress, its revolution, its technological and scientific advances. Without dissent, society would become stagnant and moribund.'

Walking the Indian political stage with revived confidence and élan, Indira went about doing what she thought was important, not caring about the voices of dissent, not even Jayaprakash. The first signs of a serious crack in their understanding had already appeared when following her decision to nationalize banks, Jayaprakash created a public furore by describing nationalization as a wrong and unwarranted step. In taking this stand, he ended up aligning himself with the likes of S. Nijalingappa, Minoo Masani[57] and the Jana Sangh—all anathema to Indira. In a press statement issued on 13 March 1973, he attacked another potentially devastating policy decision—the government's move to take over wholesale trade in grain—asking it to rescind the ill-considered policy. The policy was indeed a fiasco, as later events would show, and led to the disappearance of foodgrain from the markets as well as a sharp rise in prices.

Two really testy, flagrant areas of confrontation came up around this time. The first related to the twenty-fourth amendment to the Constitution passed in 1971 (opposed by all surviving members of the Constituent Assembly), wherein the citizen's fundamental rights and freedoms, as laid down in the Constitution, could not only be amended but also abrogated by Parliament. The second was the appointment of Ajit Nath Ray as the Chief Justice of the Supreme Court, superseding three justices technically senior to him. This was unprecedented. Jayaprakash was greatly alarmed at both these developments. He spoke about the consequences of abrogation of people's fundamental rights and freedoms. 'It should be realised that the extinction of these rights might lead to the extinction of free platform and press, of opposition parties, of all trade unions, except the official ones, of all such institutions and organisations as do not agree with the ruling party! I am not suggesting that there is an immediate danger of all this happening. I am merely pointing out the logic of unlimited power. Therefore, my earnest appeal to the prime minister and her democratic socialist colleagues is to rise above partisan considerations, look into the future and assure the present and coming generations that their liberties would remain intact.'[58]

Excoriating Indira for her arbitrary appointment of the Chief Justice, he remarked, 'The simple fact is that if appointment of the Chief Justice of India remains entirely in the hands of the prime minister, as has been the case in the present instance, the highest judicial institution of this country cannot but become a creature of the government of the day.'[59] Sounding insecure about the future, he said, 'Like millions of those who had fought and suffered for the country's freedom, I too had a golden vision of independent India. Today when I compare the reality with the vision, I am filled with sadness. And when I ponder over the future that the recent events portend, my heart sinks. I cannot believe that it can be otherwise with my fellow freedom fighters.'[60]

Indira's carefully drafted reply to the issues raised by Jayaprakash was patient, conciliatory, even a little wistful. 'It is gracious of you to assure me that you are not against me personally. It has been a privilege to have had your friendship over the years, whatever our political differences. Dissent is indispensable to democracy. Equally indispensable is a readiness to shoulder responsibilities in order to fulfil the dreams of the people. You have said that your early visions have remained unfulfilled. This is true of all battles, all quests. But the duty of working for the vision continues. It is the function of our political system and of all the organs of government—the legislature, the executive and the judiciary—to work for the vision. Frequent reversal of stand, not always in a more liberal, more humane direction, was the main difficulty with our judicial decisions in the last decade or so. There was obvious need for greater continuity of ideas and vision. The seniority principle has led to an unduly high turnover of Chief Justices. I take it that no one maintains that the rule of law is safeguarded only by the principle of seniority. In the appointment of the new Chief Justice, we have only freed ourselves of a convention which had the sanction neither of the constitution nor of rationality. Democracy, independence of the judiciary and fundamental rights are not in danger. They would be threatened if we were to allow our faith to be eclipsed by defeatism and if we help alliances of the extreme right and left.'[61] Jayaprakash, however, was far from convinced. He continued to critique the government from different platforms.

Taking the discourse beyond narrowly defined national interests, Jayaprakash, once again, raised the issue of ethics in politics. In a statement captioned 'First Things First', he derided not only the Congress but also the opposition for the fall in ethical standards. 'Not only has the fall been precipitous but there is also no sign of any slowing down of the process. There is no branch of public life—politics, government, business, education, trade unions, social work and the rest that is left untouched. The difference is only one of degree, or one of opportunity. Not only the ruling Congress but also the opposition parties are stricken with the disease, as the interregnum between 1967 and 1972 has witnessed.'[62] He rejected the invitation of Biju Patnaik to take the lead in unifying the opposition. However, he did agree to give his moral support to this cause and underscored some vital issues that needed to be adhered to. These included the necessity to be principled, and not to be consumed by negative aims such as 'Indira Hatao'.

Another related area of concern was corruption. Jayaprakash put up several appeals for putting in place effective institutional procedures to check the 'Canker of Corruption'.[63] He suggested that a beginning could be made by seriously engaging with the decade-old Santhanam Committee Report on corruption and by ensuring that the Central Vigilance Commission was empowered with statutory powers. He also asked for the Lok Pal Bill to be passed by Parliament, taking care that it was not hemmed in by restrictive provisions.

In order to protect citizen rights and democratic ethics, Jayaprakash put together a small group called 'Citizens for Democracy'. This group—consisting of people like V.M. Tarkunde, Minoo Masani, P.G. Mavalankar, A.G. Noorani, K.D. Desai and E.P.W. Da Costa—worked like a think tank on issues related to electoral reforms, defence of civil liberties and strategies to combat casteism, communalism, inequity, poverty and unemployment. He also launched a scholarly, high-impact political journal named *Everyman's Weekly*, with Sachchidananda Vatsayan as editor. A journal of ideas, *Everyman's* was used by Jayaprakash week after week to generate debates on issues like ethics in politics, erosion of moral authority of political leadership, electoral malpractices and the need for electoral reforms, besides other crucial contemporary issues. *Everyman's* also reported on global events. One of its issues carried a protest statement issued by Jayaprakash and others on political dissidents being persecuted by the Soviet Union: nuclear physicist Andrei Sakharov, the politburo's most unsparing opponent, and Alexander Solzhenitsyn, persecuted for his 1961 novella *One Day in the Life of Ivan Denisovich*, an exposé of Stalin's gulag, and the 1973 masterpiece, *The Gulag Archipelago*.

The year 1973 was one of intense tumult in Jayaprakash's personal life. It began when Prabhavati tested positive for a tumour in the uterus. Jayaprakash took her to the Tata Memorial Hospital for surgery. The tumour was successfully removed, but her fever and other related conditions persisted. By March, it became evident that the cancer had metastasized to the abdomen and liver. Even though she was in unspeakable torment, Prabhavati dealt with her terminal diagnosis calmly. She rejected palliative care in hospital and expressed the desire to return home. They returned to Patna, with a brief stopover in Delhi to meet friends at the Express House. It was a heart-rending occasion, organized by their close friend, Ramnath Goenka. Looking at her exhausted, skeletal frame, it was apparent to everyone present that her death was imminent. But as she said her goodbyes, my parents, who were by her side, recalled that her eyes were refulgent, and she seemed to radiate an inexplicable aura of peace.

Prabhavati died on 15 April 1973, surrounded by a surreal bubble occasioned by Jayaprakash's nephew Anil's wedding celebrations. The acute agony of her loss destroyed Jayaprakash. In some ways, her death felt like desertion. In life, they were bound together by exceptional camaraderie. She led his politics, underpinning it with pragmatism, and a cautious optimism, combating positions that seemed contrary to Gandhian ideas. In this period of darkness, he tried to address his grief by writing deeply personal 'broken words of worship and love' to his wife, promising to continue her work and live by her cherished ideals. 'She meant so much to me,' he said, writing to Indira who was seeking and getting regular updates from him, 'and she filled such a large part of me and my life that it does not seem possible that I can live without her.'[64] One wonders if a sense of dread shot through Indira upon Prabhavati's death. For with her death, the voice of moderation in Jayaprakash's life also died.

9

Hope in Dark Times

Writing for the *New York Times* in the 1970s, Khushwant Singh described his first meeting with Jayaprakash at the home of Minoo Masani: 'He was a strikingly handsome man, tall, sinewy. He wore coarse handspun clothes: his voice was as gentle as his speech. His accent, both in English and in Hindustani, was that of a westernised oriental professor. There were several politicians present. The last to come was Maharani Gayatri Devi of Jaipur, a member of parliament for the Swatantra Party and a renowned beauty. She gestured to the others not to disturb the proceedings and sat down on the carpet near JP's chair. He interrupted his discourse to remark, "A beautiful princess sitting at the feet of a commoner. This is indeed a revolution!"'[1]

The year 1973 closed not with a revolution but certainly the intimations of one. Indira's popularity was waning. The economy was in the doldrums. The burden of sheltering and feeding 10 million refugees from Bangladesh had taken a toll. Severe droughts in 1972 and 1973, the worst in any two successive years in recent memory, created havoc. Official statistics show a relatively minor shortfall in food production, but anomalies in procurement and distribution caused food riots at several places in Bombay, Mysore, Nagpur and Kerala. The wholesale prices of rice, wheat, pulses, oil and other essential commodities skyrocketed. Three-quarters of Indians were without assured work. There were severe inflationary pressures. Public-sector industries were working at less than half capacity, with shortages, blockages and breakdowns in every core sector. The oil shock of 1973, when OPEC quadrupled the price of crude oil, resulted in a dramatic increase in budgetary deficit and deepening of recessionary trends.

The period from 1972–74 saw large-scale industrial unrest and wave upon wave of disruptive, wildcat strikes, with more than 12,000 strikes in Bombay alone and a long and crippling nationwide strike in the railways that began on 8 May 1974. In May 1973, the Provincial Armed Constabulary of UP were up in arms against their working conditions and shortages of basic commodities. The mutiny was crushed, but not before the brutal killing of thirty rebels and the resignation of the chief minister, Kamalapati Tripathi. The anti-inflation package introduced in 1974 and the decision to take an IMF loan could not offset the crisis. The bending of rules for Sanjay Gandhi's Maruti project also triggered a tsunami of outrage. The die, in a sense, was cast, setting the stage for an era of turbulent politics.

The pivotal actors in the political drama that unfolded were young amateurs—students of Gujarat and Bihar. For the first ten weeks of 1974, there was tumult in Gujarat of proportions that even the most astute political clairvoyant could not have foreseen. Students mobilized in the tens of thousands, protesting increasing mess fees. The agitation started with riots in Rajkot, Jetpur, Porbandar and Morvi in December 1973. At the engineering college at Morvi, for instance, hundreds of students came out against the rise in mess fees. Students at the LD College of Engineering in Ahmedabad clashed with the administration on the same issue, setting fire to the college canteen and attacking the rector's residence. The administration, too, flexed its muscles. A large number of students were beaten up and arrested, and the college was shut down. But within days, several college campuses became the breeding ground of a movement that broadened its social base and began to mould itself into an agitation against artificial scarcities and rising prices of fuel, grain and groundnut oil, blamed on the pernicious collusion between politicians, traders and black marketers.

The university and college teachers' associations that rallied together in 1972 to campaign for university reforms played a transformative role in turning what was essentially a students' struggle into a people's movement against political corruption. Sarvodaya workers, opposition parties, employees of banks, insurance companies, city and state government employees, lawyers, doctors, journalists and a section of the anti-Chimanbhai faction of the Congress formed the broad phalanx of allies of the agitating students. Also at the vanguard of the movement were a group of young RSS pracharaks like Narendra Damodardas Modi. Salacious rumours about the government's secret deals with oil farmers, merchants and millers that allowed for free export of groundnut oil products from Gujarat on the condition of subscription of a part of the enormous profit to the election fund for financing elections in Uttar Pradesh were doing the rounds. Attacks on the beleaguered government headed by former economics professor Chimanbhai Patel were getting more and more vicious, as the rhetoric of reconstruction and purification of politics gained ground. Christened as the Nav Nirman movement for political regeneration on 11 January 1974, it demanded nothing less than the resignation of the government and dissolution of the assembly.

Ahmedabad was on fire. On 6 January, the Jana Sangh called for the observance of an anti-police day. Several small gangs attacked and looted shops selling foodgrains and oil, and threw stones at municipal buses and government buildings. On 10 January, during a bandh announced by students and an umbrella organization of eighty trade unions, there was a near total shutdown of the city, with the exception of textile mills. Serious riots also erupted in Surat and Rajkot. On 25 January, even as the agitators called for a Gujarat bandh, curfew was imposed in all the major cities and towns of the state. Heavily armed Border Security and Central Reserve Police forces joined the state police in containing the riots. More than a hundred people died and several thousand were injured before the army was called in on 28 January. On 4 February, when fresh riots swept across Gujarat, Indira despatched union law minister, H.R. Gokhale, to assess the situation. Five days later, Chimanbhai Patel was told to resign. His ouster, however, failed to quell the momentum of the movement.

Jayaprakash lent his support to the movement when he visited Ahmedabad on 11 February. What he saw convinced him of what he had told students in Kanpur a few days earlier, 'The country is fast heading towards a new revolution. There is another 1942 movement in sight to change the course of history.'[2] He had spent two years working on a politics of consensus, to no avail. 'The time for action is here and now'—this is what he had said to students at Paunar on 9 December 1973.[3] Gujarat was, for him, the starting point of 'Youth for Democracy', a countrywide revolutionary movement. He called upon the youth to enter the national arena and play a decisive role in establishing the primacy of the people and securing their victory over money power and the politics of falsehood and brute force.

Even though Jayaprakash advised students to remain non-violent, by 20 February full-scale riots erupted once more in Ahmedabad and spread to districts of north and central Gujarat and Saurashtra. It was a period of excesses—flash mobs went around trying to loot banks and cooperative societies, setting fire to public and private property. Several assembly members were gheraoed and forced into submitting resignations. The final spurt of agitations occurred towards the end of the first week of March. Over 1,50,000 textile and other industrial workers went on strike, redefining the support base of the movement which had until then remained largely confined to the urban middle class.

On 11 March, Morarji Desai created a polaroid moment when he began a fast unto death against the central government's alleged plans to crush the movement. On 12 March, another cycle of frenzied violence and police retaliation left a few more dead in Ahmedabad and Nadiad. Pending the dissolution of the assembly, several members of the Legislative Assembly (MLAs) resigned, with sixteen Congress (O) resignations on a single day. The drama peaked on 14 March with the majority-tipping resignation of the eighty-fifth member, former chief minister Ghanshyam Oza, known to be close to Indira. With the dissolution of the assembly announced the next day, the movement struggled to stay airborne before splitting into several warring groups and then dissipating altogether.

Whatever remained of the ties between Indira and Jayaprakash, the complexity, the pleasure, survived the volatility and unpredictability of the Gujarat movement. This is borne out by Indira's letter to him, written soon after Pakistan's recognition of Bangladesh on 27 February 1974. 'From what you told me when we last met, I was left with the impression that you were leaving Delhi. Only yesterday I learnt . . . that you have been unwell and confined to bed here. This has naturally caused me anxiety. I hope you will take complete rest and soon overcome the result of the overstrain. You must be happy, as we all are, at Pakistan's recognition of Bangladesh, even though this has come under an Islamic smokescreen.'[4] Jayaprakash replied almost immediately, addressing her as 'Indu'. 'Thanks for your letter of yesterday . . . I am better now but the recovery is rather slow. It was a case of infection of the lungs . . . I was glad to see you looking so well, spruced and charming that night. May you remain like that all your life.'[5] Four days later he sent her another intimate letter enclosing two books: Amritlal Nagar's *Manas Ka Hans* and his own rather solipsistic text, *Meri Vichar Yatra*.

History often emerges only in retrospect or so the saying goes. The Gujarat movement, with its anarchic excesses, would perhaps have quietly faded from public consciousness had it not been closely followed by the movement in Bihar. By February 1974, college and university campuses in Bihar were turning into battlegrounds and debating clubs with numerous flyers pasted on walls. Students gathered for impromptu meetings to argue and agitate and the incessant buzz of conversations about soaring prices, unemployment and corruption could be heard across campuses. On 18 February, while the agitation in Gujarat was still on, the Patna University Students' Union invited student leaders from different campuses of Bihar to come together on the same platform, the Bihar Chhatra Sangharsh Samiti, a student outfit. Their demands included an intense mix of issues—a complete shake-up of the educational system, democratization of university bodies, formation of active student unions in every college, provision of adequate scholarships and aid, jobs for the educated unemployed, check on prices, hoarding and black-market activities. They also demanded the resignation of the ministry headed by Abdul Ghafoor. From the very beginning, a left–right divide existed in the student community. The binaries were so deeply entrenched that it was difficult to get past them. The left students formed their own instrument of struggle, named the Bihar Chhatra Naujawan Sangharsh Morcha.

The Bihar Chhatra Sangharsh Samiti was a rag-tag, predominantly male group that was dominated by the Akhil Bhartiya Vidyarthi Parishad, the student wing of the Jana Sangh. Amongst the prominent members of the Samiti were Narendra Singh, Vashisht Narain Singh, Shivanand Tiwari, Ramjatan Sinha, Akhtar Hussain, Raghuvansh Narain Singh, Nitish Kumar, Ram Bahadur Rai, Gopal Sharan Singh, Bhawesh Chandra Prasad and the newly elected office-bearers of the Patna University Students' Union: its president, Lalu Yadav, general secretary, Sushil Modi and secretary, Ravi Shankar Prasad—bright, unapologetically ambitious young men. The ideological disconnect was palpable. Students affiliated with left parties like the CPI, Communist Party of India (Marxist) and CPI (ML) turned their backs on the call given by the Chhatra Sangharsh Samiti for a gherao of the Bihar Vidhan Sabha and the governor on 18 March to protest the education minister's failure in responding to their memorandum of demands.

The sudden combustion of rebellion and the upsurge of student protesters outside the Patna Assembly took the police by surprise. Students were rounded up, beaten and fired upon, setting off a severe retaliation. Flash mobs spread to different corners of the city, stoning and setting fire to shops and buildings. The building on Fraser Road housing the English daily *Searchlight* and the Hindi daily *Pradeep*, two of Patna's iconic newspapers, was also set ablaze. Jayaprakash was anguished by the sordid turn of events. 'Anyone with the least sensitivity and patriotism who was in Patna on the 18 March and knew something of what was happening would have found it difficult to withhold tears. Even as I scribble these lines . . . tears are welling up. Not only has the *Searchlight*, that beacon of the freedom movement, been destroyed but much else. It is Bihar's very soul that is torn and bleeding today.'[6]

The news of the violence in Patna and police firing and deaths spread across Bihar. The anger against police action fuelled violent student protests. Students in Motihari raided and ransacked the railway station and telephone exchange and burnt the block development officer's house. In Sitamarhi, the telephone exchange was damaged. Students set fire to the principal's office at two colleges in Arrah. At Deoghar and Madhepura, government offices were attacked. At Bettiah, violent mobs created mayhem on the streets provoking the police to open fire, leading to a couple of deaths and leaving several students injured. Students at Bodh Gaya burnt a state transport bus and a government publicity van. At Ranchi, there were attempts to burn the post office and the telephone exchange.

The Union home minister, Uma Shankar Dikshit, blamed opposition parties, the RSS and left 'adventurists' for the violence.[7] The government fought back, often with extreme brutality. The police continued to open fire at restive mobs that consisted of students and other professional groups. By 20 March, curfew was imposed in eleven towns. Nearly 2000 people were arrested. Trying to find a reason for the sustained violence, Jayaprakash said, 'The anger of the people is reaching white heat on account of their misery that is growing day by day. Reports have reached me of poor rural families selling their children to keep alive. At least one entire family . . . has preferred to die by swallowing Eldrin rather than starve inch by inch to death.'[8]

The demand for the chief minister's resignation for failure to maintain law and order came from several opposition leaders. Ram Vilas Sharma of the Congress (O) alleged that only a shameless government could feel proud of a barricaded democracy. Kailashpati Mishra of the Jana Sangh asked for immediate dismissal of the Ghafoor government as did firebrand socialists George Fernandes and Madhu Limaye.[9] What looked largely like a right-wing coalition came together on an anti-Congress platform to back the movement. It consisted of parties like the Jana Sangh, Socialist Party, SSP, Swatantra Party, Congress (O) and the Bhartiya Lok Dal (BLD). It was a strategic decision, not in small part driven by their ambition to return to centre stage after the 1971–72 electoral debacle.

The movement overcame its existential crisis on 6 April 1974 when Jayaprakash agreed to lead it and give it a constructive shape.[10] He had met student leaders while addressing students at the Wheeler Senate Hall in Patna earlier in the year, on 11 January, which was followed by meetings at the Patna College on 1 February. But this time it was revolution up close: state power versus student power, feeding on the binary of the haves and the have-nots. Not just an act of courage but the playing out of a long cherished dream of total revolution, of putting the interest of the last man and woman back on the social and political agenda—in some ways like the Bardoli struggle led by Sardar Patel.[11] Having decided that he would no longer be a 'mute spectator', Jayaprakash extracted a promise that students would keep the struggle non-violent, function in a politically non-partisan way and work under his direction.[12] The struggle regained vigour and a new sense of direction. 'He was the glue that held us all together, even as we learnt to shoehorn our individual narratives into the powerful collective narrative of the JP movement. We were his proud foot soldiers,' Ravi Shankar Prasad reminisced, in a private interview.

Jayaprakash tried to broaden the base of the movement by seeking the support of left parties like the CPM and Communist Party of India (Marxist–Leninist). Ideological constraints, however, stopped them from openly aligning with the movement. It was after months of dithering that P. Sundarayya, the general secretary of the CPM, and Promode Dasgupta, its political bureau member, agreed to sign a joint statement with Jayaprakash and socialist leader Madhu Dandavate on 18 September 1974 for frequent consultations to radicalize and intensify the movement and increase its engagement with workers and peasants. The signatories also agreed that the demand for dissolution of the Bihar Assembly would receive priority.[13]

By March end, the movement was gaining ground. There were relay fasts on street corners; 'corner midnight meetings' in university campuses; young men and women with placards moved in silent processions. A state-wide bandh was organized on 23 March. On 5 April, a 'Black Day' was observed to protest police firings that had led to several deaths. Students tied small strips of black cloth on their supporters. A group of students even managed to force a dissident Congress MLA from Banka to send a telegram to the chief minister, asking him to resign.

Lampooning Indira for 'living in a fool's paradise',[14] seventy-two-year-old Jayaprakash led a silent procession on 8 April, to protest police excesses of the previous three weeks. He was showered with rose and marigold petals. Men and women, their lips taped and hands locked behind their backs, walked from the historic Congress Maidan to Fraser Road, Ashok Rajpath, Govind Mitra Road and Ram Krishna Avenue, before returning to their starting point. Their placards had a uniform text: 'Hamla chahe jo bhi ho, haath hamara nahin uthega'. (Whatever be the provocation, we shall not raise our hands in retaliation). Prominent writers like Phanishwarnath Renu, Ramvachan Rai, Nagarjun (Vaidyanath Mishra), Ravindra Rajhans and Gopi Vallabh Sahay joined the procession and gave a new voice to the movement. When the procession crossed the city jail, hordes of detained students crammed the balconies, shouting slogans in support.

The next day, Jayaprakash addressed a large public meeting in Gandhi Maidan. 'For 27 years, I have watched events unfold, but I can stand on the side-lines no longer. I have vowed not to allow the state of things to continue.'[15] The sense that a revolution was brewing may have been naïve, but it was palpable. Twenty-six-year-old Lalu Yadav created a resonant moment when he proposed the title of 'Loknayak' for Jayaprakash. The maidan reverberated with cries of 'Loknayak Zindabad!' and 'Inquilab Zindabad!'

A five-week long people's struggle to bring down the government was launched on 9 April. In Gaya, the struggle took an untoward turn on 12 April when the police opened fire on a restive mob. Eight persons lost their lives and several were seriously injured. There were reports of lathi charges on peaceful congregations of agitating students in many other districts. But, by then, the struggle had assumed the texture of a mass movement that was unstoppable. Women and young girls formed human barricades along the national highway. Several lawyers, teachers and other professionals joined relay fasts near the secretariat and other government buildings. Work remained paralysed in most offices.

All this while, Jayaprakash was struggling with medical problems. He finally had surgery for an enlarged prostate on 23 April at the Christian Medical College in Vellore. During his absence, hunger strikes and protest marches continued unabated under the leadership of Sarvodaya leaders like Acharya Ramamurti and Narayan Desai. On 30 April, a marathon twelve-hour fast was observed all over the state. On May Day, labour unions joined students in huge processions. On 8 May, 'Dissolve Vidhan Sabha' week was announced and a signature campaign to this end was launched all over Bihar. Relay fasts in front of the residences of MLAs to secure their resignations added to the force of the protests. In the backlash that followed, three students were arrested at Muzaffarpur under the Maintenance of Internal Security Act (MISA), on the charge of forcing Congress MLA Ramai Ram to resign. Twenty-four students were also arrested at Patna City when they gheraoed the residence of Congress MLA Jamil Ahmed.

At the end of the momentous week, thirteen Jana Sangh and seven SSP assembly members submitted their resignations. Former chief minister Mahamaya Prasad Sinha was the lone Congress MLA who resigned. Resignations remained a hugely contested issue. The Jana Sangh expelled members who refused to resign. Firebrand Congress (O) leader Tarkeshwari Sinha contested the stand on resignations and the demand for dissolution of the assembly. A few MLAs who were forced to resign took back their resignations. Overall, only thirty-eight of the eighty-eight opposition MLAs resigned.

The upsurge of protests continued. To counter them, on 3 June, the CPI, which had a strong presence in Bihar and was closely aligned to the Congress, organized a mammoth march of peasants, workers, students and government employees in Patna. Its memorandum, presented to the governor, opposed the demand for the dissolution of the assembly. This was followed by another show of strength on 11 November to challenge what the party saw as a fascist mass movement designed to destroy elected assemblies, subvert parliamentary democracy and create a constitutional crisis.[16]

Everything that had been set in stone was being questioned. This included increasing government control over business with laws like the Monopolies and Restrictive Trade Practices Act 1969, and the Foreign Exchange Regulation Act 1973. Indira and her cabinet ministers were watching these developments very closely, apprehensive about their impact in other states. Aware of my father's closeness to Jayaprakash, Uma Shankar Dikshit asked him to pitch in to resolve differences. My father arrived in Patna after Jayaprakash's return from Vellore. He found the latter pensive and preoccupied with the minutiae of a huge protest rally being planned two days later, on 5 June. He recalled, 'JP looked frail. It was apparent that he was not interested in a dialogue with the government and certainly not in any settlement. He normally liked to spend hours talking to me and would insist on our having dinner together, but this time it was different. He did not ask me to stay back or even visit him the next day. It seemed to me that he was miffed that I had agreed to be the emissary of the government.' Jayaprakash spent the next day tracking the movements of his outstation supporters. The government directed the district magistrates to seal borders to prevent people from joining the rally. Even so, thousands of people from twenty-nine districts managed to reach Patna, braving extreme conditions.

On 5 June, the procession headed by Jayaprakash began its march from the Gandhi Maidan at 3 p.m. Behind his open jeep was a truck carrying bundles of papers with 5 million signatures collected from different districts, in favour of dissolving the assembly. The procession reached the governor's house at 5 p.m. Jayaprakash handed over the papers to the governor before a brief detour to the Gandhi National Museum for a little rest. As soon as he was ready to move, protesters began marching back to the Gandhi Maidan. While crossing one of the main streets, they were attacked by the 'Indira Brigade', a rogue group nurtured by a Congress MLA. The government spared no effort in scuttling the event. Several train, bus and steamer services were disrupted. Despite the impediments and the soaring June temperature, a million people gathered at the venue to listen to Jayaprakash. They were not disappointed. His speech, delivered in impeccable Hindi and strong on emotionally engaging rhetoric, was evocative of the heady revolutionary days of 1942. As Hannah Arendt wrote, 'Even in the darkest times, we have the right to expect some illumination.'[17]

In the words of my father, Jayaprakash spoke like a true revolutionary, sure of himself and his instruments. 'Friends, this is a revolution, a total revolution. This is not a movement merely for the dissolution of the assembly. We have to go far, very far . . . Nobody, Jayaprakash Narayan or anyone else can stop this movement. It was born because this system of education is rotten and the students don't see a ray of hope. It was born because the people are being crushed under high prices. There is corruption and bribery everywhere. Unemployment goes on rising both of the educated and the others. Otherwise a thousand Jayaprakash Narayans and a thousand Chhatra Sangharsh Samitis could not have created a mass movement like this.'[18] At the end of that exceptionally charged day, closeted away from the crowd, in a tired and barely audible voice, Jayaprakash said, 'Revolution has come, but now when I have grown old.'

Jayaprakash's speech had a visceral impact on Indira. Their relationship was going through one of its lowest ebbs, caught in a spiral of outrage, distrust and recrimination. It started with Indira's address at a public meeting in Bhubaneswar on 1 April, where she accused her detractors of living on the largesse of corrupt people. Her provocative remark, clearly alluding to Jayaprakash, was not a silly gaffe that could be ignored.[19] In a statement issued two days later, Jayaprakash accused her of descending to the lowest depths. Realizing that she had made a mistake, Indira tried to make amends. She wrote, 'Many friends are distressed that there should be any misunderstanding between us. I have had the privilege of your friendship for many years. The mutual regard that existed between my father and you is well known as is my mother's affection for Prabhavatiji. Even the highest personal regard and affection need not preclude an honest difference in political or philosophical outlook. You have not seen eye to eye with my father, nor now with me. We have criticised each other, but I hope we have done it without personal bitterness or questioning of each other's motives. I have consistently tried not to be confined by my office, but to reach out for ideas, for understanding and for cooperation in the task of solving problems. I shall continue to value your sympathy.'[20]

Indira's attempt to bridge the chasm did not succeed. Jayaprakash's letters to her took on a brusque, hostile tone. The form of address also changed from Indu to a formal Indiraji. His public address of 5 June further distanced them. In response, Indira wrote, 'You are angry that people from the prime minister and Shri Dikshit downwards "have the arrogance to give lessons in democracy to Jayaprakash Narayan". Would you not agree that democracy gives us the right to think and talk about it, as it does to anybody else, irrespective of position or background? May I also, in all humility, put to you that it is possible that others, who may not be your followers, are equally concerned about the country, about the people's welfare, and about the need to cleanse public life of weakness and corruption. Are you sure that all the people who today follow you and support your movement are different in their background and intentions from the people, who, according to you, have found shelter behind government?'[21] Jayaprakash chose to ignore the letter.

From 7 June, a non-violent satyagraha was launched. Jayaprakash called for the closure of all colleges and universities for a year. He also encouraged no-tax and related campaigns to paralyse the government. In the following days, several persons were arrested while picketing and offering dharna before the assembly gates. Even when the assembly session concluded on 13 July there was no let-up in the demands and agitations for its dissolution. In a spirit of defiance, Jayaprakash exhorted police personnel to be guided by their conscience rather than orders from seniors when resorting to lathi charge or firing.

Jayaprakash's call for boycott of classes and exams elicited a mixed response. Several universities and colleges remained paralysed for want of students, but the issue of boycott played on the vulnerabilities of not only the students but also their parents. When the colleges reopened on 18 July, after an inordinately long closure of four months, less than 10 per cent students abstained from exams.[22] There were instances of crude bombs being hurled at exam centres in Gaya and other towns, and disturbing reports of stoning and other forms of coercive violence against examinees in a few other districts. By the end of the year, when students began returning to their classes, Jayaprakash considerably scaled down his expectations. He gave them the option of devoting a year to the movement or even a day in a week.[23]

The first phase of the agitation concluded with the end of satyagraha before the assembly in the third week of July. The second and more intense phase began on 1 August, with the commencement of no-tax campaigns. At a time of severe famine-like conditions, farmers were advised to withhold the state levy on foodgrains meant for the public distribution system. Wine and country liquor shops were picketed. There was complete mayhem. The only exception made was for departments like post and telegraph, hospitals, courts, railways, banks and ration shops. Jayaprakash directed students to hold ten to fifteen meetings in each assembly constituency to turn public opinion against non-performing MLAs. Sons and daughters of corrupt officials, hoarders and traders were told to go on twelve-hour fasts in their own homes. Addressing a public meeting in Jamshedpur, Jayaprakash once again urged the police to disobey orders that their conscience told them were improper. He also warned, 'For the present the call is on

Gandhian lines and should not be mistaken for a call for rebellion. But a stage will come, when I will call for total rebellion.'[24]

By October, a certain fatigue seemed to have set in, even as there were increased incidences of violence and coercion in implementing the civil disobedience programme. Largely restricted to urban areas, the protests were failing to draw in poor peasants, agricultural workers and casual labourers. Touring Bihar, Nayantara Sehgal decried the gender imbalance in participation. To energize the movement and expand its base, Jayaprakash announced a new plan of action, which included intensification of struggle from 2 October. A three-day bandh was organized between 3 and 5 October. Leading the bandh, Jayaprakash marched through the streets of the state capital on 3 October with his followers. People lined the streets to support him. He ended his march at the gate of the secretariat and sat in dharna, surrounded by supporters, curious onlookers, the media and sections of the bureaucracy. Following the success of the bandh, Jayaprakash posed another direct challenge to state power. Students and Jana Sangharsh Samiti (People's Struggle Committee) volunteers were directed to move in strength to block, subdivision and district offices to paralyse their work and to set up parallel, revolutionary people's governments, or Janata Sarkars.

Patterned on the Russian democratic workers councils (soviets), these micro-organs of people's power were expected to adjudicate disputes, ensure the sale of essential commodities at fair prices, organize redistribution of ceiling-surplus land amongst the landless, prevent black market activities and hoarding, and fight against caste oppression. They were also expected to gradually bring about a shift in people's consciousness and make them reject untouchability, casteism and its symbols like the donning of the sacred thread by upper castes, patriarchy and its manifestation in early marriage and dowry.[25]

Even though Jayaprakash repeatedly said that the movement was unconstitutional but democratic and non-violent, the agitations were not entirely free of coercive violence. Shopkeepers were forced to pull down their shutters. Trains and buses were arbitrarily stopped. At Bhabua, Sasaram, Samastipur, Sitamarhi, Muzaffarpur and Danapur stations, young children blocked railway tracks. The Bihar home secretary reported twenty cases of railway sabotage, tampering with tracks and intimidation of railway workers. The police retaliated with ruthless brutality. Hundreds of students were beaten up and arrested. There were several women and girls among those arrested. They were incarcerated in the jails of Hazaribagh, Bhagalpur, Muzaffarpur, Darbhanga, Samastipur, Arrah, Bankipur and Patna. Between 2 and 5 October, the police opened fire at many places resulting in a number of deaths. In a single incident in Patna City, twenty-two rounds were fired and unofficial sources reported seventy-five deaths.

The sit-ins and protests continued. On 8 October, Jayaprakash joined the protest fast with eighty-six followers; the following day it was Narayan Desai. And that is how the momentum of protests was maintained. In the middle of all the tumult, Jayaprakash addressed a large rally in Patna on 10 October. Calling it a fight for democracy, he exhorted students to keep the movement non-violent. 'The emphasis on peaceful means is not an idiosyncrasy of the Gandhians. It is the strategy of the people's struggle. For one act of violence, the government is prepared to commit a hundred atrocities. So do not think of violence.'[26] He warned that if the assembly was not dissolved, he would hold elections for a parallel people's assembly.

Explaining why the dissolution of the state assembly in Bihar had become necessary, Jayaprakash explained, 'It seems necessary to repeat that dissolution of the state assembly has become a categorical imperative of the struggle, not only because it is with the assembly's implicit and explicit support that the present corrupt, inefficient and oppressive ministry has been functioning, but also because the style of politics set by the Congress high command has reduced the assembly to an unnecessary, burdensome and costly farce. The chief function of the legislature is to legislate. But the Bihar Assembly has abdicated its legislative powers and handed them over to the executive, which has been ruling with the help of ordinances. In one single year as many as 176 ordinances were promulgated.'[27]

In an astonishing groundswell of support, more than 50,000 men and women from different parts of the country congregated in Delhi at the Gandhi Samadhi at Rajghat on 6 October. They marched through the main streets of Delhi, joined in large numbers by teachers and students from Delhi University, Jawaharlal Nehru University and IIT, Delhi. After the march, a six-member delegation led by Acharya Kripalani met Indira to hand over a memorandum demanding dissolution of the Bihar Assembly. The prime minister remained unmoved, emphatically asserting that she would resign rather than concede to the demand. A ninety-minute meeting between her and Jayaprakash in Delhi on 1 November, that began on a poignant, personal note, also did not lead to any tangible outcome. Willing to work with him on electoral and educational reforms, and in tackling corruption, Indira said she would consider suspending the Bihar Assembly only on the condition that no similar demand would be made in other states.[28]

November 1974 was a definitive month in the history of the movement. It started with a massive rally in Patna on 4 November. Repeating the 5 June protocol, the state government ensured that all routes to Patna were sealed. Fifty-eight trains and steamer services were suspended and round-the-clock aerial patrolling over the Ganga was initiated. The entire city was barricaded. But, defying the odds, people came in large numbers, crossing the swollen river the previous night in makeshift boats made with banana stumps. They congregated at the Congress Maidan, huddled against each other, waiting for dawn. Thousands who took shelter at the Gandhi Museum were detained by the police. In the morning, even before Jayaprakash left his Charkha Samiti residence at 9 a.m., there were nearly 50,000 people, men and women, waiting for him near the Gandhi Maidan. He was in an open-air jeep, surrounded by students. Chanting revolutionary slogans, the protesters surged forward. Once they reached Gandhi Maidan, the police seized his jeep. But no one could have foreseen the events that would ensue.

Undeterred, Jayaprakash led a huge procession through Fraser Road, facing a phalanx of armed police near the income tax building. Students in the front line were dragged and brutally thrashed. The street was filled with smoke and tear gas as Jayaprakash joined students in breaking through the cordon. Just then, he was hit by a baton in the full glare of press cameras. The baton cracked two of his ribs and could have been fatal had Nanaji Deshmukh, Baburao Chandavar and Ali Haider (convener of the Gaya Sangharsh Samiti) not shielded him adequately. Ignoring the searing pain, Jayaprakash continued to walk towards the chief minister's residence. Later, he jumped in a bus crowded with detainees. Unmindful of his injuries, he drove to the Patna Medical College to meet supporters wounded by the police.

The attack on Jayaprakash, in the cosseted heart of the city, precipitated outrage. The secretary of the Patna District Congress Committee, Narmadeshwar Ranjan, resigned from the party and demanded the resignation of the prime minister for the 'naked and brutal attack on democracy'.[29] The vice chancellor of Bhagalpur University, Devendra Prasad Singh, condemned the lathi charge and urged the government to 'apologize to JP'.[30] Eminent Hindi writer Phaniswarnath Renu returned the Padma Shri awarded to him in 1970. Author and poet Nagarjun refused to accept his pensionary benefits. In a statement issued four days later, Jayaprakash remarked: 'Whether the lathi was really aimed at me or it hit me accidentally, as the prime minister has suggested, should be better known to the central government because it was the CRP men who were wielding the lathis . . . Why should so many men have been injured in trying to protect me if the CRP men had no orders to hit me? Something more than equivocation is needed to answer this question.'[31]

Jayaprakash's differences with Indira were now direct and public. Comparing her to Nehru, he said that while Nehru had been a democrat and a visionary, she was an autocrat who was killing democracy.[32] He mocked the decision of Congress to hold a razzmatazz rally in Patna on 16 November that was attended by six Union ministers. Two days later, at his own big rally at Gandhi Maidan, he accepted Indira's challenge of settling the issue of dissolution of the assembly at the next general election in February–March 1976. Reiterating that neither he nor his 'boys' were in a hurry, he said with a certain ferocity, 'Since the prime minister has dragged the conflict into the election arena, I shall take my position in the battlefield, not as a candidate, but as a leader. The contest will be only between two parties. One of those who support the struggle and the other who oppose it. This will be a new type of election, part of the struggle. The rumble of the chariot of time will be heard in Delhi after Patna.'[33] With this, the overall emphasis of the movement shifted to the defeat of Congress at the polls.

Friends of Jayaprakash and Indira tried to bring about a truce, but failed. Particularly Chandra Shekhar, who observed in an op-ed in *Young Indian* on 21 November that a purposive dialogue between Jayaprakash and Prime Minister Gandhi would most certainly find a solution to the issues that scheming persons were exploiting.[34] This was published a day after he invited Jayaprakash for a meeting with sixty Congress parliamentarians. Indira attempted to initiate a dialogue with the help of Achyut Patwardhan and her principal secretary, P.N. Dhar, with little result.[35] Finally, when they did meet, it was with some amount of cold acrimony that even the presence of Y.B. Chavan and Jagjivan Ram could not dispel. When asked to negotiate with Jayaprakash, a visibly beleaguered Indira retorted, 'I do not understand what negotiations mean. What do you negotiate about? How to destroy democracy? Is this negotiable? The other main point is to "remove Indira Gandhi". How can I negotiate about that?'[36]

The time for dialogue was clearly up. Congress leaders like D.K. Barooah began a slanderous campaign against Jayaprakash, calling him a fascist and alleging that there were well-known corrupt people amongst his supporters.[37] Another frequent allegation was that he was aligned with fascist forces like the Jana Sangh.[38] The assassination of Union minister Lalit Narayan Mishra on 3 January 1975 resulted in a fresh bout of attacks and counter-attacks. CPI leader S.A. Dange said that the murder was the outcome of the politics of violence let loose in the country by Jayaprakash and his followers. This would not be the last murder, he said, 'they want to settle the politics of their total revolution through the politics of assassination'.[39] Indira echoed almost the same words in a condolence meeting in Delhi. Jayaprakash pulled no punches in saying that Indira was trying to whip up a climate of hysteria to justify large-scale repression and the eventual imposition of authoritarian rule.[40]

Jayaprakash's association with Vinoba Bhave took a serious blow when the latter indicated that he wanted Sarvodaya workers to follow a policy of neutrality towards the Congress. This transpired during Jayaprakash's visit to his ashram in Paunar. The conflict that this stand generated caused a permanent rift within the Sarvodaya movement. However, several eminent Gandhians like Dada Dharmadhikari,

Manmohan Choudhry, Acharya Ramamurti, Siddharaj Dhadda, Thakurdas Bang and Narayan Desai continued to support Jayaprakash. V.M. Tarkunde and other leaders of the Radical Humanist movement also joined him.

Political resistance took many forms. It created ground-breaking political art and literature. 'Time will inscribe the crimes of those who remain silent,' remarked Renu, encouraging young writers and poets to create subaltern protest spaces. The poetry of protest was seen in graffiti across the heartland. Satish Anand, Vasant Kumar, Uma Shankar and a few other theatre activists launched a street-theatre movement, staging trailblazing productions in front of Quality Corner, at the Boring Road crossing in Patna. A random space in front of the Lucknow Sweet House became the venue of nukkad art exhibitions. There was no looking back. The Coffee House in Patna metamorphosed into the adda of revolutionary writers, poets, artists, theatre activists, and visiting journalists like Ajit Bhattacharjea, Kuldip Nayar and Dharamvir Bharati. It was also the favourite dig of Chandra Shekhar and B.P. Koirala and a bunch of Jayaprakash's scholar friends, Amlan Datta, Rajni Kothari, L.C. Jain, Meera Chakravarty and J.D. Sethi.

As the unrest entered its next landmark phase, there was a sense of urgency to carry the ideas of the Bihar movement to other states. Jayaprakash convened a meeting of leaders of opposition parties like the Jana Sangh, Congress (O), BLD, SSP and Akali Dal, in Delhi, on 25 November 1974, to give shape to a national coordination committee. The committee was asked to assess the significance of the movement and its prospects in other states. He rejected the suggestion of leading a new national party. The struggle, he said, was not for capture of power, but for purification of politics, including that of the opposition, and for fashioning instruments and conditions to control unbridled centralized power. A forty-member committee of students and youth leaders, with Arun Jaitley and Anand Kumar as conveners, was also formed.[41] Consequently, pro-Indira journalists like Sham Lal remarked that Jayaprakash was creating a political climate propitious not for revolution, but for anarchy. Jayaprakash ignored the scurrilous comments and continued to mobilize new supporters. Some of his detractors nearly lynched him near Karnal, when he was heading for a meeting in Kurukshetra, accompanied by Madhu Limaye, Narayan Desai and a bunch of students. There was another attempt to harm him at Ludhiana station. Jayaprakash saw these incidents as examples of the stripping away of democratic spaces.

The loss of faith in parliamentary democracy was also exemplified by the resignation of Jana Sangh leader Atal Bihari Vajpayee from the Lok Sabha on 8 December, on the grounds that it was no longer an effective instrument to serve the people. Responding to the righteous indignation of many young parliamentarians about the death of democracy, Jayaprakash appealed to Jagjivan Ram, Y.B. Chavan and other senior leaders to restore internal democracy in the Congress. The Young Turks in the Congress, committed to democratic renewal, saw ominous portents in the escalating tension between Indira and Jayaprakash. Their insistence on a dialogue for political reconciliation, however, did not work. Rather, in what can only be seen as a crude example of collateral damage, Mohan Dharia, a vocal, independent voice, was stripped of his ministerial portfolio. Seeing this as yet another example of the erosion of democracy, Jayaprakash observed, 'By forcing him out of her ministry Mrs Gandhi has not only shown how hollow is her desire for discussion and accommodation with the opposition, which indeed are imperatives of democratic politics, but also how determined she is to destroy the Congress itself as a democratic political party.'[42] It was a chilling presentiment of what would happen within a year.

Jayaprakash's obsession with total revolution continued. Towards this end, on New Year's Eve, he formed a new non-partisan youth corps named Chhatra Yuva Sangharsh Vahini. Its membership was restricted to young men and women below thirty who would commit to keep away from the politics of power and work within an inclusive, non-hierarchical, non-violent framework. To this group was entrusted the responsibility of working on JP's dream of a total revolution—social, economic, political, cultural, ideological, educational and ethical. Jayaprakash also issued directions for broadening the coverage of Janata Sarkars in the entire state by 5 June 1975, the 'Total Revolution Day'.[43] He travelled extensively throughout the country, speaking on the need for total revolution for the reconstruction of society on the basis of equality, and elimination of poverty, oppression and exploitation. Warning his supporters that it was not going to be an easy ride, he asked them to be prepared for lathi attacks, bullets and long periods of incarcerations.

The violence in parts of rural Bihar prompted Jayaprakash to note with great anguish, 'What is more shocking is the open collusion between the administration and the land owners. It appears as though under the pretext of fighting Naxalites the police forces, both armed and civil, have been placed at the disposal of the rural power structure to terrorise the low-caste agricultural labour and to ruthlessly suppress even the most peacefully articulated demands for increase in the prevailing dismally low farm wages.'[44]

On 6 March 1975—another memorable day in the life of the movement—Jayaprakash led a 'People's March' to Parliament. The 8-kilometre-long procession of thousands of people, reminiscent, in his words, of the Dandi March, was the biggest anti-government outpouring in years. People present at the occasion at the Boat Club reported seeing at least 1,00,000 to 3,00,000 men and women carrying placards with the poet Dinkar's immortal words, '*Singhasan khali karo, ki janta aati hai*' (vacate the throne, the people are coming). Overcome with emotion, Jayaprakash spoke in a faltering voice, 'I do not go about setting fires all over the country—the fire is already smouldering under the rulers' seats. If I or the students are guilty, it is only of giving direction to the fire so that it does not destroy but purifies the country and renews it.'[45]

The evening ended with the presentation of a people's charter to the Speaker of the Lok Sabha and chairman of the Rajya Sabha. The charter was a radical rejection of key aspects of the prevailing policy regime. Its core demands included the call for fresh elections in Bihar and Gujarat, need-based minimum wages and income, restoration of democratic rights and civil liberties, revocation of the emergency imposed during war, and withdrawal of draconian laws like MISA and the Defence of India Act (DIR), and governance by ordinance. The grossly outsized role of money in elections was to be countered through mandatory submission of election expense returns by all parties. A few of its other core components included the right to recall, universal primary and adult education within a five-year framework, raising the quality and content of education, decentralization of power and appointment of high-powered judicial tribunals with powers to inquire into allegations against persons in high positions, including the prime minister.

The impact of the march and the charter shook Indira. However much she raged against it, the movement in Bihar continued to be a political force. Another massive demonstration was held before the Vidhan Sabha on 18 March. Under siege, embattled from all sides, Indira focused on the merger of Sikkim with the Indian Union. The Indian army marched into Gangtok on 8 April. Six days prior, there had been another attempt on Jayaprakash's life. This time in Calcutta University where he was greeted with black flags by students instigated by Youth Congress leaders Priya Ranjan Dasmunsi and Subroto Mukherjee. The car in which he was sitting was badly damaged. Such hooliganism, Jayaprakash felt, was not possible without the government's complicity.

Jayaprakash's call for ending all forms of exploitation, distribution of ceiling-surplus land and the radical transformation of the public health and education structures also came in the form of a meticulously researched document called 'Manifesto for a New Bihar'. It began with a critique of the political economy of Bihar and its appalling regime of inequality. It spoke about the urgent need to educate sharecroppers, marginal and small cultivators, agricultural labourers and the urban poor about their rights. The manifesto distanced itself from any single ideology. 'The fault of an ideology is that it insists that certain values, such as social and economic equality, can be achieved only within its own framework and no other. Whereas, my contention is that once the goal is fixed and the values defined, it is a question for science to determine how the goal can be reached within the given value framework.'[46]

Amongst the student volunteers who worked on the socio-economic aspects of the manifesto was twenty-four-year-old Anand Patwardhan, an avant-garde filmmaker, who had just returned to India after participating in a peace movement in the US. The possibility of a genuine social, economic and political revolution, in not so distant a future, exhilarated him. 'The people were genuinely excited about the potential for change.'[47]

Every so often, moving away from the politics being played out in the full glare of media and the detailed algorithms being worked out behind closed doors, Jayaprakash returned to his roots in rural Bihar to reconnect with people. Sitting on a charpai, he listened to their woes and talked to them for hours, ignoring the heat, the monsoon rains, the cold winds, and accepted their gift of red hibiscus flowers in moments that reawakened hope. These were periods of relative calm, before the stormy days of June 1975, when everything would change all at once.

10

The Death of a Dream

Jayaprakash's movement continued to pose a huge challenge for Indira. But it was not the only one. In her own party, the Young Turks were getting restive, while another group led by Jagjivan Ram was fomenting dissent. By 12 June 1975, it was evident that she was sitting on a tinderbox. The news from Gujarat was deeply disquieting. In the assembly elections held on 10 June, the Janata Front, a coalition of opposition parties backed by Jayaprakash and led by Morarji Desai, managed to win eighty-seven seats as against the Congress tally of seventy-five. Even though the Congress got 41 per cent of the votes cast to the Janata Front's 34, it was the latter that formed the government after forging an alliance with Chimanbhai Patel.

A much more disquieting and ominous foreshadowing of all that followed was the Allahabad High Court judgment on an election petition filed by Raj Narain, the candidate who had lost to Indira in the Raebareli parliamentary election of 1971. Her election was rendered null and void. Indira was held guilty of 'corrupt practices'—availing of the services of a government official (Yashpal Kapoor) to further her election prospects and the use of government-built rostrums from which she spoke. The 'offences' were laughable, especially in view of the fact that Yashpal Kapoor had already put in his papers, but the conviction barred her from elective office for six years. Jayaprakash celebrated the judgment and said that she had forfeited her moral right to continue as prime minister.[1]

Indira failed to get the relief she had expected from the Supreme Court, which only gave her a conditional stay.[2] The opposition created an uproar. Indira sidestepped the pressure for her resignation with a flash of arrogance. Openly contemptuous of opinions that ran contrary to hers, she decided she would stay, if only to spite the opposition. Speaking to her biographer Dom Moraes about her decision, she said, 'After my judgement in 1975, what could I have done except stayed? You know the state the country was in. What would have happened if there had been nobody to lead it? I was the only person who could, you know. It was my duty to the country to stay, though I didn't want to.'[3]

On 13 June, nearly all opposition parties, with the exception of the CPM, staged an agitation in front of the President's office, demanding Indira's immediate resignation. Present at the venue, Piloo Mody of the Swatantra Party added a touch of slapstick humour by wearing a medallion around his neck that said, 'I am a CIA agent.'[4] The Congress parliamentary party that met on 18 June reiterated its full faith and confidence in Indira's leadership. Contesting the party's resolution, Jayaprakash issued a strong press statement the next day, dripping with acrimony and sarcasm: 'Yesterday's resolution of the Congress parliamentary party is yet another instance of the unabashed political immorality of the Congress leadership and of its mischievous attempt to mislead the people. The point at issue is not whether Congress MPs have faith in Mrs Gandhi's leadership but whether there is a rule of law in this country and whether it applies equally to everyone high or low. Mrs Gandhi must go. Her nine years' rule has already ruined the country's economy and its public and political life and completely degraded the values for which Swaraj was fought and won at so much cost.'[5]

The opposition joined the chorus. They accused Indira of committing a constitutional impropriety by holding on to office, an assessment stripped of nuances. One by one all the anti-Indira cards were put in place, setting the stage for the final denouement. Jayaprakash announced the formation of a five-member Lok Sangharsh Samiti, a people's struggle group headed by Morarji Desai and Nanaji Deshmukh to launch a countrywide movement to secure Indira's resignation. The Sangharsh Samiti unfolded a mega-plan of week-long, countrywide civil disobedience campaigns and demonstrations outside the prime minister's residence, ending with the gherao of her residence by several lakh volunteers. In a rally held on 22 June, Morarji Desai evoked the 1942 'Do or Die' spirit to oust Indira's regime. The Congress too toughened its rhetoric and staged several 'rent-a-crowd' rallies outside Indira's residence.

During this period of volatility, Jayaprakash quietly retreated to Bihar. More than a little wary of being sucked into the ghetto of party politics and known for his contrariness, he turned his attention to the task of strengthening the young, avant-garde Sangharsh Vahini. He joined a group of Vahini volunteers on a tour of the Naxalite areas of Bihar. Appalled by what he saw, he warned the government that the aspirations of the economically oppressed agricultural labourers could no longer be suppressed under the garb of eliminating Naxalism.

It took some amount of persuasion to coax Jayaprakash back to Delhi to champion the anti-Indira front. Leading a skewering attack on Indira at a massive rally at the Ramlila Maidan on 25 June, Jayaprakash called for a prolonged and widespread civil disobedience movement against her. 'Be prepared for a long and arduous struggle to avert such a possibility (of her dictatorship). I shall also be with you in this struggle.' Praising the Young Turks for their courage in telling the truth, he urged Jagjivan Ram and Y.B. Chavan to admit that it was not in the interest of the country or the party that Indira should continue as prime minister. He appealed to the armed forces and the police to refrain from carrying out illegal orders and openly dared the government to try him for treason for making the appeal. He also urged government employees to ponder over 'their duty' and asked students to go to jail rather than to classes in the weeks and months ahead. Lashing out at the television and radio for turning into government propaganda machines, he incited people to gherao the minister of information and broadcasting.[6] Once again, the maidan resonated with the echoes of Dinkar's powerful words, *'Singhasan khali karo, ki janta aati hai.'*

Jayaprakash's powerful, emotive speech and the overwhelming response it elicited became the cause célèbre of much of what followed. His appeal to the armed forces and the police was treated as nothing less than treason. Interestingly, in the 1930s, Indira's grandfather,

Motilal Nehru, moved a similar resolution urging the police to disobey illegal orders. The Allahabad High Court allowed an appeal by those convicted for distributing leaflets carrying the resolution; ruling that there was nothing wrong in asking the police to not obey illegal orders.

Indira handed over control to Sanjay and his hand-picked cabal of pugnacious bullies. The rest is history, so well known that it almost defies the need for recapitulation. The imposition of Emergency, bypassing the cabinet, came like a thunderbolt, subverting recognized norms of parliamentary democracy. A few minutes before midnight on 25 June, Indira, accompanied by Siddhartha Shankar Ray, went to Rashtrapati Bhavan to direct the suitably servile President, Fakhruddin Ali Ahmed, to sign the proclamation that invoked Article 352(1) of the Constitution to impose Emergency. The cabinet met at 6 a.m. to approve it. The supply of electricity to Bahadur Shah Zafar Marg—the street where leading newspaper presses, with the exception of a couple like *Hindustan Times* and the *Statesman*, were located—was suspended from midnight. For many Indians, the first source of information about the imposition of Emergency was the BBC's radio broadcast at 7.30 on the morning of 26 June. This was the beginning of a repugnant politics of paranoia, delusion and deception that justified human rights violations, censorship, suppression of freedom of speech, ruthless demolitions, forced sterilizations and the incrimination of those protesting it.

In a predawn swoop on 26 June, dozens of opposition leaders and Congress dissidents, college and university teachers, journalists, trade unionists and student leaders were arrested using the notorious 1971 law MISA that provisioned for arrest without trial for a period of two years. Among those arrested were Jayaprakash, Morarji Desai, Charan Singh, Asoka Mehta, Atal Bihari Vajpayee and about thirty MPs, including Young Turks like Chandra Shekhar and Mohan Dharia. At 8 a.m. the same day, in an unscheduled address to the nation on All India Radio, Indira said that the President had proclaimed Emergency to meet an internal threat to security. She also said that there was nothing to panic about. The narrative got a little wilder later as she alluded to a conspiracy of foreign powers—drawing analogies between her situation and that of Salvador Allende, the moderate socialist president of Chile who went down fighting during a coup in September 1973. (More like General Pinochet, as some of her victims would later lament!)

Jayaprakash was bundled out from his spartan room at the Gandhi Peace Foundation before dawn at 3 a.m. on 26 June. His secretary managed to send word to Chandra Shekhar who arrived within minutes, only to be arrested as well. Jayaprakash was taken to a tourist lodge at Sohna in Haryana. Morarji was also brought there and kept in an adjoining room. They were not allowed to meet. The following day, Jayaprakash began to show symptoms of a heart condition. He was brought back to Delhi and taken to AIIMS for cardiological investigations. Once the cardiologists gave the green signal, he was flown to Chandigarh in an Air Force plane on 1 July to serve his period of incarceration.

Jayaprakash's place of detention was a room in the third-floor ward of the Postgraduate Institute of Medical Education and Research (popularly known as PGI). It was not a grubby, blank-walled cell, but a clean room with a small bed, an air conditioner, a writing table, cupboard and armchairs. The district magistrate and inspector general prisons of Chandigarh, M.G. Devasahayam, who was also present to receive him at the air force base, was his custodian. The latter recalled that on the day of Jayaprakash's arrival, Chief Minister Bansi Lal called him past midnight to instruct that no visitors would be allowed and no calls would be permitted. The friendly young officer, however, managed to sneak in an occasional visitor: Prabhavati's brother Shivnath, Jayaprakash's siblings and nephews, his friends Sugata Dasgupta and Tarkunde, his secretary Abraham and his long-time personal attendant, Gulab. With time, some other small concessions were made. He was allowed to stroll in his balcony and receive a newspaper. He was also given access to lawyers like P.N. Lekhi, J.P. Goyal and Pranav Chatterjee. But it was largely an insular world of silence, interrupted by occasional visits, a time, perhaps also, of a little rest and renewal.

During this period, Jayaprakash's correspondence with Indira was limited. In words that simmered with rage and anguish, his first letter dated 21 July was an acerbic critique of her speeches and interviews. 'Having muzzled the press and every kind of public dissent, you continue with your distortions and untruths without fear of criticism or contradiction. You are reported to have said that democracy is not more important than the nation. Are you not presuming too much, Madam Prime Minister? . . . Please do not destroy the foundations that the fathers of the nation, including your noble father, have laid down. There is nothing but strife and suffering along the path that you have taken. You inherited a great tradition, noble values and a working democracy. Do not leave behind a miserable wreck of all that. It would take a long time to put all that together again. Dear Indiraji, please do not identify yourself with the nation. You are not immortal, India is.' The long tirade ended with what seemed like a proposal for conditional truce: 'You have accused the opposition and me of every kind of villainy. Let me assure you that if you do the right things, take the opposition into confidence, heed its advice, you will receive the willing cooperation of every one of us. For that you need not destroy democracy. The ball is in your court. It is for you to decide.'[7] As expected, there was a wall of silence on the other end that no amount of words could penetrate.

Described as 'The Siege' in Shashi Tharoor's *The Great Indian Novel*, the Emergency showed how the personal crisis of a leader could metamorphose into the political crisis of the state.[8] Unacceptable behaviour was legitimized as arrests, while torture and other forms of miscarriage of justice became the order of the day. The Shah Commission, set up to probe the excesses, put the number of people detained and arrested under MISA and DIR at more than one lakh. Even freedom fighters like Acharya Kriplani and Sushila Nayyar were not spared. Legitimate, opposition-ruled governments in Tamil Nadu and Gujarat were toppled, as Indira, with her pitch-perfect ear for conspiracy theories, went about dismantling constitutional safeguards one by one. Accusations and counter-accusations were hurled liberally from both sides. According to Jayaprakash, the Emergency was a hidden communist plot engineered by Indian communists working as stooges of the Soviet Union. Citing his brief flirtation with the Council for Cultural Freedom, a notorious anti-communist organization, his detractors alleged that Jayaprakash's movement was in cahoots with the CIA.

Two months later, reading in the *Tribune* that Sheikh Abdullah had offered to mediate, Jayaprakash was ready to seek the path of conciliation. He did not waste time in writing to his old friend, even if it was with some amount of trepidation. 'You have said that the PM is more than keen to end the emergency. Well, the first test of her keenness will be whether this letter is allowed to be delivered to you and whether you are permitted to see me.'⁹ Indeed, the letter reached the prime minister's office (PMO), but remained there undelivered. It was rumoured that efforts at mediation were being sabotaged by Sanjay and his coterie. But in this case, it seemed more likely that Indira did not want the Sheikh to play the role of negotiator. She did, however, open a channel of communication through her principal secretary, P.N. Dhar. Dhar, in turn, sent Jayaprakash's close associate, the director of Varanasi's Gandhian Institute, Sugata Dasgupta, to mediate. But this time, it was Jayaprakash's turn to act tough. 'I told Sugata that obviously Dhar could not expect me, after all that had happened, to support or cooperate with Mrs Gandhi. For the rest, the course of my future action would depend on the situation outside. I was quite clear in my mind that if parliamentary elections were to be held at the scheduled time, I would advocate ending confrontation with the government and call for an all-out effort to win the elections.'¹⁰

The noose of dictatorship was considerably tightened. On 27 June, a presidential order suspended the right to move the courts for enforcement of fundamental rights guaranteeing equal protection of the law and ensuring immunity against deprivation of life or liberty except by procedure established by law. The meeting of five or more persons was banned. Following ordinances amending MISA, an individual could be detained without disclosure of grounds for detention. On 22 July, both houses passed the 38th Amendment Bill, prohibiting judicial review of the proclamation of Emergency and associated curbs on freedom. On 18 August, Parliament passed the 39th Amendment Bill, placing elections of the President, vice president, prime minister and Speaker outside the purview of the judiciary. MISA was put in the 9th Schedule, giving it judicial immunity. Two major amendments brought about sweeping changes in the Constitution. The 41st Amendment prohibited filing any case, civil or criminal, against the President, vice president, prime minister or governor. The 42nd Amendment gave unrestrained powers to Parliament to amend or change any part of the Constitution. On 8 January 1976, the president suspended 'the seven freedoms' guaranteed by Article 19 of the Constitution and on 28 April, reversing orders passed by seven high courts, a Supreme Court bench led by Chief Justice A.N. Ray ruled that no one could move a writ petition for habeas corpus or the judicial questioning of the Emergency. The sole dissenting voice of Justice H.R. Khanna remained unheard.

The notorious 42nd Constitutional Amendment led to a huge barrage of protests. A large conclave organized by opposition parties in Delhi on 16 and 17 October 1976 resolutely opposed the bill. On 25 October, a memorandum titled 'Nation-Wide Demand', signed by India's leading scholars, writers, artists and prominent public personalities, was presented to the President. The signatories included Lotika Sarkar, S. Gopal, Romila Thapar, Raj Krishna, Mrinal Datta Chaudhuri, V.M. Dandekar, Andre Beteille, Mulk Raj Anand, Vijay Tendulkar, J. Swaminathan, Mrinal Sen, Romesh Thapar, B.G. Verghese, Nikhil Chakravarty, M.C. Chagla, V.M. Tarkunde and Soli Sorabjee.[11] They argued that a significant constitutional amendment such as this could only be passed after extensive public debate. They also argued that since the existing Lok Sabha had outlived its term, it had no political or moral authority to enact fundamental changes in the Constitution. The Supreme Court Bar Association too joined the protests.

A significant number of high court judges stood up for civil rights by upholding the right of judicial review in cases that came before them. Justice Rangarajan and Justice Agarwal of the Delhi High Court accepted Kuldip Nayar's appeal in September 1975—convinced that the courts retained the rights to review detention cases even under the Emergency. Justice Jal Rustomji Vimadalal and Justice Krishna Gawde of the Bombay High Court stood up for the rights of detenus to decent treatment in jail. There were many more such instances of vocal condemnation of repressive laws even as Indira continued to justify her moves to cripple democracy by taking recourse to petulant, post-factual rationalizations such as this: 'My intention is not to destroy but strengthen democracy. Let it not be said that Jawaharlal Nehru's daughter will ever think of undoing what her great father strove for all his life.'[12]

Whatever the provocation, Nehru would never have gagged and censored the press as Indira did. Nearly a hundred journalists met at the Press Club in Delhi on 29 June to move a resolution deploring the imposition of censorship. The government hit back by arresting Kuldip Nayar, one of the main organizers of this historic meet. In December 1975, an ordinance repealed editors' and publishers' immunity from civil and criminal action on the publication of accounts of parliamentary proceedings. Another ordinance abolished the Press Council. In another draconian measure, the government merged the four independent news agencies—the Press Trust of India, United Press of India, Samachar Bharati and Hindustan Samachar—into one single news agency functioning directly under its control. Accreditation was withdrawn from more than fifty-four reporters, cartoonists and photographers who dared to push at the boundaries of what the censors were ready to tolerate. Altogether, 253 journalists were sent to jail.

Many journals closed or suspended their operations: Jayaprakash's *Everyman's*, Shankar's *Weekly*, *Mainstream*, *Quest*, *Seminar*, *Frontier*, *Himmat* and several others. The BBC withdrew its correspondent, Mark Tully. A few reputed journals like the *Economic and Political Weekly* and the *Marxist Review* escaped the guillotine but foreign correspondents of *The Times* (London), the *Daily Telegraph*, the *Washington Post* and *Los Angeles Times* were expelled. Reporters of *The Economist* and the *Guardian* were also forced to leave. Newspapers like the *Indian Express* faced abominable intimidation in the form of raids, court cases, withdrawal of bank loans and advertisements.

The Emergency evoked mixed responses. M.F. Husain's painted mural depicting Indira as Goddess Durga astride a tiger may have been over the top, but a section of the middle class was pleased with the end of agitations, fall in crime rates, the running of trains on time and the crackdown on hoarders and tax evaders. A bountiful monsoon resulted in record output of foodgrains and edible oils during 1975–76 and put the economy back on track. Certainly, the Emergency saw none of the excesses of Nazi Germany or Mussolini's Italy, the two countries it would be later compared to. 'We collapsed without struggle in the face of the mildest possible dictatorship,' wrote Arun Shourie despairingly.[13]

For industrialists there were tax incentives and sops, like improvement in industrial relations, labour discipline and banning of strikes. The clampdown on strikes resulted in a drastic decrease in workdays lost: from 40.3 million in 1974 to 12.8 million in 1976. Lockouts and retrenchments were allowed with impunity. Over 8,00,000 workers lost their jobs in the first year of the Emergency. Protest was no longer an option. Three of the five major trade union organizations—the All India Trade Union Congress, Indian National Trade Union Congress and the Hind Mazdoor Sabha—supported the Emergency.[14] Hence, it was not surprising that industrialists like J.R.D. Tata, a supporter of Jayaprakash till the early years of the 1970s, welcomed the imposition of Emergency with open arms. 'You can't imagine what we've been through here—strikes, boycotts, demonstrations. Why, there were days I couldn't walk out of my office into the street. The parliamentary system is not suited to our needs.'[15]

Indira claimed that not even a dog barked during the Emergency.[16] With most of the opposition leaders in prison, the anti-Congress movement was certainly on the back foot. However, led by angry and despairing men and women, there was a strong underground movement brewing in Bihar and other parts of the country. Approximately 7000 persons, mainly students, were arrested for circulating clandestine literature. There were individual, much ballyhooed cases of underground resistance by leaders like George Fernandes. In Karnataka, C.G.K. Reddy helped political and cultural activists come together in organized dissent. There were impromptu protests at railway stations, bus stands and outside government offices in the most unlikely of towns and cities. The Lok Sangharsh Samiti staged satyagraha at busy street intersections in Bombay, drawing attention to the serious flaws of the Emergency. Maniben Patel, daughter of Vallabhbhai Patel, led protesters on a march to Dandi, taking the same route as Gandhi had more than forty-five years ago.

Cultural resistance to the Emergency took different forms. Eminent artists like Vivan Sundaram, Ghulam Mohammed Sheikh, Gieve Patel and Rameshwar Broota reclaimed their right to protest through radical artwork. Anand Patwardhan organized secret screenings of *Waves of Revolution*, his banned film on the 'JP Movement'. Sarveshwar

Dayal Saxena's bitter political satire *Bakri* was staged surreptitiously in university campuses. Nagarjun's poem 'Indiraji' and Dharamvir Bharati's 'Munadi' were part of the resistance narrative. In rural Karnataka, allegorical performances of Yakshagana were staged through the night to educate people. Street theatre was used as a popular form of protest in Bihar, Kerala, Karnataka, Tamil Nadu, West Bengal and other states. The spools of Amrit Nahata's film *Kissa Kursi Ka*, a spoof, with thinly veiled references to Indira and Sanjay, were picked up from the processing lab in Bombay and ferried to the Maruti factory in Gurgaon to be burnt.

Global protests marked the imposition of the Emergency and Jayaprakash's arrest. Starting with 'Free Jayaprakash' campaigns in the UK and the US, advertisements signed by intellectuals and scholars like Philip Noel-Baker, A.J.P. Taylor, W.H. Morris-Jones, E.F. Schumacher and Fenner Brockway appeared in *The Times* (London) and the *New York Times* carrying the caption: 'Today is India's Independence Day. Don't Let the light go out on India's Democracy. Free Jayaprakash Narayan.'[17] On 26 January 1976, several people marched in London in an alliance against 'Fascist Dictatorship' in India. On 5 March the same year, eighty American Nobel laureates and prominent intellectuals like Noam Chomsky, Linus Pauling and Allen Ginsberg signed an appeal for the restoration of Fundamental Rights. On 20 September, a group called 'Indians for Democracy' began a long march from Liberty Bell, Philadelphia, that ended on 1 October at the United Nations headquarters in New York. The Emergency was also condemned by the former German chancellor Willy Brandt and the Socialist International.[18] Amongst its few supporters were Britain's Labour Party leaders Michael Foot and Jennie Lee and Conservative leader Margaret Thatcher who later became Britain's prime minister.

Jayaprakash's *Prison Diary* gives insight into the workings of his mind during these tumultuous times. He found his isolation mind-numbing initially. There are poignant entries in his diary that reveal his torment. 'There was nobody to whom I could confide my inner feelings. This lack of company I suffered most till the end.'[19] He complained that he was treated better by the British Imperial Government when he was a prisoner at the Lahore Fort, where after a while, he was allowed to meet Lohia for an hour every day. He was ebullient on days he was allowed visitors: peppering them with questions, chewing over the current state of affairs over coffee.

On 6 August, Shivnath brought the news that Parliament had approved the proclamation of Emergency at a special session convened for the purpose. He also spoke about the amendments to the Constitution that barred the judicial review of the proclamation. Jayaprakash was devastated. Saying that the situation was intolerable, he wrote to Indira that he would protest by fasting till his release or death, whichever came earlier. It was left to Devasahayam to persuade him to drop the idea. Jayaprakash was also shattered by the harrowing details of the floods that ravaged Bihar in August. He asked for parole for a month to be able to address the humanitarian crisis citing the analogy of the epochal Bihar earthquake of 1934, when Rajendra Prasad was released to support relief work. The government predictably turned a deaf ear.

On 18 September, Jayaprakash was moved to a guest house in the hospital campus. He used its green lawns for short strolls and seemed happier. The team of doctors attending to him earlier was deputed there as well. The staff was warm and caring. A big bouquet of flowers from the jail superintendent greeted him on his birthday. The denial of parole may have rankled, but Devasahayam found Jayaprakash free of resentment against Indira. He did, however, frequently remark that it was an irony of fate that the daughter of Nehru, one of the greatest democrats of the twentieth century, had destroyed democracy.

His diary became a space to incubate ideas. It was also a space to delve into questions of violence and non-violence and whether the opposition was committed to his revolutionary goals. He wrote unflinching accounts of the movement's darkest moments when MLAs were roughed up by protesters and a constable was killed by a violent mob. He also wrote a short summary for a proposed book that would bring together the theses propounded by him at different times. But above all, the diary voiced his concern about the future of democracy. 'The state swells up, the people shrink', an evocative quotation picked up from Professor Bertram Wolfe's book *Khrushchev and Stalin's Ghost*, was the leitmotif of much of his writing. The entries were erratic after 26 October, ending abruptly on 4 November.

Towards the end of October, Jayaprakash began experiencing serious medical issues. He was taken back to his room in the hospital ward area for close monitoring. Within days he was completely bedridden with chronic fatigue and severe abdominal pain, so acute that he could not even turn in bed. In one of his last diary scribbles on 29 October, he wrote: 'Have gone through hell these last days—continuous pain in the lower abdominal region. Felt miserable, all kinds of investigations were done but nothing has been found . . . Have no appetite. There is a total aversion to food.'[20] Several investigations followed before he was informed that his kidneys were severely damaged.

Rumours spiralled about his worsening condition. His hands and legs were bloated. There were swollen bags under his eyes. He could not keep his eyes open for more than a moment and would lapse into a stupor in the middle of a sentence. The official report on his condition was sent to the PMO on 7 November 1975. His brother Rajeshwar addressed a personal note to Indira on 10 November asking her whether it would be in her government's interest if Jayaprakash died in detention. The forebodings were ominous. On 12 November, the government dispatched a team of doctors from AIIMS to report his condition. On the same evening, the chief secretary of Delhi arrived in Chandigarh with two orders, one for Jayaprakash's unconditional parole and the other for release. The release order was a backup, to save the government from possible embarrassment in the event of his refusal to be freed on parole.

Jayaprakash was flown to Delhi on 16 November and taken to AIIMS. From there, at his brother's insistence, he was moved to Jaslok Hospital on 22 November. He flew to Bombay accompanied by doctors, Rajeshwar and Minoo Masani. He was placed under the care of the chief of the renal unit at Jaslok, Dr M.K. Mani and eminent cardiologist Dr A.B. Mehta. Jayaprakash was informed by Dr Mani that his kidneys could have been partially saved had he reached the hospital a couple of weeks earlier.[21]

Jayaprakash's condition provoked bitter insinuations and angry rebuttals. The Alva Commission set up by the Janata government to probe allegations of medical negligence held hearings in camera. Some of the leaks made sensational cover stories, much to the delight of cub reporters like Shekhar Gupta who was interning with the Chandigarh edition of the *Indian Express* at that point. The stories created a furore even as the commission wound up abruptly, with no sense of closure.

Jayaprakash was put on a regimented protocol of dialysis. The procedure took several agonizing hours, but he began to show signs of improvement and, within a few weeks, was able to manage brief walks. A dialysis machine was bought for him through money collected from an appeal for the donation of a rupee. The response to the appeal was stupendous. The donations surged to reach the magic figure of Rs 3 lakhs in no time. Indira's contribution of money from the prime minister's relief fund was given a polite go-by. His secretary Abraham, and daughter-like Sarvodaya activist Janaki, learnt to handle the machine, equipping him fully for his long-awaited journey home.

Jayaprakash's return to Patna on 20 July 1976 was not without considerable political tumult. Thousands of people thronged the streets of Patna to see him. The paranoid government imposed Section 144 of the Indian Penal Code that laid down punitive measures for anyone who was part of an unlawful assembly or carrying a weapon. Loudspeakers were used to announce that persons moving towards the airport would be arrested under the DIR. Several people were detained, including three of Jayaprakash's closest relatives, who were kept in detention for many hours. Shocked beyond belief, Jayaprakash despairingly described the city as a 'prison house'. He accused the police of keeping a strict watch on his residence. But the vigil failed to stop the swirling crowds. On a visit from Calcutta on his birthday on 11 October, poet and novelist Maitreyi Devi was stunned to see hundreds of visitors. She was equally amazed at the volume of letters and telegrams received daily. 'Two to three volunteers were needed to sort them out.'[22]

A team of senior doctors—C.P. Thakur, Narendra Prasad, Indu Bhushan Sinha and R.V.P. Sinha—was appointed to monitor Jayaprakash's physical condition. What was more worrying to Jayaprakash was the incomplete task of forging unity between opposition parties at a time when their leaders were in jail, or, out on parole, to build a national political alternative. He believed, rather naively, that the leaders, being thrown in prison together, would have resolved their differences. His initial meetings with the Congress (O), the BLD, the Jana Sangh and the SSP seemed to be going nowhere. He had to deal with fragile egos and cagey self-interests. Ideological polarities made the task even more difficult. Jayaprakash did what was necessary, tenaciously, doggedly, demonstrating an astonishing strength of spirit. But even by May 1976, his effort to dissolve differences by presenting a blueprint of the merger plan evoked a churlish response from some quarters.

Reacting to Jayaprakash's press conference on this subject on 25 May, Charan Singh said, 'Your statement before the press conference on May 25 speaks of all the four parties dissolving their identities after the new party has been formally launched . . . Now, this amounts to putting the cart before the horse.'[23] He reminded Jayaprakash of his efforts to bring about a merger in 1974. 'I had told you that a motley crowd consisting of widely different, even conflicting political elements, will hardly add up to an organisation which would carry an agitation through a successful end, or win an election. Valuable time has been lost and it is not possible to make up for this lost time by rushing things.'[24]

Jayaprakash was also disappointed by the attitude of opposition MPs who refused to resign from the Lok Sabha when its term expired in March 1976, extended twice until February 1977. Several of them were hedging their bets and playing for time even as the Congress (O) and the BLD leaders were in secret parleys with the Congress, a move abhorred by the socialists.

It would take a few more months for a cohesive plan for a new, united party to materialize. Differences between Charan Singh and Asoka Mehta continued to rise mainly over the insistence of the Congress (O) on retaining its existing name and flag and its obduracy on the question of leadership. Other parties too kept bringing to the table near-impossible conditions for merger. Several questions continued to be raised on the role of the RSS in the new party. There was a broad consensus that the RSS would be kept out of the orbit and dual membership would not be allowed. Worried that RSS leaders 'still believed in the concept of Hindu Rashtra', Jayaprakash advised them to embrace the idea of Indian nationhood, 'which is a secular concept and embraces all communities living in India'.[25]

A year into the Emergency, the political climate became increasingly febrile. This, despite the release of a number of political leaders on parole and a clever attempt on Indira's part to combine socialist rhetoric with realpolitik. It was a fractious summer of discontent. The economy, that had seen perceptible growth, slackened. Inflation was back with a 10 per cent increase in prices by year end. By Indira's own admission, the administration went back to its laid-back ways.[26] On the corruption front too, the initial gains were reversed. Threat-based extortions grew momentously with a rampant abuse of power. The personality cult built around Indira began to be matched by Sanjay. As a result, his hold over the party grew exponentially. Sanjay's 5-point programme rivalled his mother's 20-point programme, and was cross-pollinated with ideas from Jayaprakash's Charter of People's Demands. There were serious bureaucratic misdemeanours in crucial appointments. The bulldozing of slums, the killing of squatters resisting removal, and forced sterilization campaigns were illustrative of the extent to which democracy was threatened.

Alarmed at the erosion of civil liberties and human rights, Jayaprakash founded the People's Union for Civil Liberties and Democratic Rights in October 1976 with Tarkunde as president and Krishna Kant as general secretary. Meant to complement the work of Citizens for Democracy, the organization went about uncovering serious cases of human rights violation. The highly politicized environment forced it to tread the finest of lines. The organization was rechristened as People's Union of Civil Liberties in November 1980. The exponential rise in encounter killings of Naxalites in the states of West Bengal, Orissa, Bihar, Kerala and Andhra led Jayaprakash to found the Andhra Pradesh Civil Rights Committee, with people of the stature of Tarkunde, Arun Shourie, Nabakrushna Choudhury and B.G. Verghese as its members. The committee's reports on custodial deaths provoked widespread outrage,

Jayaprakash remained steadfast in his belief that a united democratic opposition was the only thing that would stem the tide of totalitarianism.[27] For some time his efforts at unity were enveloped in a fog of fractious political see-sawing. He was despondent one moment, blithely optimistic the next. It was not until November 1976 that internal differences were somewhat resolved. Representatives of parties other than the BLD met on 11 November to pass a unanimous resolution to form a new opposition party. Charan Singh stayed away from this meeting but wrote to Jayaprakash that his party would be the first to join the proposed merged party.[28] Several notes were exchanged between different leaders, echoing their apprehensions and bargaining stands. BLD pitched for leadership for Singh, citing his rural orientation and centrist ideological disposition. Seeing red, the Congress (O) said it was not prepared to go beyond thinking of a united front. The parties that were willing to merge unconditionally at this stage were the Jana Sangh and the Socialist Party. Vajpayee beseeched Jayaprakash to seal the issue. He said, 'If we do not unite even now, history will never forgive us.'[29]

The inveterate dithering continued even after the resolution was passed. The socialists began to feel that they had overcommitted to an electoral merger with the 'diabolical JS-BLD-Congress (O) leadership'.[30] A week before the formation of the Janata Party, Singh was still exploring possibilities of a dialogue with Indira through her envoy Mohammad Yunus.[31]

The situation reversed on 18 January 1977. In an unexpected and rather dramatic move, Indira dissolved the Lok Sabha and called for elections in March. Singh, Asoka Mehta, Vajpayee, Surendra Mohan and others met at Morarji Desai's house on the cold, windy morning of 19 January for the final round of negotiations. The 'Janata Party' was formally launched four days later, on 23 January, with Desai as chairman, Singh as deputy chairman and Jayaprakash as its éminence grise. It entered into tactical seat arrangements with parties like the Shiromani Akali Dal in Punjab, the DMK in Tamil Nadu and the CPM in Bengal. The party received a huge boost when Jagjivan Ram left the Congress and joined the alliance.[32]

The announcement of elections revived and energized Jayaprakash. Speculating on what could have led to this momentous decision, Jayaprakash observed, 'The increasing restiveness of the people and criticism from abroad has persuaded the government to take this decision. It feels it is bound to win, not because it is popular, but because the opposition parties have been given hardly any time to reorganise their shattered party cadres, raise funds and make the extensive arrangements required to fight elections.'[33] The election campaign was launched on 30 January, Martyrs' Day. Addressing a massive rally at Gandhi Maidan, a visibly emotional Jayaprakash told the people that he had returned from the jaws of death to join them in the struggle to save democracy. On 4 February, he appealed to the youth to uproot dictatorship.[34] On 13 March, he issued another strong appeal captioned 'Defeat the Dictators', which became one of the tag lines of his campaign.

Jayaprakash was irrepressible. Advised by Dr Mani to not skip dialysis for more than three days at a stretch, he flew hundreds of miles to address meetings and rallies in Patna, Calcutta, Hyderabad, Ratlam, Indore, Poona, Bombay and Chandigarh with an electric energy that surprised his admirers and even his detractors. He spoke with certitude, in a voice that still retained its ability to inspire. Dr Mani called it 'an odyssey unparalleled in the history of haemodialysis'.[35] Tens of thousands of people took to the streets to campaign as Jayaprakash took upon himself the task of overseeing the minutiae.

The Congress was trounced, facing its worst defeat in thirty years, winning only 154 of the 492 contested seats, almost wholly from Maharashtra, and the southern states of Andhra, Karnataka, Tamil Nadu and Kerala. Indira lost her Raebareli seat and Sanjay lost Amethi. Sanjay publicly apologized for his role in the electoral debacle. On behalf of her colleagues, Indira accepted the people's verdict unreservedly. At least at this point. Allowing himself a cautious optimism after the results were declared on 21 March, Jayaprakash reflected, 'The people have made their choice. They have opted for liberty. All eyes are now focused on the Janata Party. Every step it takes is being watched by the people.'[36] The Janata's manifesto was titled 'Both Bread and Liberty'. Its three revolutionary charters were a summation of JP's Gandhian Socialist vision. He was confident that the Janata leaders would work selflessly to actualize that vision. For the romantics, the Janata victory came with the promise of a second revolution, comparable to the attainment of freedom from colonial rule in 1947.

What people saw was certainly not what they wanted to see. Three leaders on three different trajectories tried to stake a claim to prime ministership of India's maiden non-Congress government: Charan Singh, Jagjivan Ram and Morarji Desai. The decision makers were Jayaprakash and J.B. Kripalani. Jayaprakash briefly toyed with the idea of proposing Chandra Shekhar for the job, but finally eighty-one-year-old Desai, who had twice missed becoming prime minister, got the nod. Singh was given the weighty home portfolio while Ram settled rather reluctantly with defence. Chandra Shekhar became the party president with Madhu Limaye, Nanaji Deshmukh and Rabi Ray as general secretaries. The coveted external affairs charge was given to Vajpayee. On 24 March, Desai took the oath as prime minister. The newly elected members of Parliament took a pledge at Rajghat to uphold the rights of the people, to promote national unity and harmony, and to practise austerity and honesty in personal and public life.

Jayaprakash went to meet Indira soon after the pledge-taking ceremony at Rajghat. It was an emotional meeting, drenched in tears. Not much was said. Sensing that Indira was worried about Sanjay's fate, Jayaprakash assured her that there would be nothing like a witch-hunt. In a similar spirit of reconciliation, the newly formed government invited veteran Congressman Y.B. Chavan, the newly elected leader of the opposition, for a radio broadcast to the nation. In the euphoria of the results, Jayaprakash did not forget his promise of total revolution. Speaking on behalf of the people, in a broadcast on AIR, he repeated his pledge to work for total revolution as soon as his physical condition would permit.

For a while, there was an intoxicating sense of a new consensus being born. Within days of being sworn in, the new government led by law minister Shanti Bhushan began work on the restoration of Fundamental Rights. It revoked the external emergency proclaimed at the time of the Bangladesh war, and amidst raucous cheers in the Lok Sabha repealed the Publication of Objectionable Matter and the Parliamentary Proceedings Protection Acts. The 43rd and 44th amendments were in the pipeline when, in a move that did not remain uncontested, nine Congress-ruled states were brought under President's rule. Seven weeks later, in June 1977, the election to state legislative assemblies reaffirmed the Janata Party's hold over the electorate in northern India with the exception of West Bengal where the CPM won 178 seats to Janata's twenty-nine.

By March end, Jayaprakash was teetering on the brink of a full-on health crisis, On the advice of his Jaslok doctors, he was flown to Seattle on 30 April, for a graft operation at a super-speciality centre that had the best vascular surgeons. He was accompanied by Dr Mani and Abraham. The Indian ambassador received him at the airport with a warm message from President Carter. Jayaprakash remained in hospital for ten days, feted and spoilt by the doctors and nurses and an unstoppable tide of democrats, scholars, activists and friends, who came to see him during the visiting hours. His niece Jyoti who lived in Seattle was part of the team of caregivers. Jayaprakash recovered rapidly and by the middle of May was declared fit for discharge.

He boarded the flight to India on 18 May, with stopovers in New York and London, oblivious to the unseemly wrangling for tickets for state assembly elections that had taken place in his absence. By the time he returned, the chaos in the party was nearly soap operatic. What surprised him was that not only had major developments been kept from him, but that none of the key leaders were present at the airport to receive him. The flat-out erasure of his presence upset him. He felt let down and reportedly confided in close friend Kuldip Nayar that it was apparent that he had ceased to matter to the Janata leaders.[37] He was also pained by scurrilous stories planted in newspapers about his failing memory, that were strongly rebutted by his physicians.[38]

Masking his emotional bruises, Jayaprakash remained zealously protective of the party. He combated the media storm surrounding the out-of-control events by condoning the party's missteps and drawing the media's attention to the important steps taken to restore civil liberties and provide constitutional safeguards against the subversion of democracy. But the feuds and foibles of the Janata leaders and their attempt to make him irrelevant did not go unnoticed. Speaking to the correspondents of *Sunday*, Surendra Pratap Singh and Shobha Kilachand, he said despairingly, 'No one comes from Delhi to seek my advice. Karpooriji [Karpoori Thakur, chief minister of Bihar] is here. Occasionally he comes to see me, but he does not come with his problems. Sometimes, I suggest something . . .'[39] When asked how it felt to be labelled the Mahatma of 1977, the founder of the second liberation, he said rather self-deprecatingly that he hated the title and that he was only a humble fighter for freedom.

The news that came from Delhi was of disunity, indiscipline, groupism and nepotism, leading to an alarming decline in the popularity of the party.[40] Physically distanced from the raucous politics, encumbered by tormenting thoughts, and exhausted by the long illness, Jayaprakash retreated more and more into himself. My father spent some heart-wrenching moments with him in the last week of August. Their conversations, spread over three warm and humid afternoons, constitute the last chapter of my father's book on Jayaprakash's selected writings, named, *A Revolutionary's Quest*. My father found him both forthright and withdrawn. He was scrupulous about skirting questions directly related to the convulsive politics of the party fathered by him, saying that the party needed a year before it could be judged. Drawing him into conversation about development of agro–industrial communities, the need for electoral reforms, the necessity of enshrining the right to work in the Constitution as a fundamental right and of prioritizing improvements in irrigation and agriculture, rural health and education was easier. Jayaprakash set aside his rectitude, speaking also about the need to form people's committees at the grassroots and district, state and national level to act as watchdogs: an idea whose time had come, not a moment too soon. His site of resistance and organ of protest against injustice, the Sangharsh Vahini, dominated much of the conversations.[41]

The failure of Janata leaders to seize the moment cleared the way for Indira's revival. The political moment that she was looking for came when eight Dalits and three persons from other deprived communities were brutally killed by landowners in Belchi, a nondescript village not far from the state capital of Patna, in July 1977. She journeyed there, travelling by train, jeep, tractor and finally on an elephant in torrential rain, walking through slush and waist-deep water, establishing her position as the only hope of the poor and destitute. It was a brilliant move: an amalgamation of Machiavellian politics with a humane twist that seemed to legitimize even the darker side of the Emergency.

She completed her historic trip with a stopover in Patna, to see Jayaprakash. His Charkha Samiti home was resonant with memories of that memorable visit. Indira spent nearly an hour, fussing over him, just as a daughter would.

Threatened by Indira's soaring popularity, Charan Singh ordered her arrest along with four former cabinet colleagues, on 3 October, on charges of misuse of authority and corruption. After several hours of drama, from the time the police arrived at her residence at 12, Willingdon Crescent to the point of her refusal to post bail, the magistrate before whom she was produced dismissed the charges and ordered her unconditional release. Shanti Bhushan admitted that the evidence presented for Indira's prosecution was hopelessly flimsy and contrived. This was the moment of martyrdom that Indira was looking for, and she made the most of it, using it to fan a sympathy wave in her favour. Even foreign newspapers bitterly critical of the Emergency, like the *Guardian*, saw the arrest as a perilous decision. Everywhere she went, people welcomed her with exceptional warmth.

There were, however, signs of a crisis brewing within the Congress, with several erstwhile Indira loyalists testifying before the Shah Commission—a commission of inquiry set up in May 1977, one of eight, to investigate the misuse of power, excesses and malpractices committed during the Emergency—that they were forced to act wrongfully. Feeling that Indira was a serious political liability, party president Brahmananda Reddy expelled her from the Congress on 1 January 1978. The party split into two factions. Indira Congress was born with fifty-four Lok Sabha members. Her name as suffix augured well for what would be a spectacular political comeback.

Jayaprakash watched these developments with trepidation. He was pleased when the government announced the creation of a commission to provide institutional safeguards to minorities. He did not doubt the sincerity of the Janata leaders in the steps taken to restore democracy, noting with satisfaction the move to bring in the 43rd and the 44th amendments by law minister Shanti Bhushan in December 1977 and May 1978. He also appreciated the increased focus on agriculture and projects aimed at expanding employment in rural areas, but the factional infighting within the party triggered an avalanche of negative emotions. A letter dated 9 May 1978, to Chandra Shekhar, voiced his sense of disquiet. 'What you friends have done in the last one year is by no means insignificant. It is unnecessary to go into details here. But it cannot also be overlooked that the great hope and enthusiasm that had been generated amongst our people at the time of the last Lok Sabha elections has, more or less, wholly cooled down by now and instead a feeling of hopelessness is growing among the people. It is sad that so far we had not been able to grasp this opportunity. Even at this late hour we should begin to ponder deeply on this matter and devise ways and means whereby this awakened aspiration of our people can be fully utilized in the reconstruction of India.'[42]

Jayaprakash recalled the question that Chandra Shekhar frequently asked during the days of the Bihar movement; if the Congress was replaced with a government of the opposition, would that government do any better? The words of Chandra Shekhar came back to haunt him.

As the storm clouds gathered, no one bothered to seek Jayaprakash's opinion. In a sense, it was history repeating itself, with his predicament not very different from Gandhi's in 1947. Even when the Desai–Singh feud began to take apocalyptic proportions he was not asked to mediate. It came to a point when Singh resigned from the Janata national executive and its parliamentary board and began labelling his own government impotent for failing to arrest Indira in the wake of the Shah Commission's findings. Fingers were also being pointed at Desai because of his son, who was reportedly closing one deal after another. By June 1978, Singh, Raj Narain and four ministers of state from the BLD were out of the cabinet, further accentuating the crisis. Madhu Limaye rushed to Patna to apprise Jayaprakash of the situation. In a desperate effort to rein in the crisis, Jayaprakash wrote separate letters to Ram, Desai and Singh. His letter to Ram, who had quietly acquiesced to Desai's authority, spelt out his core worry. 'The crisis in the party is not an ordinary one. The destiny of the country is linked with it. If the party breaks up, the centrifugal forces will acquire strength, thereby endangering the unity of the country and the future of democracy which we all have saved with so much effort . . .'[43] He appealed to both Desai and Singh to resolve the crisis. He told Desai that he depended on his leadership, and expected him to maintain the unity and discipline of the party in ways that would be acceptable to Singh.

Hurt by Desai's statement that the crisis was an internal matter of the ruling party and that he would not tolerate any outside interference, Jayaprakash poured out his heart to J.B. Kripalani. 'You and I might have nominated Morarji Desai for the prime ministership of India, but I doubt very much that he feels any obligation or is inclined to consider our advice seriously . . . In all these past months since he has become prime minister not once has he cared to consult me personally or even by correspondence.'[44]

In what would be called her second coming, Indira won the high-decibel Chikmagalur by-election by 70,000 votes and was back in Parliament by the end of the year. Within a fortnight of her victory, she was held guilty of breach of privilege and contempt of the House for having blocked a parliamentary inquiry into the affairs of her son's company. She used the floor of the House to apologize for Emergency excesses, before going on the offensive. She accused the government of epochal misdeeds; provoking civil strife, weakening the secular base, surrendering the country's right to nuclear technology and inviting multinationals to what had up till that point been a heavily controlled economy. She was stripped of her membership of Parliament, arrested and sent to Tihar Jail. Her arrest, a major political gaffe, sparked unprecedented outrage.

The internal squabbles of the Janata Party also continued to make headlines. In the closing days of the 1977 election campaign, Indira compared the Janata to an orange; the moment it would be peeled off, it would fall apart in segments, a prescient statement, given what ultimately befell the party. Jayaprakash tried to mediate, but no one listened. Singh did visit him briefly in November, but by then the battle line was drawn. Supported by the chief ministers of Bihar, Haryana and Uttar Pradesh, Singh organized a mammoth rally on 23 December. The show of strength worked in his favour. He was reinducted into the cabinet as finance minister and deputy prime minister on 24 January 1979. Ram was elevated as the second deputy prime minister.

Jayaprakash was immensely relieved. Speaking to a correspondent of the *Indian Express* the same day, he said: 'I am happy that at last a formula has been found that has given satisfaction to all sides concerned. It augers well for the future of our democracy.'[45] However, after a brief truce, the warring factions renewed their fight. Singh's coruscating attacks on the RSS took on a certain ferocity as did the issue of dual membership.

Trying to make sense of the enduring tumult, Jayaprakash addressed a letter to Desai on 1 March, placing all his worries and apprehensions on the drawing board. His worries were not just centred on the toxic polarization that had overtaken the party. He was equally upset that, despite being the 'child of revolution', the government was monumentally corrupt. Using sharp words about wasted economic and social potential, he pointed out that people's participation in governance was as abysmal as before. What troubled him most was that social inclusiveness remained a pipe dream as did his vision of economic decentralization. He also wrote with anguish about the increasing oppression of Dalits and about the 'demon of communalism' that was raising its head. With equal anguish, he wrote about the unemployment of crores of people. He felt that it was a matter of deep regret that the government had failed to channelize youth power. Ending the letter with his characteristic tone of righteousness, he chided the prime minister: 'The Janata Party had begun as a joint family and you had been elected head of that family . . . Instead of this, it is a divided family today. I feel that it was your duty to see that the constituent units did not function as factions either within or outside.'[46]

With class and caste conflicts accelerating dangerously, Jayaprakash felt that the exploited classes had no alternative but to unite and assert their rights. His dream of building up a real people's movement was increasingly centred on the Sangharsh Vahini, the foot soldiers of Total Revolution. The momentum created by them in 1978, propelled by their struggle against the mahants of the Shaivite math (a monastery-cum-temple complex) of Bodh Gaya, put Jayaprakash's socialist ideas back in circulation. The Vahini joined the struggle of landless labourers and sharecroppers for rights in land they had cultivated for decades. Approximately 9575 acres of land spread over 138 villages was held by the mahants. Following the Vahini protocol for people's struggle, young Vahini members camped in villages, in the huts of people from the Bhuiyan caste who were at the bottom of the caste and class hierarchy. In a move towards something altogether more vital and visceral, they formed labour organizations, ready to take on the might of the oppressive mahants. The movement rested on a knife-edge when Jayaprakash visited Bodh Gaya to lend it his support.

The Bodh Gaya struggle pushed women's issues into the mainstream and awakened a deeper understanding of gender relations. Encouraged by fiery activists like Manimala, women tilled the land, challenging gender norms. At the heart of the feminist struggle was their resistance to oppression at multiple levels, their lack of agency, domestic violence, their exclusive responsibility for housework, discrimination against girl children, trafficking and child marriage. They challenged alcoholism and the sale of liquor. No longer acquiescent, they too struggled for land rights.

The spirit of the movement was infectious. This was something Jayaprakash had foreseen: 'I do not see any prospect for total revolution without a long-drawn-out struggle and without the masses participating in such a struggle.'[47] In 1980, the activists seized 3000 acres of land and completed the sowing operations, using the catchy slogan '*Jo zameen ko boye jote, woh zameen ka malik hai*' (the one who sows and reaps is the owner of the land). The government was eventually forced to identify 1000 acres of land for redistribution. But women, other than widows, were kept out of the redistribution list. Their struggle for independent rights on land continued. It was only after three years of unabated struggle that their rights were recognized. The Vahini that was earlier confined to Uttar Pradesh and Bihar spread to other states, even as Jayaprakash issued an appeal to 'Naxalite friends' to join hands to help build a peoples' movement based on the Gandhian technique of peaceful protest.[48]

One of Jayaprakash's last recorded letters was to the chief minister of Bihar, Ramsundar Das, on the subject of state repression in Bodh Gaya. He drew the chief minister's attention to the merciless assault on Vahini activists in police lockups, after labelling them Naxalites, and the equally disturbing attempt to involve them in fabricated cases.

Dealing with end-stage renal issues, Jayaprakash was in and out of his Bombay hospital. During one such critical spell of hospitalization at Jaslok, beginning 18 March, the government committed a terrible faux pas. Jayaprakash was swerving between life and death when, based upon a careless report of the Intelligence Bureau, the AIR interrupted its regular programme to announce his death. This was on 23 March 1979 at 1.10 p.m. No one bothered to confirm the news from the hospital, or even from Chandra Shekhar who was camping at the hospital. At 1.15 p.m., the Speaker of the Lok Sabha, K.S. Hegde, broke the news to a shocked House. The hospital was in a state of siege as reporters, photographers and hundreds of restive mourners, undone by grief, tried to break through the security cordons. A large media contingent was flown into Patna, even as the state government began to barricade the roads leading to the cremation ground on the riverfront.

For Jayaprakash, his faux death worked as a metaphor at different levels—the smothering of his dream of revolution and the death of a promise that his closest protégés failed to keep. The news of the communal carnage in Jamshedpur in mid-April sliced his soul. He was also disturbed by the news of mutiny in the Central Reserve Police Force, the rising mayhem in the North-East, spiralling inflation and labour unrest. His period of recuperation was long. Part of it was spent at the penthouse of Express Tower, where he was looked after by his close friend, Ramnath Goenka. Tagore's poems on death and the afterlife absorbed him and helped him come to terms with his own mortality.

Jayaprakash returned home on 7 July. He looked frail and was constantly fatigued, every ounce of energy sucked out. He was struggling with insomnia, made worse by news of the full-on governance crisis. The frequent dialysis was also wearing him out. He could not read much. A mass of incomplete writing piled up on his desk. If he was holding up, it was not in small part due to a dedicated team of caregivers. His foster daughter Vibha reminisced, 'He found solace in poetry. We sat by his bed-side reciting portions from *Madhushala* and *Rashmirathi*. Equally, he found succour in the psalms of Nicaraguan liberation poet Ernesto Cardenal Martinez and poems from the Octavio Paz collection, *The Labyrinth of Solitude*. Reading a few pages from the *Ramcharitmanas* was a daily evening ritual. He enjoyed listening to Sahir's lyrics from *Pyaasa*. He also seemed to enjoy my rendition of "Raghupati Raghav", and other Gandhian songs, and Tulsidas's immortal song, "Tu Dayalu Deen Ho".'

'Ganga babu [Ganga Sharan Singh] was with us every evening, giving dada [Jayaprakash] the day's news, while his attendant Gulab fussed over him, coaxing him to eat a small portion of grilled fish or chicken. He chewed on his food slowly, using, as always, a fork and knife. Abraham and Sachchidanand, his secretaries, remained within calling distance. His brother-in-law Shivnath, friends and long-time associates like Dayanand Sahai, Devendra Singh, Ramanand Tiwari, Madhu Limaye, Razi Ahmed, Agyeya, Renu, Upendra Maharathi and his daughter Gopa, Acharya and Sucheta Kripalani, frequently congregated at his place. But he was never pain-free, and looking at his sad, pensive face all we wanted to do was to alleviate his physical and existential suffering. Santosh Bhartiya, who came often, tried to bring back dada's incandescent smile by inviting tabla maestro Lachchu Maharaj to perform at his place. Dada made me sing a song from our revolutionary days. The song was "Jayaprakash ka Bigul Baja". During the rendition, he put his head on the pillow and covered his eyes. The pillow was drenched with tears when we finished.' The rules of politics were being rewritten to eviscerate everything Jayaprakash stood for. All that remained were broken shards of a dream.

The rapprochement between Desai and Singh was extremely short-lived. As the party hurtled from one major crisis to another, the political stage seemed set for another change. June was an action-packed month. Health minister Raj Narain, popularly perceived as a tetchy political gadfly, was removed from the party's national executive when he publicly attacked the government and exhorted people to gherao the MPs of their area. His ouster triggered massive defections. Narain staged an ideological coup by forming the Janata Party-Secular to distinguish it from the Janata, which he dubbed communal. The socialists had already kicked the hornet's nest by bringing up the issue of dual membership. The stage was set for their taking a hard line by walking out of the party and the government.

Jayaprakash appealed to everyone in the party to find some way to save democracy and ward off instability and chaos.[49] He wrote to Chandra Shekhar, saying that he felt Desai needed to step down from the leadership of the party, and make way for Jagjivan Ram, to save the country from anarchy and dictatorship.[50] It was a damning critique of Desai's leadership, set to create a permanent rift.

He sent a letter with the same text to Desai. In a bizarre incident, a Xeroxed copy found its way to the Patna station of AIR, much before the original reached Desai. The latter was outraged. His stinging reply was reflective, my father felt, of his egregious vanity: 'I was surprised and stressed to receive your letter of July 18 1979, the contents of which had already been flashed by news agencies long before the letter was delivered to me late in the evening yesterday. What caused me even greater unhappiness was that in a matter of great importance to the country and the Janata Party, you formed a judgement, without having personal discussions with me . . . In this difficult hour, I owe a duty to the country and the party, and in performing it, I have necessarily to rely on my own judgement.'[51]

The political skulduggery reached its apotheosis when Y.B. Chavan, leader of the opposition, moved a no-confidence motion against the government on 11 July 1979. On 14 July, Desai was asked to step down as leader of the House by the Janata Parliamentary Board. Industry minister George Fernandes resigned after doing his best to defend the government during the no-confidence debate. Pressure mounted on Desai to resign. Less than two weeks later, on 27 July, Desai stepped down as head of the party and was replaced by Ram.

Watching the unravelling of the Janata Party with pleasure, Indira inched closer to her goal of staging a comeback. She set about wooing Singh, even while she was briefly incarcerated in Tihar Jail, sending flowers on his birthday. Sanjay did his bit by holding parleys with Narain. After Desai lost a confidence vote in the Lok Sabha on 28 July, the Indira faction of the Congress extended outside support to the Singh-led coalition, consisting of Janata Party (Secular) and Congress (Urs). Indira's support came with an unspoken rider; that, as quid pro quo, Singh would withdraw the special courts set up to prosecute her and Sanjay. Singh seemed to be in a hurry to set up a commission chaired by B.P. Mandal to recommend caste quotas, with the exclusion of all else. His laid-back, non-committal attitude on burying the Special Courts Act was probably what led Indira to withdraw support within twenty-one days, on 20 August. Singh preferred to resign rather than face the ignominy of facing a vote of confidence in the Lok Sabha. Rejecting Jagjivan Ram's contention that he, as the opposition leader, would be able to muster the support of other parties, President Neelam Sanjiva Reddy dissolved the Lok Sabha two days later and ordered elections. In the seventh general election held in January 1980, Indira was voted back to power with an absolute majority.

Stripped of every vestige of self-worth, Jayaprakash died a sad death. What aggrieved him particularly was that his poor physical condition prevented him from taking proactive steps to change the political narrative or even challenge it effectively. 'How should I rest on the shore, when the waves are beckoning me,' he wallowed in the poetic excess of his favourite Bachchan verse. My father saw him about a month before his death. He was not even a pale shadow of himself and seemed to have lost his will to live. In acute pain and slightly delirious, while being readied for his dialysis, he whispered, 'How much should I do to just remain alive.' His voice was barely audible.

His condition kept worsening. A few days later, when Achyut Patwardhan arrived to see him and asked him how he was doing, he replied, 'Just waiting to pass away.' He told S.M. Joshi, another intimate friend, 'I want to sleep and forget all that has gone before.' Sleep seemed to elude him. He worried about the severe drought conditions in Bihar, the continued existence of pervasive, seemingly ineradicable inequality, and increasing attacks on Sangharsh Vahini members. He died at dawn on 8 October.

Reminiscing about his last hours, Vibha told me, 'He was gasping for breath on the previous day, so had to be put on dialysis a day before it was scheduled. He seemed a little better after the procedure, lulling us into a false sense of security. That night I left his room later than usual, around midnight. An hour later, Gulab knocked on my door to wake me up and urged me to return to the room. I found dada in a twilight zone. Clearly his life was ebbing away. His wife's absence hovered over him like an overwhelming presence. "Prabha was here just now," he whispered. "She smiled and spoke a few words . . ." I tried to calm him, stroked his fragile limbs, hummed a little, leaving the room when he seemed a little rested and reposeful.'

Indira and Sanjay joined the troika of Janata leaders and President Neelam Sanjiva Reddy in offering floral tributes to Jayaprakash's mortal remains kept at Patna's Shri Krishna Memorial Hall, but were not allowed to go near him. He was cremated on the banks of the Ganga in the presence of thousands of young students and villagers convulsed with emotions, who walked through the night or sat on bus and train roofs to reach Patna. Long queues of Dalit musahar women from Gosain parsa, Piperahatta, Sekhwara and other villages of Bodh Gaya, whom the state treated as agent provocateurs, patiently waited to catch a glimpse of their hero. In death, as in life, he belonged to them. Not all of them were directly touched by the revolution of 1974, but in that year of hope and renewal, they found their simmering and unspoken aspirations mirrored, and given a name.

Jayaprakash's best obituary, which was not intended to be one, was written by the *India Today* collective, Minhaz Merchant, Dilip Bobb, Arul Louis, Sunil Sethi, Prabhu Chawla and Farzand Ahmed, a few weeks after Jayaprakash was erringly declared dead and more than a few months before he eventually passed on. 'Even in his illness, Jayaprakash remains the country's foremost dissenter, critic, visionary and fighter for lost causes which never lose their value. He has always been one "ism" out of step, one generation too early or too late.'

Acknowledgements

Many years in the making, this book has been an incredible leap of faith, the keeping of a silent promise made to my father, Bimal Prasad. After nearly an entire life spent in academia, at the age of ninety he turned down the volume on other overriding commitments to initiate work on JP's biography. So determined was he to write this work, that even in the blitzkrieg of severe pneumonia and a broken hip, he asked for his notebook and pen. The long shadow cast by his death was dappled by my decision to take his work forward. His room had nearly everything I needed—handwritten notes, stacks of reference books (many his own), and the precious ten volumes of JP's selected works, their pages marked with orange and green Post-its. My mother's affectionate and deceptively simple book on JP's wife, Prabhavati, helped me explore the arc of their tumultuous relationship. *The Dream of Revolution* is, above all, my requiem for my father and my mother, Asha.

For understanding my emotional need of embarking on this very personal journey, and connecting all the vital dots, I owe a huge debt of gratitude to Kanishka Gupta, my dynamic literary agent. I am grateful to Milee Ashwarya and her team at Penguin, especially Vineet Gill, my copy editor, who brought it all together and showed remarkable tolerance to my rather wayward tryst with deadlines.

I warmly thank Himmat Singh, Jayoo Patwardhan, Razi Ahmad, Devi Prasad Tripathi, Vibha Sinha, Anand Kumar, Mahashweta Maharathi, Ajay Kumar, Alakh Narayan Sharma and Ravi Shankar Prasad for showing me rare glimpses of JP's inner life and movements, some of which are not more than historical footnotes. For their love and interest in the book, my wonderful community of friends, especially Syeda Apa, Yogesh Jain and Margaret Chatterjee, who encouraged me to continue even as I came perilously close to abandoning it midway; Simar, for her line edit; Oroon, who tantalized me with spectacular cover page options; and Raghu Rai, for his exceptional magnanimity in letting me use his photo essay on the decisive moments of the Bihar movement.

It feels strange to thank people one takes completely for granted. My siblings, Jayant and Sanjay, read through the many iterations of the manuscript with infinite patience. Tripurari, my closest friend and partner, taught me to deal with my lingering sense of inadequacy and warmed up the early drafts with his comments. My son, Vivan, took over the quotidian aspects of my life that I felt I could no longer deal with and was my go-to person for counselling and advice. Meghna, my surrogate daughter, generously shared her editorial expertise, paragraph after paragraph, and helped me nail the chapters. My niece Aastha offered to type whenever she could while on sabbatical from Oxford. Our large cohort of dogs—Tara, Trotsky, Harper and Chutki—created eruptive, joyous moments that made me survive the dullest phase of writing. I am in their debt. This book is for you: Meghna, Karan, Gitanjali, Vivan, Meghna Bal, Satyam, Aastha and our munchkin Samaa.

Sujata Prasad

Notes

Chapter 1: The Formative Years

1. For instance, Shambhu Sharan, a reputed lawyer; Anugraha Narain Sinha and Ram Charitra Singh, prominent Congress state-level ministers; and Ram Navmi Prasad, an ardent Gandhian. Shri Krishna Sinha, who went on to become the chief minister of Bihar, was also a temporary resident of the hostel.
2. He was given a generous but rationed amount of money for his expenses every day, a sum of three 'annas' (there being sixteen annas in a rupee then). He spent one anna on an 'ikka', a horse carriage, for commuting to his school, which was located at a distance of 3 miles from home, one anna on the return journey and the remaining anna on some delicacy during lunchbreak. Rambriksh Benipuri, *Jayaprakash Narayan: Ek Jivan* (Hindi), Kitab Ghar, New Delhi, 2005.
3. In the oral history recorded by the Nehru Memorial Museum and Library (NMML), Jayaprakash gave a different date. He said that the wedding took place at Prabhavati's ancestral village in Chhapra in June 1919.
4. Jayaprakash Narayan, 'From Socialism to Sarvodaya', in Bimal Prasad, ed., *A Revolutionary's Quest: Selected Writings of Jayaprakash Narayan*, Oxford University Press, New Delhi, 1980, p. 183.
5. Founded on 6 February 1921, with Rajendra Prasad as principal, Maulana Mazharul Haq and later Braj Kishore Prasad as its vice chancellor.

6. Chauri Chaura, a town near Gorakhpur, witnessed a violent incident on 4 February 1922 when a mob set fire to a police chauki, killing around twenty-two policemen.
7. A north Indian custom associated with child marriage, marking the ceremonial entry of a girl into her husband's home on reaching puberty.
8. Jayaprakash could not recollect their full names (as per his reminiscences recorded by NMML's oral history project).
9. Jayaprakash Narayan, *From Socialism to Sarvodaya*, Akhil Bharat Sarva Seva Sangh Prakashan, Rajghat, Kashi, 1959, p. 10.
10. Ibid.
11. Ibid.
12. The application of sociology to the ends of social reform.
13. 'Cultural Variation: A Thesis Presented for the Degree of Master of Arts', Ohio State University, 1929, part of the Brahmanand Papers, NMML (Prof. Nageshwar Prasad obtained a copy of this thesis from Ohio in 1966).
14. From NMML's Oral History Series.
15. The texts of the testimonials are part of the Bimal Prasad papers at Rajendra Bhawan, Delhi. Cited also in Ajit Bhattacharjea, *Jayaprakash Narayan: A Political Biography*, Vikas Publishing House, 1975, p. 42.

Chapter 2: Evolution of Political Life

1. Ajit Bhattacharjea, *Jayaprakash Narayan: A Political Biography*, Vikas Publishing House, 1975, p. 109.
2. *Young India*, 5 January 1928, cited in S. Gopal, *Jawaharlal Nehru: A Biography*, Vol. I, OUP, 1976, p. 112.
3. Chores were shared by all the ashram inmates: these included Gandhi's closest associates and confidantes such as Mahadev Desai, Narayan Khare, Narhari Parikh, Ramniklal Mehta, Chhaganlal Joshi, Pandit Sanadhya, Miraben and Abdul Kadir Bavazeer, popularly known as Imam Saheb, who lived there with his daughter Ameena, and many others including his nephew Maganlal. Maganlal played a vital role in the running of the ashram and died of typhoid in April 1928.
4. The Oral History Project of NMML, p. 141.

5. Gandhi to Prabhavati, 23 November 1928, cited in Asha Prasad, *Kasturba, Kamala, Prabhavati*, Vani Prakashan, New Delhi, 2003, p. 226.
6. Undated from the archive of Mahila Charkha Samiti, Patna.
7. Gandhi to Prabhavati, 26 November 1928, Archive of Mahila Charkha Samiti, Patna.
8. Ibid., 27 November 1928.
9. Gandhi to Prabhavati, 3 March 1936, cited in Asha Prasad, *Kasturba, Kamala, Prabhavati*, Vani Prakashan, New Delhi, 2003, p. 217.
10. Undated, Archive of Mahila Charkha Samiti, Patna.
11. Ibid.
12. Gandhi to Prabhavati, Wardha, 11 November 1939, cited in Asha Prasad, *Kasturba, Kamala, Prabhavati*, Vani Prakashan, New Delhi, 2003, p. 226.
13. Gandhi to Prabhavati, Borsad, 8 May 1931, cited in ibid., p. 214.
14. There is a certain ambiguity about the place where they met. Nearly all the available sources mention Wardha but in Jayaprakash's own words, recorded for NMML's Oral History Project, he first met Nehru in Lahore during the Congress session in December 1929.
15. The Oral History Project, NMML, p. 75.
16. Cited in Bimal Prasad, ed., *Jayaprakash Narayan: Selected Works*, Vol. III, NMML, 2003, p. 41.
17. Gandhi papers (Gandhi National Museum, New Delhi). Original in Hindi, 11 January 1930.
18. 25 June 1933, cited in Asha Prasad, *Kasturba, Kamala, Prabhavati*, Vani Prakashan, New Delhi, 2003, p. 133.
19. 10 January 1934, cited in ibid., p. 126.
20. 30 April 1934, cited in ibid., p. 127.
21. The All India Trade Union Congress was established in 1920. Its chief objective was to cooperate with and coordinate the activities of all labour organizations in the country and to give a lead for extension of trade unionism in areas where it had not penetrated.
22. Letter to Gandhi, 24 February 1930, Gandhi Papers, Gandhi National Museum, New Delhi.
23. The Oral History Project of NMML, pp. 82–84.
24. Circular 14, Bombay, AICC Papers (NMML), 11 June 1932.
25. M.R. Masani Papers (NAI), 19 August 1945.

26. 'Life as a Socialist Agitator', abridged chapter from Minoo Masani's political memoir *Bliss Was It in That Dawn*, socialistpartyindia. blogspot.com/2017

27. Yusuf Meherally, *Jayaprakash Narayan: Towards Struggle*, Bombay, 1946, p. 7.

Chapter 3: The Congress Socialist Years

1. Quoted by Minoo Masani, 'No Deviations, Right or Left', *Congress Socialist*, Vol. VI, 10 March 1935.

2. Resolutions on Economic Policy and Programme, 1924–54, AICC Papers (NMML).

3. John Patrick Haithcox, *Communism and Nationalism in India: M.N. Roy and Comintern Policy, 1920-1939*, OUP, 1971, p. 217–18.

4. Congress Leaders and their Policy, Nehru Papers (NMML), August 1934.

5. Statement on Congress Working Committee Resolution, 22 June 1934, cited in Bimal Prasad, ed., *Jayaprakash Narayan: Selected Works*, Vol. I, NMML, 2000, p. 64.

6. Bimal Prasad, ed., *Jayaprakash Narayan: Selected Works*, Vol. I, NMML, 2000, p. 68.

7. Ibid., p. 69.

8. Jawaharlal Nehru, *A Bunch of Old Letters*, Bombay, Asia Publishing House, 1958, p. 118.

9. Gandhi to Nehru, Wardha, 17 August 1934, cited in Stanley Wolpert, *Nehru: A Tryst with Destiny*, OUP 1996, p. 172.

10. Gandhi to Patel, September 1934, cited in ibid., p. 173.

11. E.M.S. Namboodiripad, 'The Congress Socialist Party and the Communists', *The Marxist*, Vol. III, No. 4, October–December 1985.

12. John Patrick Haithcox, *Communism and Nationalism in India: M.N. Roy and Comintern Policy, 1920-1939*, OUP, 1971, pp. 230–31.

13. Cited in Bimal Prasad, ed., *Jayaprakash Narayan: Selected Works*, Vol. I, NMML, 2000, p. 142.

14. Jayaprakash Narayan, 'Why Socialism?', All India Congress Socialist Party, 1936.

15. The entire text of Jayaprakash Narayan's *Why Socialism?*, published in January 1936, is available in Bimal Prasad, ed., *Jayaprakash Narayan: Selected Works*, Vol. II, NMML, 2001, pp. 1–89.

16. Ibid.

17. Full text available in Appendix 2. Ibid.

18. 'Appeal to Support the Congress Socialist', Jayaprakash Papers (NMML), 25 January 1937.

19. Lectures were delivered by Ram Manohar Lohia, Asoka Mehta, Minoo Masani, M.L. Dantwala and Yusuf Meherally.

20. Minoo Masani, *Bliss Was it in that Dawn*, Arnold-Heinemann, New Delhi, 1977, p. 89

21. Bhola Chatterji, *Conflict in Jayaprakash's Politics*, Ankur Published House, New Delhi, 1984, p. 17.

22. Ibid.

23. *Tribune*, 11 April 1938, cited in Bimal Prasad, ed., *Jayaprakash Narayan: Selected Works*, Vol. II, NMML, 2001, p. 212.

24. Sarvepalli Gopal, *Jawaharlal Nehru: A Biography*, Vol. I (1889-1947), OUP, 1976, p. 200.

25. Interview to press, 14 April 1936, cited in Bimal Prasad, ed., *Jayaprakash Narayan: Selected Works*, Vol. II, NMML, 2001, p. 106.

26. Sarvepalli Gopal, *Jawaharlal Nehru: A Biography*, Vol. I (1889-1947), OUP, 1976, p. 207.

27. R. Palme Dutt, *India Today*, Peoples Publishing House, 1949, p. 258.

28. 'Political Earthquake in Bihar', *Congress Socialist*, 6 February 1937.

29. Lecture on 'The Task Before Us', 30 January 1938 at the Socialist Study Centre, Patna, published in *Searchlight*, 3 February 1938, and *Congress Socialist*, 19 February 1937, cited in Bimal Prasad, ed., *Jayaprakash Narayan: Selected Works*, Vol. II, NMML, 2001, p. 153.

30. Notes on Faizpur Congress, *Congress Socialist*, 9 January 1937, cited in Bimal Prasad, ed., *Jayaprakash Narayan: Selected Works*, Vol. II, NMML, 2001, pp. 46–48.

31. Cited in Bimal Prasad, ed., *Jayaprakash Narayan: Selected Works*, Vol. II, NMML, 2001, p. 193.

32. *Searchlight*, 19 January 1938.

33. Ibid. p. 196.

34. Letter to Nehru, 23 November 1938, Jawaharlal Nehru Papers, NMML.

35. *Congress Socialist*, 7 August 1937.

36. 'From Faizpur to Haripura', *Congress Socialist*, 19 February 1938.

37. 'Lessons of Haripura', *Congress Socialist*, 26 February 1938.

38. 'A Haripura Diary', *Congress Socialist*, 12 March 1938.
39. 'Lessons of Haripura', *Congress Socialist*, 26 February 1938.
40. 'Victory of Rajaji over Gandhiji', M.R. Masani, *Congress Socialist*, 23 October 1938.
41. Bose's re-election stung Gandhi to the quick, so much so that he came out with the historic statement that the defeat of Subhas's rival was his own defeat. Pattabhi Sitaramayya, *The History of the Indian National Congress*, Vol. 2 (1935-1947), Padma Publication, Bombay 1947, p. 106.
42. Cited in Bimal Prasad, ed., *Jayaprakash Narayan: Selected Works*, Vol. III, NMML, 2003, pp. 26–28.
43. Charu Banerji, a Bengal socialist, in a letter dated 16 April 1939 to Jayaprakash available at the Nehru Memorial Museum and Library.
44. Ajit Jha, *Some Aspects of Congress Politics: 1934-39*, Department of History, University of Delhi, February 1997, p. 266.
45. Yusuf Meherally Papers Cited in Bimal Prasad, ed., *Jayaprakash Narayan: Selected Works*, Vol. III, NMML, 2003, p. 1.
46. 'The Fundamental Issues at Stake', 10 May 1940, Statement to the Press by Jawaharlal Nehru, *Hindustan Times*, Document No. 4, cited in K.N. Panikkar, ed., *Towards Freedom: Documents on the Movement for Independence in India 1940*, Part I, Indian Council of Historical Research, OUP, p. 6.
47. The Dutt–Bradley thesis, brought out by R. Palme Dutt and Ben Bradley, was published on 29 February 1936. Cited in Ajit Jha, *Some Aspects of Congress Politics: 1934-39*, Department of History, University of Delhi, February 1997, p. 244.
48. Joint appeal by Jayaprakash and P.C. Joshi to celebrate Communist Party day, 19 March 1939, cited in Bimal Prasad, ed., *Jayaprakash Narayan: Selected Works*, Vol. II, NMML, 2001, p. 303.
49. Ibid., p. 308.
50. Cited in Bhola Chatterji, *Conflict in JP's Politics*, Ankur Publishing House, 1984, p. 20.
51. 'War Circular No.2' of December 1939, cited in Bhola Chatterji, *Conflict in JP's Politics*, Ankur Publishing House, 1984. p. 21.
52. Madhu Limaye, *Communist Party: Facts and Fiction*, Chetna Prakashan, Hyderabad, 1951, pp. 48–49.
53. Ibid., p. 38.

Chapter 4: The Making of a National Hero

1. Statement in the court of the DC, Chaibasa, 15 March 1940. The statement ends with the following passage: 'If the people of Great Britain remove their present rulers and renounce imperialism with its capitalist parent, not only India but the freedom loving people of the whole world would exert themselves to see the defeat of Nazism and the victory of freedom and democracy. In the present circumstances, however, India has no alternative but to fight and end British imperialism. Only in that manner can it contribute to the peace and progress of the world.' Cited in Bimal Prasad, ed., *Jayaprakash Narayan: Selected Works*, Vol. III, NMML, 2003, pp. 46–47.

2. *Harijan*, 16 March 1940. Cited in *Collected Works of Mahatma Gandhi*, LXXI, New Delhi, 1978, p. 322.

3. S. Gopal, ed., *Selected Works of Jawaharlal Nehru*, New Delhi, 1971, p. 347.

4. Letter to Minoo Masani, 14 June 1940. Cited in Bimal Prasad, ed., *Jayaprakash Narayan: Selected Works*, Vol. III, NMML, 2003, p. 105.

5. He further wrote, 'Let us form a new revolutionary party out of the C.S.P., the Anushilan, the Forward Bloc, the Labour Party and other such groups or elements. A party based squarely on Marxism-Leninism, independent of all other political organisations and parties. I think this is eminently possible if you only wish it. The C.S.P. may or may not be kept going merely as a cover and platform for the new party and particularly to function within the Congress as long as we consider it feasible to do so.' Undated letter from prison sent to Subhas Bose sometime in 1940 and preserved in the archives of Netaji Research Bureau, Calcutta. Cited in Bimal Prasad, ed., *Jayaprakash Narayan: Selected Works*, Vol. III, NMML, 2003, pp. 53–55.

6. The Hindu Mahasabha also welcomed the offer of dominion status as practicable, clear and definite. The Muslim League was opposed to the idea. Jinnah believed that it was unsuitable for a multireligious country like India and feared that it would result in the rule of the majority community.

7. Cited in Brahmanand Papers, NMML, p. 51.

8. He goes on to say, 'Some people get exercised over the question if we should leave or remain in the Congress. To me the question is of

secondary importance. The main thing is that for us the Congress no longer remains as instrument for revolutionary action and therefore we must prepare an independent basis for such action. We may continue in the Congress as long as it serves any useful purpose. But we cannot continue to ask the masses to look to the Congress for their economic and political emancipation. To keep the masses tied up to the Congress is to do them the greatest disservice and to sabotage the revolutionary.' Cited in Bimal Prasad, ed., *Jayaprakash Narayan: Selected Works*, Vol. III, NMML, 2003, pp. 53–55.

9. Viceroy's Statement, 8 August 1940, Linlithgow Papers, NAI, Document No. 57, cited in K.N. Panikkar, ed., *Towards Freedom: Documents on the Movement for Independence in India 1940*, Indian Council for Historical Research, OUP, pp. 173–74.

10. The Revolutionary Socialist Party was founded by the heroes of the famous Chittagong armoury raid in 1938.

11. Letter to Minoo Masani, from M.R. Masani papers, National Archives, 4 January 1942.

12. Letter to Ganga Sharan Singh. Cited in Bimal Prasad, ed., *Jayaprakash Narayan: Selected Works*, Vol. III, NMML, 2003, p. 95.

13. Deoli Papers. cited in Bimal Prasad, ed., *Jayaprakash Narayan: Selected Works*, Vol. III, NMML, 2003, pp. 80–81.

14. Ibid.

15. Mahatma Gandhi's statement on the government's publication of Jayaprakash's Deoli letters cited in *Collected Works of Mahatma Gandhi*, Vol. III, LXXV (1941-42), Delhi, p. 34.

16. Ibid., p. 34.

17. Ibid., p. 35.

18. Letter addressed to Gandhi from Deoli Detention Camp, 28 October 1941.

19. Mahatma Gandhi to Jayaprakash Narayan (Telegram), 12 November 1941, cited in Appendix 21, Bimal Prasad, ed., *Jayaprakash Narayan: Selected Works*, Vol. III, NMML, 2003.

20. 'To All Fighters for Freedom', cited in Bimal Prasad, ed., *Jayaprakash Narayan: Selected Works*, Vol. III, NMML, 2003, p. 110.

21. Ibid., p. 111.

22. Ibid., p. 113

23. Ibid., 1 September 1943, p. 119.

24. Ibid., p. 122.

25. Ibid., p. 128.

26. Ibid., p. 131.

27. Ibid., p. 135.

28. Ibid., p. 136.

29. He began by saying, 'I address you as one who loves America only next to his own motherland. I spent the best part of my youth in your great country and seven of my happiest years. I went there as a student and learnt much not only from its universities but also from its factories and farms where I worked as an ordinary labourer in order to pay my way through college. Having studied at California, Iowa and Wisconsin, I finally graduated from Ohio. There may be men among you from these Universities. To such of you I send my fraternal greetings.' 'To American Officers and Soldiers in India', cited in Bimal Prasad, ed., *Jayaprakash Narayan: Selected Works*, Vol. III, NMML, 2003, pp. 138–44.

30. Vijaya Patwardhan, interview given to *Naya Sangharsh*, 11–12 October 1992, p. 90.

31. It was possible to track the brief but definitive period of Vijaya Patwardhan's life from her family archives with the help of Jayu Patwardhan, her niece-in-law.

32. Intelligence Bureau File No. 3/64/43: Home Poll (I), cited in Partha Sarthi Gupta, ed., *Towards Freedom, Documents on the Movement for Independence in India 1943-44*, Part I, Indian Council for Historical Research, OUP, p. 64.

33. Intelligence Bureau: Extract from Bihar Special Branch Report dated 28 June 1943 cited in ibid., p. 93.

34. This letter was published with the following note by Jayaprakash under the title 'This was Lahore Fort', *Inside Lahore Fort*, Socialist Book Centre, Madras, 1959: 'My "interrogation" had been completed by then. As I was at that time a State prisoner, the Home Secretary to the Provincial Govt. Mr. A.A. MacDonald used to visit me every month. He came to see me first in the middle of December 1943 when he told me that the Punjab C.I.D. had given me up as "hopeless". It was then that I had asked him for permission to make a written complaint to the Provincial Government. He said then that he would think over the matter. When he came again he told me that I had permission to

write to the Government whenever I wanted. But there was a further delay of a couple of weeks. For in spite of the Home Secretary's orders, I was not provided with the necessary writing materials till the beginning of February. This letter was written to the Punjab Government early in February, 1944. There was no formal reply from the Government to my representation: only Mr. MacDonald informed me, when he came to see me next, that my letter was "sent up", as I had wished, and was "sent down" again.' Cited in Bimal Prasad, ed., *Jayaprakash Narayan: Selected Works*, Vol. III, NMML, 2003, pp. 145-48.

35. To Home Secretary, Government of Punjab, Lahore, February 1944, cited in Bimal Prasad, ed., *Jayaprakash Narayan: Selected Works*, Vol. III, NMML, 2003, p. 146.

36. Random Jottings, 'A Visitor Comes to My Cosmos', 25 October 1944, cited in Bimal Prasad, ed., *Jayaprakash Narayan: Selected Works*, Vol. III, NMML, 2003, p. 232.

37. Ibid.

38. Letter to Gandhi, 6 October 1945, cited in Bimal Prasad, ed., *Jayaprakash Narayan: Selected Works*, Vol. III, NMML, 2003, p. 275.

39. Random Jottings, 25 October 1944, cited in Bimal Prasad, ed., *Jayaprakash Narayan: Selected Works*, Vol. III, NMML, 2003, p. 233.

40. Most of them were brought out in a book form in 1947 by Sahityalaya, Patna, and have been incorporated in Bimal Prasad, ed., *Jayaprakash Narayan: Selected Works*, Vol. III, NMML, 2003, pp. 149–247.

41. Cited in Bimal Prasad, ed., *Jayaprakash Narayan: Selected Works*, Vol. III, NMML, 2003, p. 202.

42. Ibid., pp. 202–03.

43. Ibid., p. 156.

44. Ibid., p. 157.

45. This is the third petition Jayaprakash made to the Lahore High Court on 2 January 1945 (the texts of his two earlier petitions could not be found anywhere). JP's purpose in filing these petitions was to draw the court's attention to the brutalities to which political prisoners like him were subjected in the Lahore Fort so that those taken to that place after him could be saved from similar tortures. However, the

concerned judge failed to take note of it and rejected the petition on the ground that the central government had informed the court that JP was soon to be transferred to an ordinary prison outside the Punjab (he was actually transferred to the Agra Central Jail the next day).

46. Anirban Mitra, 'Freedom on the Waves: The Indian Naval Mutiny, 70 Years Later', TheWire.in, 18 February 2016, thewire.in/history/freedom-on-the-waves-the-indian-naval-mutiny-70-years-later

Chapter 5: Parting of Ways

1. Cited in Bimal Prasad, ed., *Jayaprakash Narayan: Selected Works*, Vol. IV, NMML, 2003, p. 2.
2. Ibid.
3. Ramdhari Singh Dinkar was one of the most iconic modern Indian poets. Known for his revolutionary, nationalist poetry he was awarded the Padma Bhushan in 1959. His book *Sanskriti ke Char Adhyaya* won him the Sahitya Akademi Award.
4. Cited in Bimal Prasad, ed., *Jayaprakash Narayan: Selected Works*, Vol. IV, NMML, 2003, pp. 4–5.
5. Ibid., p. 20.
6. Ibid., p. 30.
7. 'To all Fighters for Freedom III', 28 July 1946, cited in Bimal Prasad, ed., *Jayaprakash Narayan: Selected Works*, Vol. IV, NMML, 2003, p. 33.
8. Interview to Press, 13 September 1946, cited in Bimal Prasad, ed., *Jayaprakash Narayan: Selected Works*, Vol. IV, NMML, 2003, p. 57.
9. Ibid.
10. Diary entry on 8 May 1944, Bhagalpur Jail, cited in Asha Prasad, *Kasturba, Kamala, Prabhavati*, Vani Prakashan, New Delhi, 2003, p. 175.
11. Diary entry on 12 April 1946, Bhagalpur Jail, cited in ibid., p. 181.
12. Gandhi's letter to Prabhavati, cited in ibid., p. 181.
13. Address to students at Patna, 8 November 1946, cited in Bimal Prasad, ed., *Jayaprakash Narayan: Selected Works*, Vol. IV, NMML, 2003, p. 71.
14. Cited in Bimal Prasad, ed., *Jayaprakash Narayan: Selected Works*, Vol. IV, NMML, 2003, p. 71.

15. Interview on 4 November 1946. Cited in Bimal Prasad, ed., *Jayaprakash Narayan: Selected Works*, Vol. IV, NMML, 2003, p. 72.

16. Statement on disturbances in Punjab, 21 March 1947, cited in Bimal Prasad, ed., *Jayaprakash Narayan: Selected Works*, Vol. IV, NMML, 2003, p. 118.

17. At this point, Ramanand Tiwary was heading the 'Inqualabi Sipahi Dal' (Revolutionary Policemen's Association), an organization formed in 1942 when he himself was a constable.

18. Sir H. Dow to Field Marshal Viscount Wavell, DO No. 299-G.B., 26 October 1946. Cited in Nicholas Mansergh, ed., *The Transfer of Power 1942-47*, Vol. VIII, OUP, 1979, p. 812.

19. An established writer before 1947, Saadat Hasan Manto was amongst the greatest chroniclers of Partition.

20. 'My picture of Socialism', 24 November 1946, cited in Bimal Prasad, ed., *Jayaprakash Narayan: Selected Works*, Vol. IV, NMML, 2003, p. 81.

21. Ibid., p. 86.

22. 'The Transition to Socialism', *National Herald*, 26 January 1947, cited in ibid., p. 110.

23. Ibid.

24. 'The Transition to Socialism', article in *Janata*, 26 January 1947, cited in ibid.

25. Interview with Muslim workers in Bombay, published in *Janata*, 9 February 1947, cited in ibid., p. 114.

26. Vallabhbhai Patel to Jayaprakash Narayan, 17 October 1946, cited in ibid.

27. From letter dated 23 October 1946, part of JP Papers, NMML.

28. Letter to Louis Fischer, 24 March 1947, JP Papers, NMML.

29. Address at Coimbatore District Textile Workers' Conference, 18 April 1947, cited in Bimal Prasad, ed., *Jayaprakash Narayan: Selected Works*, Vol. IV, NMML, 2003, p. 136.

30. Letter from Vallabhbhai Patel, Sardar Patel Correspondence, NAI.

31. Letter to Vallabhbhai Patel, 17 May 1947, from the Sardar Patel Collection, NAI.

32. Vallabhbhai Patel to Jayaprakash Narayan, 23 May 1947, Sardar Patel Correspondence, NAI.

33. Cited in Bimal Prasad, ed., *Jayaprakash Narayan: Selected Works*, Vol. IV, NMML, 2003, p. 153.

34. Statement to Press regarding Sardar Patel's offer, 11 August 1947, cited in ibid., p. 177.
35. The full text of the statement is as follows: 'The assassin is not one person, not even a team of persons, but a big and wide conspiracy of a foul idea and of organisations that embody it. On Hindu Mahasabha, Rashtriya Swayamsevak Sangh and Muslim League and such like organisations rest the responsibility for this twofold crisis of the spirit and the State. In accordance with the approved norms of democracy, Government must formally resign in symbolic atonement of the evil deed, and, on reconstitution, the Home and Information Ministries must change. The Home Ministry must be entrusted to the care of a minister who will have no other portfolios to administer and who will be able and willing to curb and crush the organisations of communal hate.' Cited in ibid., p. 211.
36. Speech at a public meeting in Bombay, 28 February 1948, cited in ibid., p. 218.
37. Speech at a meeting of the AICC, adapted from *National Herald*, 22 February 1948, cited in ibid., p. 216.
38. Address at a public meeting in Patna, 31 October 1947, cited in ibid., p. 187.
39. Speech at a public meeting in New Delhi, 2 February 1948, cited in ibid., p. 210.
40. Letter to Nehru, 11 January 1948, JP Papers, NMML.
41. Appendix 18, Draft Constitution of Indian Republic by the Socialist Party, cited in Bimal Prasad ed., *Jayaprakash Narayan: Selected Works*, Vol. IV, NMML, 2003.
42. Cited in Bimal Prasad, ed., *Jayaprakash Narayan: Selected Works*, Vol. IX, NMML, 2008, pp. 203–04.
43. Rakesh Ankit, 'Jayaprakash Narayan, Indian National Congress and Party Politics, 1934-1954', *Studies in Indian Politics* 3(2): 149–63, Sage Publications, p. 157.
44. Annual Report of the General Secretary, Socialist Party Conference (Organisational), Nasik, 19–21 March 1948, cited in Bimal Prasad, ed., *Jayaprakash Narayan: Selected Works*, Vol. IV, NMML, 2003, Appendix 23.
45. Ajit Bhattacharjea, *Jayaprakash Narayan: A Political Biography*, Vikas Publishing House, 1975, p. 99.

Chapter 6: Emergence of New Fault Lines

1. Ajit Bhattacharjea, *Jayaprakash Narayan: A Political Biography*, Vikas Publishing House, 1975, p. 98.
2. Annual Report of the General Secretary, Nasik, 19 March 1948, cited in Bimal Prasad, ed., *Jayaprakash Narayan: Selected Works*, Vol. IV, NMML, 2003, p. 229.
3. Letter to Nehru, 27 March 1948, Brahmanand Papers, NMML.
4. Sarvepalli Gopal, *Jawaharlal Nehru: A Biography*, Vol. II, Jonathan Cape Ltd, 1984, p. 67.
5. Ibid.
6. Nehru quoted by Louis Fischer in Sarvepalli Gopal, *Jawaharlal Nehru: A Biography*, Vol. II, Jonathan Cape Ltd, 1984, p. 66.
7. Nehru to Jayaprakash, 19 August 1948, Sarvepalli Gopal, *Jawaharlal Nehru: A Biography*, Vol. II, Jonathan Cape Ltd, 1984, p. 67.
8. Bimal Prasad, ed., Jayaprakash Narayan: Selected Works, Vol. V, NMML, 2005, pp. 37–38.
9. 'Towards Fascism', *Janata*, 4 July 1948. Cited in Bimal Prasad, ed., *Jayaprakash Narayan: Selected Works*, Vol. V, NMML, 2005, p. 39.
10. 'Lessons from the UP Elections', 11 July 1948, Bimal Prasad, ed., *Jayaprakash Narayan: Selected Works*, Vol. V, NMML, 2005, p. 43.
11. The full text of the report was published as a pamphlet under the title 'Democratic Socialism, the Ideal and the Method'. Bimal Prasad, ed., *Jayaprakash Narayan: Selected Works*, Vol. V, NMML, 2005, pp. 416–40.
12. For full text, see Appendix 26, Bimal Prasad, ed., *Jayaprakash Narayan: Selected Works*, Vol. V, NMML, 2005, pp. 505–17.
13. Debate on the General Secretary's Report, 9 July 1950, Bimal Prasad, ed., *Jayaprakash Narayan: Selected Works*, Vol. V, NMML, 2005, p. 497.
14. Ibid., p. 492.
15. Ibid., p. 493.
16. Ibid., p. 494.
17. Ibid., pp. 492–503.
18. On the demise of Yusuf Meherally, Bombay, 3 July 1950, JP Papers, NMML.

19. Ajit Bhattacharjea, *Jayaprakash Narayan: A Political Biography*, Vikas Publishing House, 1975, p. 104.
20. Kamaladevi Chattopadhyay, *Inner Recesses Outer Spaces*, Navrang, New Delhi, 1986, p. 286.
21. Letter to Nehru, 10 December 1948, Brahmanand Papers, NMML.
22. JP Papers, NMML.
23. Bimal Prasad, ed., *Jayaprakash Narayan: Selected Works*, Vol. V, NMML, 2005, p. 51.
24. Letter to Nehru, 10 December 1948, Brahmanand Papers, NMML.
25. Ibid.
26. Ibid.
27. Statement to the press, Patna, 26 May 1949, Bimal Prasad, ed., *Jayaprakash Narayan: Selected Works*, Vol. V, 2005, p. 226.
28. Letter to Patel, 19 August 1950, Brahmanand Papers, NMML.
29. Letter to Nehru, 18 October 1950, Sarvepalli Gopal, *Jawaharlal Nehru: A Biography*, Vol. II, Jonathan Cape Ltd, 1979, p. 68.
30. Nehru to Patel, 30 June 1949, Ajit Bhattacharjea, *Jayaprakash Narayan: A Political Biography*, Vikas Publishing House, 1975, p. 68.
31. Letter to Aruna Asaf Ali, 6 August 1949, JP Papers, NMML.
32. Address to students of Lucknow University, 16 December 1948, Bimal Prasad, ed., *Jayaprakash Narayan: Selected Works*, Vol. V, NMML, 2005, p. 125.
33. Speech at public meeting in Patna, 29 March 1950, Bimal Prasad, ed., *Jayaprakash Narayan: Selected Works*, Vol. V, 2005, p. 361.
34. Sarvepalli Gopal, *Jawaharlal Nehru: A Biography*, Vol. II, Jonathan Cape Ltd, 1979, p. 162.
35. Address at an election meeting in Jalandhar, 20 December 1951, Bimal Prasad, ed., *Jayaprakash Narayan: Selected Works*, Vol. VI, NMML, 2005, p. 206.
36. Intervention in the debate on the General Secretary's Report at the Pachmarhi Convention, 24 May 1952, Bimal Prasad, ed., *Jayaprakash Narayan: Selected Works*, Vol. VI, NMML, 2005, p. 226.
37. Lohia's Presidential Address at the Pachmarhi Convention, 23 May 1952, Appendix 21, Bimal Prasad, ed., *Jayaprakash Narayan: Selected Works*, Vol. VI, NMML, 2005, pp. 469–502.
38. Ibid.

39. Ibid, p. 234.
40. To Nehru, 25 May 1952, JP Papers, NMML.
41. From Nehru, 27 May 1952, Brahmanand Papers, NMML.
42. Jayaprakash felt that he had let down post and telegraph workers by conveying government assurances, which had not been fulfilled. The idea of a self-purification fast had emerged with the breakdown of the negotiations with the communication minister, Rafi Ahmad Kidwai.
43. Jayaprakash fasted at Dr Dinshaw Mehta's Nature Cure Clinic in Pune.
44. Letter from Nehru, 8 July 1952, Brahmanand Papers, NMML.
45. Letter to Nehru, 10 July 1952, JP Papers, NMML.
46. Letter from Nehru, 12 July 1952, Brahmanand Papers, NMML.
47. Ibid.
48. Letter from Nehru, 23 September 1952, Brahmanand Papers, NMML.
49. 'Aphrodisiacs vs. Real Vitality, Plain-speaking to the Comrades', 10 August 1952, Bimal Prasad, ed., *Jayaprakash Narayan: Selected Works*, Vol. VI, NMML, 2005, p. 261.
50. 'Incentives for Goodness', 12 October 1952, cited in Bimal Prasad, ed., *Jayaprakash Narayan: Selected Works*, Vol. VI, NMML, 2005, p. 282.
51. 'The Ideological Problems of Socialism', Rangoon, 7 January 1953. Bimal Prasad, *A Revolutionary's Quest: Selected Writings of Jayaprakash Narayan*, New Delhi, 1980, pp. 158–72.
52. Ibid.
53. Letter to Nehru, 4 March 1953, JP Papers, NMML.
54. Sarvepalli Gopal, *Jawaharlal Nehru: A Biography*, Vol. II, Jonathan Cape Ltd, 1979, p. 200.
55. To Nehru, 4 March 1953, JP Papers, NMML.
56. Ibid.
57. From Nehru, 17 March 1953, Brahmanand Papers, NMML.
58. Ibid.
59. Press conference related to talks with Nehru, 18 March 1953, New Delhi, cited in Bimal Prasad, ed., *Jayaprakash Narayan: Selected Works*, Vol. VI, NMML, 2005, p. 328.
60. Intervention in the debate on the General Secretary's Report, Betul, 16 June 1953, cited in Bimal Prasad, ed., *Jayaprakash Narayan: Selected Works*, Vol. VI, NMML, 2005, p. 345.

61. Ajit Bhattacharjea, *Jayaprakash Narayan: A Political Biography*, Vikas Publishing House, 1975, p. 118.

Chapter 7: From Socialism to Sarvodaya

1. *Janata*, 27 June 1954, cited in Bimal Prasad, ed., *Jayaprakash Narayan: Selected Works*, Vol. VII, 2007, NMML, p. 16.
2. Speech at the Bhoodan Workers Training Camp, Mokamah, 21 November 1953, cited in Bimal Prasad, ed., *Jayaprakash Narayan: Selected Works*, Vol. VII, NMML, 2007, p. 384.
3. Asha Prasad, *Kasturba, Kamala, Prabhavati*, Vani Prakashan, 2003, p. 229.
4. Address to PSP workers, Bombay, 15 May 1954, Brahmanand Papers, NMML.
5. Interview given to Press Trust of India, Bombay, 16 November 1954, cited in Bimal Prasad, ed., *Jayaprakash Narayan Selected Works*, Vol. VII, 2007, p. 41.
6. Jayaprakash asked every Sarvodaya worker to take the Jeevandan pledge approved by Vinoba Bhave. The pledge included the spinning and wearing of khadi and using articles produced by village industries.
7. Letter to Rajendra Prasad, 28 June 1955, JP Papers (NMML).
8. Letter from J.R.D. Tata, 11 December 1954, JP Papers (NMML).
9. Letter to J.R.D. Tata, 24 December 1954, JP Papers (NMML).
10. Their reactions were mentioned in Minoo Masani's letter to Jayaprakash on 11 December 1954, part of JP Papers at NMML.
11. Allan and Wendy Scarfe returned to India in December 1971 to work on a biography of Jayaprakash Narayan. Their biography, published in 1975, had details of Jayaprakash's life till 1973. In 1997, their personal reminiscences came out in the form of another book, *Remembering Jayaprakash*.
12. From Nehru, 5 September 1955, Rajendra Prasad Papers (NAI).
13. Letter to Nehru, 20 February 1956, Nehru Papers, Files at Home (NMML).
14. Letter to Morarji Desai, 29 March 1956, JP Papers (NMML).
15. Letter to Nehru, 1 May 1956, Nehru Papers, Files at Home (NMML).
16. Letter from Nehru, 3 May 1956, JP Papers (NMML).
17. Ibid.

18. Published as a pamphlet and in several newspapers and political journals. Cited in Bimal Prasad, ed., *Jayaprakash Narayan: Selected Works*, Vol. VII, 2007, NMML, p. 141.
19. Speech in Bombay, 11 November 1956, cited in Bimal Prasad, ed., *Jayaprakash Narayan: Selected Works*, Vol. VII, 2007, NMML, p. 151.
20. Sarvepalli Gopal, *Jawaharlal Nehru: A Biography*, Vol. II, Jonathan Cape Ltd, 1979, p. 292.
21. Gerald Priestland, 20 November 1956, cited in Sarvepalli Gopal, *Jawaharlal Nehru: A Biography*, Jonathan Cape Ltd, 1979, p. 296.
22. Statement to the press, 23 January 1961, JP Papers (NMML).
23. Speech at Tibet Convention, 9 March 1959, JP Papers (NMML).
24. Press statement, Patna, 3 February 1957, cited in Bimal Prasad, ed., *Jayaprakash Narayan: Selected Works*, Vol. VII, 2007, NMML, p. 163.
25. From Nehru, 3 April 1957, Brahmanand Papers (NMML).
26. 31 July 1957, Nehru Papers, Files at Home (NMML).
27. From Nehru, 3 April 1957, Brahmanand Papers (NMML).
28. To Nehru, 14 July 1957, Brahmanand Papers (NMML).
29. From Nehru, 18 July 1957, Brahmanand Papers (NMML).
30. To Nehru, 27 October 1957, JN Papers, Files at Home (NMML).
31. From Nehru, 30 October 1957, Brahmanand Papers (NMML).
32. Comments on the possibility of a single socialist party, Lucknow, 15 July 1957, cited in Bimal Prasad, ed., *Jayaprakash Narayan: Selected Works*, Vol. VII, 2007, NMML, p. 186.
33. To Ganga Sharan Sinha, 25 July 1957, Brahmanand Papers (NMML).
34. Letter to Achyut Patwardhan, 22 August 1957, JP Papers (NMML).
35. From 'Socialism to Sarvodaya', 25 October 1957, cited in Bimal Prasad, ed., *Jayaprakash Narayan: Selected Works*, Vol. VII, 2007, NMML, pp. 227, 254.
36. 'A Plea for Reconstruction of Indian Polity', 30 September 1959, cited in Bimal Prasad, ed., *Jayaprakash Narayan: Selected Works*, Vol. VII, 2007, NMML, pp. 434–99.
37. Bimal Prasad, ed., *A Revolutionary's Quest*, Oxford University Press, 1980, p. xlv.
38. Address to MPs, 23 September 1958, JP Papers (NMML).
39. Speaking at a public lecture delivered at the Indian Institute of Public Administration, New Delhi, on 26 July 1961, Jayaprakash

commented, 'Powers are being given and it is being said that self-governing institutions are being created at three levels within certain spheres. But when you come to look at the resources that are being placed at their disposal, you find that they are entirely dependent on the State Government.' Cited in Bimal Prasad, ed., *Jayaprakash Narayan: Selected Works*, Vol. VII, 2007, NMML, p. 162.

40. 'Swaraj for the People', Varanasi, 15 March 1961, Bimal Prasad, ed., *Jayaprakash Narayan Selected Works*, Vol. VIII, 2007, pp. 81–110.

41. Mentioned in the convocation address at the University of Mysore, 29 November 1965, cited in Bimal Prasad, ed., *Jayaprakash Narayan: Selected Works*, Vol. VIII, 2007, NMML, p. 580.

42. Reproduced in *The Hindu*, 10 June 1958, cited at Appendix 50, Bimal Prasad, ed., *Jayaprakash Narayan: Selected Works*, Vol. VII, 2007, NMML, pp. 633–37.

43. In an address to the Sarva Seva Sangh, Patna, 9 April 1962, cited in Bimal Prasad, ed., *Jayaprakash Narayan: Selected Works*, Vol. VIII, 2007, NMML, p. 232.

44. Address to members of Parliament, 23 September 1958, JP Papers (NMML).

45. 'Violence against Muslim Citizens: A Denial of Nation God and Man', New Delhi, 26 March 1964, JP Papers (NMML).

46. 14 April 1964, J.J. Singh Papers (NMML).

47. Press interview, New Delhi, 29 October 1969, cited in Bimal Prasad, ed., *Jayaprakash Narayan: Selected Works*, Vol. IX, 2007, NMML, 2008, p. 476.

48. 'The Need to Re-think', 11 May 1964; published in *Hindustan Times* on 15 May 1964, JP Papers (NMML).

49. Ibid.

50. Issuing a strong statement, Jayaprakash had said, 'It seems to me that after such a national tragedy the least that the Indian Government could do was to institute a proper and impartial enquiry into the whole affair. In the meanwhile it does not seem proper for the Prime Minister to pronounce judgement on such a controversial subject and to attempt to whitewash the guilt of those who seem to deserve severe punishment.' Lucknow, July 1953, cited in Bimal Prasad, ed., *Jayaprakash Narayan: Selected Works*, Vol. V, 2005, NMML, p. 361.

51. Balraj Puri, 'JP's role in Jammu and Kashmir', 26th JP Memorial Lecture, 23 March 2006.

52. Sarvepalli Gopal, *Jawaharlal Nehru: A Biography*, Vol. III, Jonathan Cape Ltd, 1984, p. 263.

53. The demand for arrest came from the president of the UP Congress, A.P. Jain. Reacting cryptically to his remarks, Jayaprakash said, 'Personally I would welcome that as an opportunity to snatch some rest and do some reading. But the crucial point to ponder is: If a person of Shri Jain's position throws about threats in this manner, can it be surprising that irate young men should go about muttering assassination.' 'The Need to Re-think', 11 May 1964, JP Papers (NMML). Twenty-seven Congress MPs also issued a statement asserting the primacy of law over moral and human values.

54. Speech in Poona, 22 August 1964, cited in Bimal Prasad, ed., *Jayaprakash Narayan: Selected Works*, Vol. VIII, 2007, p. 464.

55. Statement on behalf of India–Pakistan Conciliation Group issued to *Indian Express*, 13 September 1964, cited in Bimal Prasad, ed., *Jayaprakash Narayan: Selected Works*, Vol. VIII, 2007, p. 470.

56. Letter to Lal Bahadur Shastri, 11 June 1965, JP Papers (NMML).

57. Even though Jayaprakash believed that it was possible for India and Pakistan to live as friends, he was circumspect enough to say that if Pakistan wanted war with India because of being denied a hand in the Kashmir issue, conciliation would have to wait. Patna, 17 September 1965, JP Papers (NMML).

58. Balraj Puri, 'JP's role in Jammu and Kashmir', 26th JP Memorial Lecture, 23 March 2006.

59. To Indira Gandhi, 23 June 1966, JP Papers (NMML).

60. 'Need for Settlement in Kashmir', Srinagar, 10 October 1968, JP Papers (NMML).

61. Speaking on the right of self-determination, Jayaprakash said that it was not an unlimited right and that if it were to be enforced indiscriminately, very few of the modern nations would remain intact; 12 August 1966, Kohima, JP Papers (NMML).

62. Saying that the military intervention had cost India international regard and tarnished India's image as a peace-loving country, Jayaprakash said, 'As a member of the UN, we were committed not to use armed force against another member, and we broke that commitment in a manner that came as a shock.' Convocation Address at the University of Mysore, 29 November 1965, cited in Bimal

Prasad, ed., *Jayaprakash Narayan: Selected Works*, Vol. VIII, 2007, p. 582.

63. From Gopal Krishna Gandhi, 16 September 1964, Brahmanand Papers (NMML).

64. To Gopal Krishna Gandhi, 28 October 1964, JP Papers (NMML).

65. 'A Plea for Settling India–China Dispute through Arbitration', Bombay, 7 March 1962, cited in Bimal Prasad, ed., *Jayaprakash Narayan: Selected Works*, Vol. VIII, NMML, 2007, p. 226.

66. Nehru's comments, New Delhi, 22 March 1962, cited in Bimal Prasad, ed., *Jayaprakash Narayan: Selected Works*, Vol. VIII, NMML, 2007.

67. 'India's Policy of Appeasement', Patna, 26 October 1962, cited in Bimal Prasad, ed., *Jayaprakash Narayan: Selected Works*, Vol. VIII, NMML, 2007, p. 263.

68. Jayaprakash's reference was to the 1954 treaty between China and India proclaiming Tibet as a region of China.

69. Statement issued at Patna on 21 May 1963, cited in Bimal Prasad, ed., *Jayaprakash Narayan: Selected Works*, Vol. VIII, 2007, p. 294.

70. Letter from Bhutto, 11 June 1963, JP Papers (NMML).

71. Convocation Address at the University of Mysore, 29 November 1965, cited in Bimal Prasad, ed., *Jayaprakash Narayan: Selected Works*, Vol. VIII, 2007, p. 578.

72. 'Reconvene Nepalese Parliament', Patna, 12 February 1961, cited in Bimal Prasad, ed., *Jayaprakash Narayan: Selected Works*, Vol. VIII, NMML, 2007, p. 78.

73. Asha Prasad, *Kasturba, Kamala, Prabhavati*, Vani Prakashan, 2003, p. 193.

74. Ibid.

75. Ibid.

76. Tribute to Nehru, Calcutta, 27 May 1964, cited in Bimal Prasad, ed., *Jayaprakash Narayan: Selected Works*, Vol. VIII, NMML, 2007, p. 405.

77. From Indira Gandhi, 12 June 1964, JP Papers (NMML).

78. Offering Indira his warmest congratulations, Jayaprakash wrote, 'You have taken on a tremendous burden, and my heart goes out to you in this hour of trial and anxiety. In Bhai, you had an unequalled preceptor, and Lal Bahadurji by this success both in war and peace has lightened

somewhat the heavy burden.' Cited in Bimal Prasad, ed., *Jayaprakash Narayan: Selected Works*, Vol. VIII, NMML, 2007, p. 601.

79. Homage to Lohia, New Delhi, 12 October 1967, cited in Bimal Prasad, ed., *Jayaprakash Narayan: Selected Works*, Vol. IX, NMML, 2008, p. 180.

80. Calling for review of the use of DIR on 29 August 1965, Jayaprakash said, 'If this policy is not given up, I am afraid it will do much harm to the democratic institutions of the country.' Cited in Bimal Prasad, ed., *Jayaprakash Narayan: Selected Works*, Vol. VIII, NMML, 2007, p. 563.

81. Letter to J.J. Singh, 6 March 1964, JP Papers (NMML).

Chapter 8: The Sting in the Tail

1. Ramchandra Guha, *India After Gandhi: The History of the World's Largest Democracy*, Picador, 2007, p. 418. Translated, this reads: 'Give up smoking bidis, give your vote to the Jana Sangh, the bidi contains tobacco, Congressmen are bandits.'

2. A few of these statistics come from Ankit Mittal's analysis in the *Mint*, 24 January 2016, in an article titled 'India and Liberalization: There was a 1966 before 1991'.

3. Reported in the *Times of India*, 13 June 1966.

4. Jairam Ramesh in discussion with Elizabeth Roche on his book *Intertwined Lives: P.N. Haksar and Indira Gandhi*, Mint, 16 June 2018.

5. From Indira, New Delhi, 6 July 1996, JP Papers (NMML).

6. Cited in Bimal Prasad, ed., *Jayaprakash Narayan: Selected Works*, Vol. IX, Manohar, 2008, p. 60.

7. To Indira, Sitabdiara, 21 November 1967, JP Papers (NMML).

8. From Indira, New Delhi, 25 November 1967, JP Papers (NMML).

9. Paul R. Brass, 'The Political Uses of Crisis: The Bihar Famine of 1966-67', *The Journal of Asian Studies*, Vol. 45, No. 2 (Feb 1986), pp. 245–67.

10. 'Ranchi Riots: Some Serious Questions', 18 September 1967, cited in Bimal Prasad, ed., *Jayaprakash Narayan: Selected Works*, Vol. IX, Manohar, 2008, p. 171.

11. Ibid.

12. Ibid., p. 175.

13. Presidential Address at the Eleventh National Convention against Communalism, New Delhi, 28 December 1968, JP Papers (NMML).

14. Megha Kumar, *Communalism and Sexual Violence in India: the Politics of Gender, Ethnicity and Conflict*, I.B. Tauris & Co. Ltd, 2016.

15. Bimal Prasad, ed., *Jayaprakash Narayan: Selected Works*, Vol. IX, Manohar, 2008, p. 472.

16. To Frank Moraes, New Delhi, 19 September 1972, JP Papers (NMML).

17. Princeton, 2 April 1968, JP Papers (NMML).

18. Allan and Wendy Scarfe, *J.P.: His Biography*, Orient Blackswan, 1998, p. 207.

19. Bimal Prasad, ed., *Jayaprakash Narayan: Selected Works*, Vol. IX, Manohar, 2008, p. 802.

20. 'Thoughts on Gandhi Centenary', talk delivered on All India Radio, 1 October 1968, JP Papers (NMML).

21. This song was recorded in 1971. The relevant portion of the lyrics go: 'You may say I'm a dreamer, But I'm not the only one, I hope some day you'll join us, And the world will be as one.'

22. *Voluntary Action*, Volume 2, July–August 1969, pp. 3–9.

23. Ibid.

24. 'Face to Face', Musahari, 5 November 1970, cited in Bimal Prasad, ed., *Jayaprakash Narayan: Selected Works*, Vol. IX, Manohar, 2008, p. 566.

25. Protest against Security Arrangements, Musahari, 20 June 1970.

26. 'Current Agrarian Situation in Bihar', Asian Development Research Institute, Bihar, 2008, p. 58.

27. Ibid., p. 57.

28. Press Statement, Musahari, 23 December 1970, JP Papers (NMML).

29. Address to the National Conference of Voluntary Agencies, New Delhi, 8 June 1969, JP Papers (NMML).

30. 'Face to Face', Musahari, 5 November 1970, cited in Bimal Prasad, ed., *Jayaprakash Narayan: Selected Works*, Vol. IX, Manohar, 2008, p. 572.

31. Gair majurwa is cultivable land for which the government holds the title. Literally, it is land without a deed, i.e., land that does not have legal papers to prove an individual's ownership of it.

32. 'The Land Grabbers', Patna, 4 August 1970, JP Papers (NMML).
33. Ibid.
34. From Indira Gandhi, New Delhi, 9 December 1970, JP Papers (NMML).
35. To Indira, Sitabdiara, 13 March 1971, JP Papers (NMML). Original in Hindi.
36. From Indira, New Delhi, 14 April 1971, JP Papers (NMML). Original in Hindi.
37. Bimal Prasad, ed., *Jayaprakash Narayan: Selected Works*, Vol. IX, Manohar, 2008, p. 145.
38. Report of the Study Team on Jammu and Kashmir, 15 July 1968, Appendix 62, Bimal Prasad, ed., *Jayaprakash Narayan: Selected Works*, Vol. IX, Manohar, 2008.
39. Description given by Balraj Puri in 'Jayaprakash Narayan's role in Jammu and Kashmir', 26th JP Memorial lecture, 23 March 2006, organized by the PUCL.
40. Ibid.
41. Ibid.
42. 'Democracy Needs Fair and Free Elections', Patna, 26 January 1972, JP Papers (NMML).
43. Letter to Indira, Sitabdiara, 26 March 1971, JP Papers, NMML.
44. Press Statement II, Sitabdiara, 27 March 1971, JP Papers, NMML.
45. Press Statement, New Delhi, 28 July 1971, JP Papers, NMML.
46. 'Bangladesh: My Mission Overseas', Press Statement, New Delhi, 29 June 1971, JP Papers, NMML.
47. Article published in the *Indian Express*, 28 October 1971.
48. Jonathan Kandell, *New York Times*, 7 November 1971.
49. 'Recognition of Bangladesh', Statement to Press, Patna, 6 December 1971, JP Papers, NMML.
50. Interview with Minoo Masani, *Illustrated Weekly of India*, 11 June 1972.
51. Sudipta Kaviraj, *Trajectories of the Indian State: Politics and Ideas*, Permanent Black, 2010, p. 130.
52. Bhola Chatterji, *Conflict in JP's Politics*, Ankur, 1984, p. 237.
53. Ibid.
54. 'Elections in Kashmir', Patna, 12 February 1972, JP Papers (NMML).

55. Bipan Chandra, *In the Name of Democracy*, Penguin Books, 2003, p. 22.
56. 'Prospects of Democracy in India: A Hopeless Situation', August 1972, JP Papers (NMML).
57. At this point the president of the right-wing Swatantra Party.
58. Statement to the press, New Delhi, 15 May 1973, quoted in Bimal Prasad, ed., *Jayaprakash Narayan: Selected Works*, Vol. X, Manohar, 2009, p. 114.
59. Ibid.
60. Ibid., p. 112.
61. From Indira, New Delhi, 9 June 1973, JP Papers, NMML.
62. 'First Things First', 28 July 1973 cited in Bimal Prasad, ed., *Jayaprakash Narayan: Selected Works*, Vol. X, Manohar, 2009, p. 140.
63. 'How to Check the Canker of Corruption', 1 September 1973, *Everyman's*, Vol. I, No. 9, p. 7.
64. Letter to Indira, Patna, 24 April 1973, JP Papers, NMML.

Chapter 9: Hope in Dark Times

1. Khushwant Singh, 'A New Wave from the Old India', *New York Times*, 30 March 1975.
2. Address to students at Kanpur, 3 February 1974, JP Papers, NMML.
3. 'Youth for Democracy', Paunar (Wardha), 9 December 1973, JP Papers, NMML.
4. Letter from Indira, New Delhi, 27 February 1974, JP Papers, NMML.
5. Letter to Indira, New Delhi, 28 February 1974, JP Papers, NMML.
6. 'Happenings at Patna', Patna, 18 March 1974, JP Papers, NMML.
7. Lalan Tiwari, *Democracy and Dissent: A Case Study of the Bihar Movement, 1974–75*, Mittal Publications, 1987, p. 28.
8. Statement to Press, 30 March 1974, JP Papers, NMML.
9. Lalan Tiwari, *Democracy and Dissent: A Case Study of the Bihar Movement, 1974–75*, Mittal Publications, 1987, p. 28.
10. The specific date was 6 April. The president of the Patna University Students' Union and some other student leaders met Jayaprakash and requested him to assume leadership of the movement.
11. Jayaprakash made the comparison of the Bihar struggle with the Bardoli struggle while inaugurating the All India Youth Conference at Allahabad on 23 June 1974.

12. The date was 6 April 1974. The president of the Patna University Students' Union and some other student leaders met Jayaprakash and requested him to take over the leadership of the movement.
13. Jyoti Basu, ed., *Documents of the Communist Movement in India*, Vol. XVI (1973-74), 1998, p. 464, cited in Bipin Chandra, *In the Name of Democracy*, Penguin Books, 2003, p. 56.
14. Riposte to Indira Gandhi's remarks at a public meeting at Bhubaneswar on 1 April 1974, published in *Everyman's*, 6 April 1974, JP Papers, NMML.
15. Quoted in Allen and Wendy Scarfe, *J.P.: His Biography*, 1977, p. 422.
16. Indradeep Sinha, 'Red Face of JP's Total Revolution', Communist Party Publication No. 16, November 1974, pp. 4, 25.
17. Hannah Arendt, *The Crisis of the Republic*, Harcourt Brace Jovanovich, 1972.
18. 'Towards Total Revolution', Patna, 5 June 1974, published in *Everyman's*, JP Papers, NMML.
19. Lalan Tiwari, *Democracy and Dissent: A Case Study of the Bihar Movement, 1974–75*, Mittal Publications, 1987, p. 116.
20. From Indira, New Delhi, 22 May 1974, JP Papers, NMML.
21. Letter from Indira, New Delhi, 29 June 1974, JP Papers, NMML.
22. Ghanshyam Shah, *Economic and Political Weekly*, 14 December 1974, p. 116.
23. Only 300 of the 13,000 students of Patna University opted for the first option and 2500 for the second. Similarly, when Jayaprakash called for 5000 volunteers to become total revolutionaries, few responded. Bipan Chandra, *In the Name of Democracy: JP Movement and the Emergency*, Penguin Books, 2003, p. 54.
24. *Times of India*, 29 July 1974.
25. By 26 January 1975, the Jana Sangharsh Samitis claimed to have formed parallel governments in Madhubani, Saharsa, Bhagalpur, Deoghar, Godda, Sahebganj and other areas in the Santhal Parganas.
26. Address at public meeting, Patna, 10 October 1974, cited in Bimal Prasad, ed., *Jayaprakash Narayan: Selected Works*, Vol. X, Manohar, 2009, pp. 370–72.
27. Press Statement issued at Patna, 15 September 1974, JP Papers, NMML.

28. As revealed by Jayaprakash in a conversation with Bimal Prasad in January 1975.

29. *The Indian Nation*, 6 November 1974, p. 3.

30. Ibid.

31. Patna, 13 November 1974, JP Papers, NMML.

32. *Statesman*, 6 January 1975, p. 1.

33. 'The Rumble of the Chariot of Time Soon Be Heard in Delhi', Patna, 18 November 1974, cited in Bimal Prasad, ed., *Jayaprakash Narayan: Selected Works*, Vol. X, Manohar, 2009, p. 319.

34. Cited in Bhola Chatterji, *Conflict in JP's Politics*, Ankur, 1984, p. 285.

35. Bipan Chandra, *In the Name of Democracy: JP Movement and the Emergency*, Penguin Books, 2003, p. 58.

36. Interview with *Blitz* in December 1974, cited by Bipan Chandra, *In the Name of Democracy: JP Movement and the Emergency*, Penguin Books, 2003, p. 60.

37. Lalan Tiwari, *Democracy and Dissent: A Case Study of the Bihar Movement, 1974–75*, Mittal Publications, 1987, p. 105.

38. *Everyman's*, Vol. II, No. 42, 20 April 1975.

39. *Statesman*, 6 January 1975, p. 1.

40. Patna, 9 January 1975, JP Papers, NMML.

41. At that point, Arun Jaitley was a law student in Delhi and a prominent leader of the ABVP, and Anand Kumar was a Free Thinker at JNU.

42. Cited in Bimal Prasad, ed., *Jayaprakash Narayan: Selected Works*, Vol. X, Manohar, 2009, p. 420.

43. The Janata Sarkars were to be governed by a six-point minimum programme. The programme included formation of Janata courts, distribution of essential commodities, distribution of Bhoodan and government land, verification of electoral rolls, campaign for cleanliness and fight against dowry.

44. Press statement issued at Patna, 22 May 1975, JP Papers, NMML.

45. Bipan Chandra, *In the Name of Democracy: JP Movement and the Emergency*, Penguin Books, 2003, p. 62.

46. 'Manifesto for a New Bihar', 11 May 1975, JP Papers, NMML.

47. Quoted from an interview given by film-maker Anand Patwardhan to *India Today*, 1 April 2015.

Chapter 10: The Death of a Dream

1. 'On Justice Sinha's Historic Judgement', press statement issued at Arrah, 12 June 1975, JP Papers, NMML.

2. The court allowed her to attend Parliament but not vote until her appeal was heard and judged.

3. Quoted in Dom Moraes, *Indira Gandhi*, 1980, p. 220, cited in Bipan Chandra, *In the Name of Democracy: JP Movement and the Emergency*, Penguin Books, 2003, p. 67.

4. Seema Chishti, 'Calling Attention', *Indian Express*, 27 November 2014, indianexpress.com/article/india/india-others/calling-attention/

5. 'Mrs Gandhi and Allahabad High Court Decision', press statement, Patna, 19 June 1975, JP Papers, NMML.

6. References from speech delivered at the rally in New Delhi on 25 June 1975, cited in Bimal Prasad, ed., *Jayaprakash Narayan: Selected Works*, Vol. X, Manohar, 2009, pp. 464–66.

7. To Indira Gandhi, Chandigarh Detention Centre, 21 July 1975, cited in Bimal Prasad, ed., *Jayaprakash Narayan: Selected Works*, Vol. X, Manohar, 2009, p. 473.

8. Sudipta Kaviraj, *Trajectories of the Indian State Politics*, Orient Blackswan, 2010, p. 283.

9. Letter to Sheikh Abdullah, Chandigarh Detention Centre, 22–23 September 1975, cited in Bimal Prasad, ed., *Jayaprakash Narayan: Selected Works*, Vol. X, Manohar, 2009, p. 545.

10. From Jayaprakash's *Prison Diary*, in an entry made on 10 October, cited in Bimal Prasad, ed., *Jayaprakash Narayan: Selected Works*, Vol. X, Manohar, 2009, p. 556.

11. As cited in *In the Name of Democracy: JP Movement and the Emergency*, Penguin Books, 2003, p. 169.

12. 'Dismay in India', *New York Times*, 9 April 1976.

13. Arun Shourie, 'Role of the Intellectual During and After the Emergency', in Balraj Puri, *Revolution, Counter-Revolution*, 1978, p. 20, cited in Bipan Chandra, *In the Name of Democracy: JP Movement and the Emergency*, Penguin Books, 2003, p. 183.

14. Most of these figures have been taken from Bipan Chandra, *In the Name of Democracy: JP Movement and the Emergency*, Penguin Books, 2003, pp. 226–27.

15. Reported by J. Anthony Lukas in the *New York Times*, reproduced in Ramchandra Guha, *India After Gandhi*, Picador, 2007, p. 304.

16. Kuldip Nayar, 'JP's Quest', 24th JP Memorial Lecture, *PUCL Bulletin*, May 2004.

17. Quoted at several places, can be found in Ramchandra Guha, *India After Gandhi*, Picador, 2007, p. 496.

18. Ramchandra Guha, *India After Gandhi*, Picador, 2007, p. 520.

19. 'A Letter to the people of Bihar', 28 August 1976, cited in Bimal Prasad, ed., *Jayaprakash Narayan: Selected Works*, Vol. X, Manohar, 2009, p. 597.

20. From Jayaprakash's 'Prison Diary', Bimal Prasad, ed., *Jayaprakash Narayan: Selected Works*, Vol. X, Manohar, 2009, p. 561.

21. Ibid.

22. Maitreyi Devi in Vibha Sinha, ed., in a commemorative volume on Jayaprakash, published by Bihar Hindi Granth Academy, p. 50.

23. Letter from Charan Singh, New Delhi, 1 June 1976, JP Papers, NMML.

24. Ibid.

25. In an interview to *Samayika Varta*, 13 September 1977, cited in Bhola Chatterji, *Conflict in JP's Politics*, Ankur, 1984, pp. 191–92.

26. Address to a conference of chief secretaries on 7 May 1976, cited in Bipan Chandra, *In the Name of Democracy: JP Movement and the Emergency*, Penguin Books, 2003, p. 185.

27. Letter to Asoka Mehta, Patna, 30 November 1976, JP Papers, NMML.

28. Letter from Charan Singh, 8 November 1976, JP Papers, NMML.

29. Letter from Vajpayee, 6 December 1976, JP Papers, NMML.

30. Rakesh Ankit, 'Janata Party (1974-77) Creation of an All-India Opposition', *History and Sociology in South Asia*, Sage Publications, 11(1) 39-54, 2017, p. 51.

31. Ibid.

32. Jagjivan Ram formed the Congress for Democracy (CFD) with Bahuguna and Nandini Satpathy after quitting the Congress.

33. Statement to press, New Delhi, 23 January 1977.

34. Appeal to the Youth, Patna, 4 February 1977, cited in Bimal Prasad, ed., *Jayaprakash Narayan: Selected Works*, Vol. X, Manohar, 2009, p. 640.

35. Quoted in Janaki Venkataraman, 'JP and Dr. Mani', *Madras Musings*, Vol. XXVII, No. 1, 6–30 April 2017.

36. 'On the Victory of the Janata Party', Patna, 21 March 1977.

37. Kuldip Nayar, 'JP's Quest', 24th JP Memorial Lecture, *PUCL Bulletin*, May 2004.

38. Bimal Prasad, ed., *Jayaprakash Narayan: Selected Works*, Vol. X, Manohar, 2009, Appendix 97.

39. Conversations with correspondents of *Sunday*, Surendra Pratap Singh and Shobha Kilachand, 14 August 1977, quoted in Bimal Prasad, ed., *Jayaprakash Narayan: Selected Works*, Vol. X, Manohar, 2009, p. 661.

40. Letter from Balraj Madhok to Jayaprakash, cited in 'Janata Party (1974–77) Creation of an All-India Opposition', *History and Sociology in South Asia*, Sage Publications, 11(1) 39-54, 2017, p. 54.

41. 'The Task Ahead: Conversations with Bimal Prasad', Patna, 28-30 August 1977, in Bimal Prasad, ed., *Jayaprakash Narayan: Selected Works*, Vol. X, Manohar, 2009, p. 679.

42. Letter to Chandra Shekhar, Patna, 9 May 1978, JP Papers, NMML.

43. Letter to Jagjivan Ram, Patna, 2 August 1978, JP Papers, NMML.

44. Letter to Kripalani, Patna, 20 August 1978, JP Papers, NMML.

45. Interview with the *Indian Express*, Patna, 24 January 1979, JP Papers, NMML.

46. Letter to Morarji, Patna, 1 March 1979, JP Papers, NMML.

47. Conversations with Bimal Prasad, Patna, 28-30 August 1977, cited in Bimal Prasad, ed., *Jayaprakash Narayan: Selected Works*, Vol. X, Manohar, 2009, p. 689.

48. 'Appeal to the People to Lend Support to Total Revolution', Patna, 15 November 1977, JP Papers, NMML.

49. 'On the Deepening Crisis in the Janata Party', Patna, 15 July 1975, JP Papers, NMML.

50. Letter to Chandra Shekhar, Patna, 18 July 1979, JP Papers, NMML.

51. Letter from Morarji Desai, New Delhi, 19 July 1979, cited in Bimal Prasad, ed., *Jayaprakash Narayan: Selected Works*, Vol. X, Manohar, 2009, p. 981.

Index